140 MILES OF LIFE

140 Miles of Life

A Remarkable Journey to Self-Acceptance & Love

A memoir

by

VERONICA CARRERA

BOOKS

Adelaide Books
New York / Lisbon
2021

140 MILES OF LIFE

A Remarkable Journey to Self-Acceptance & Love

A memoir

By Veronica Carrera

Copyright © by Veronica Carrera

Cover design © 2021 Adelaide Books

Published by Adelaide Books, New York / Lisbon

adelaidebooks.org

Editor-in-Chief

Stevan V. Nikolic

For any information, please address Adelaide Books
at info@adelaidebooks.org

or write to:

Adelaide Books
244 Fifth Ave. Suite D27
New York, NY, 10001

ISBN: 978-1-956635-04-1

Printed in the United States of America

To all those who seek the light within

Contents

IRONMAN PART 3.

I was surprised when a good-looking married couple, the husband from Spain and the wife from Mexico, approached me after our South African post-marathon celebration. I hadn't spoken that much to them, only seen them running. They took turns telling me, "You did very well in the race. It was a completely challenging route!" I politely thanked them. Then the Spaniard looked into my eyes and paused for a couple of seconds before he spoke, "Have you ever thought about doing an Ironman?"

"An Ironman? What is that?" I asked.

He was quiet for a minute, as if going over some private thoughts, and then he said kind of passionately, "I just feel you would do very well! I think you should do it."

His wife nodded her agreement.

"But what is it?" I asked, anxious to know.

He proceeded to tell me that he and his wife had just completed an Ironman before flying to South Africa for this Marathon.

"It is a 140 Mile Race," he said. **"You swim for 2.4 Miles, then bike for 112 Miles and finally run a full marathon for 26.2 miles.** It's raced in that order and without a break. That's an Ironman. You have 17 hours to complete it."

"17 Hours?!!!" I was dumbfounded.

I was astonished at its length and trying to comprehend what kind of crazy race that might be. Would that even be fun? Masochistic? What? Then he interrupted my thoughts, "Doesn't it sound amazing? It is truly epic!" He had such fire and certainty about it. I didn't quite get it.

"Well," I said, laughing, "I can't do it anyway."

"Why not?" he asked.

"I don't know how to swim."

He looked at me in a way as if wanting to light an unknown fire in me and said, "I don't agree. You and I have the same look in our eyes. You can do it."

I shook my head and said, "You don't understand. I am terrified of the water. I think it's because I almost drowned as a child and that was it for me," and then I shook their hands and wished them well.

"Think about it," he said.

A few days later, I said goodbye to all the wonderful athletes I had met in South Africa at the marathon, and all the kind and beautiful South African people who'd made me feel so at home. I was on my way back to New York.

As I sat on the plane, I could feel myself returning to my "normal" life, but I felt renewed by this journey. I'd seen a wonderful new country; I'd done extremely well in the marathon and I had made many new friends. It was yet another time when I realized how each experience opens our eyes to the beauty of life, rekindling the light within us and chiseling out more of our inner strength and character. It made me sit back and recall what a race I had been running all my life. One that had had more than its share of obstacles and victories, one that had already tested my resilience and faith. But in some ways, such a circuitous and difficult race had been a privilege.

I moved my seat to reclining, and began to wonder, "If I could survive all that, maybe I could do an Ironman. "And then I closed my eyes and began to remember.

Chapter 1.

We have to go

I can still recall, even though I was only four years old, how my mother woke me up as I lay fast asleep. She wrapped me in a blanket and whispered, "We're going." It was still dark; it must have been around 4 in the morning. "Mama, donde vamos?"

She hushed me softly and asked me to be quiet.

Then I asked, "Y mi papi?"

She didn't answer.

Everyone seemed to be sleeping. We finally reached the front door and a cab was out front waiting for us. We quickly got in. It seemed that everything had been carefully planned, carefully orchestrated. The cab took us to an elderly couple's home with whom my mother, I eventually learned, had made arrangements to become their helper in exchange for room and food for both of us. It was light by the time we walked in, and I saw an old man in a wheelchair and his equally elderly wife standing next to him. There was nothing warm about her. She seemed to have a harsh and cold energy. We had barely put our luggage down, when this old woman authoritatively asked my mother to go and buy some things for her right now.

As my mother started to walk toward the front door, I immediately followed, but the old lady screamed, "And where do you think you are going? You stay here!"

I saw my mom's eyes immediately turn towards me, desolate and teary. Then the woman screamed again, rushing my mom to move on. Mom seemed hesitant to leave me behind but, as she heard the old woman squeal again, she opened the door. I started to scream, "Mama! No me dejes aqui! Llevame contigo." She looked back, but left.

I began to cry and scream even louder. I found myself alone with these two strangers – thrown in like a tossed stick of wood. They started to follow me around the room to make me stop crying. I felt frightened alone with them; I was busy trying to get away. As the old couple were trying to find a way to grab me, I suddenly made it to the front door and escaped. I don't believe they followed me outside. This little 4-year-old me replicated an escape of her own.

As I walked around lost in that unfamiliar neighborhood, I remember asking random people, "Have you seen my mom?" There was a butcher at the corner wearing a white uniform and a tall white hat, someone you might see in a movie and I asked him, "Usted ha visto mi mama?" I tried to describe her, "Ella es negra, alta, y bonita. Y esta vestida con Jeans." He replied, "Ah, the black lady?"

I did not know that being black in the vibrant city of Guayaquil, Ecuador was something unusual and, I later was to learn, something to be ashamed of. One didn't see black people walking around in the city very much at all. Being born with dark skin and light hazel eyes, my mom stood out in a crowd. That is why this man was able to answer me, "Oh yeah, I saw a black lady head that way..." I started walking the streets in the direction he pointed me to and all I remember is getting on a bus, not sure in my child mind where I thought I was heading, but I was determined to find my only real lighthouse in this vast sea of life. I got on that bus with the blind faith of a child who would walk through anything to find the one person who could make me feel protected and loved.

I don't have any memories of what happened after getting on the bus or the moment my mother found me, but by some miracle of God she found me hours later. I remember getting off the bus by myself, wearing a light summer white dress and small leather black shoes with a horizontal strip across the front of my feet. A man standing by the door helped me jump out, and held my hand and suspended me in air as he then placed me on the ground, and there was my mom waiting at the bus station. Her eyes met mine in relief, and she ran towards me and hugged with the desperation of a mother who had lost her heart and suddenly found it again.

I was overjoyed to see my mom. We headed back to the old people's home, and without any explanation, she picked up our few belongings and we hastily left them, too. I was glad I never had to see them again. I had no idea where we were heading next. My mom, it seemed, had become unpredictable, but despite the instability, I felt safe with her.

The next thing I recall, we were taking a bus to another city. My mother bought a sandwich, opened it and gave it all to me. We were on the bus for hours and my mother hadn't eaten. I wish I would have had the capacity as a child to understand that that was all we had, but I was only four. In retrospect, I realize mothers are those imperfect restless angels that God has put on this earth to take care of our souls and, for the most part, God has gifted them with this unbreakable endless love. Because even with broken wings, they'll walk many miles until their last breath to rescue us and encircle us with their love.

We got to a new home...this time, a happy home. I don't remember many details. But it seems that the woman who lived there was friends with my mother. Their children became my friends. I felt loved and embraced by this family. I wish I could remember their names, who they were. But all I know is that I was happy. One day, after a year, my mother said we had to go back to the main city, Guayaquil.

This made me sad. As a child, you can't verbalize your sorrow, you just feel it and I couldn't make sense of all this uncertainty around me. "Mami, por que nos vamos? Nos podemos quedar aqui? Me gusta mucho estas aqui...Please mom!" She didn't even acknowledge my questions. She just continued packing our belongings and we left again.

"Why do we have to go?" I would ask but I never learnt the answer. All I knew was that sense of joy and stability left me again. As a child who did not yet have any consistency, I just wanted to grab those moments of joy and hope and keep them. But it wasn't to be like that- There was just this constant impermanence.

This new change of a home would leave a big mark on my life, in my heart. This next home is where the first chapter or miles of my life ended, where perhaps I got my deepest wounds.

I don't know how my mother met "Mrs Teresa." She and her husband were wealthy and were from Lebanon. They had two daughters and one son, and I became very close to Anita, the youngest one. Anita followed me everywhere and she made me feel that I was closer to her than even her own siblings. She had a brother and a sister, and we used to play Indians and Cowboys. Her brother and sister would team up and be the Cowboys. They were white and had light eyes. So, I naturally gravitated to playing the Indian warrior in this game and, although Anita looked like her family, she would always want to be on my team, which made me feel her unspeakable love and loyalty. I was her protector in every way. In my mind, I was the invincible Indian warrior who would be an emperor one day.

Their father was cold and unapproachable, but Mrs Teresa made up for it with her generosity and friendship with my mother. They had several maids. Julia was one of them, a big curvaceous black woman with a warm heart and there was also Elsa, a light skin Ecuadorian, who was also a close friend of my mother.

My mom had a unique situation, she was the cook, but she was also Mrs Theresa's close friend. I was the daughter of the cook, but I was also integrated in some ways into the family. I didn't go to the same prestigious private school that the other girls went to, but I did attend a really good private Catholic school. Mrs Teresa became informally my godmother. I remember her attending a few parents-teacher meetings at my school and how her elegant confident presence made me dream in those moments that I was also important like her.

My mother never taught me religion, but she showed me a lot about giving. Every day after lunch, she would save leftovers for the homeless. I still remember each homeless person who came to our house. They were not undesirable strangers; they were real people with dignity. No matter how poorly or in rags they were dressed, my mother treated each one with gentleness and respect. I still remember the face of one of the men. He looked beaten down by life, with unkempt hair, dirty clothes, but there was a simple pure kindness all over his face.

I have many difficult but also fond and beautiful memories of my childhood in Ecuador, that small country right on the equator in South America, known primarily for its Galapagos Islands which Darwin made famous in his evolutionary theories.

My mom came from Esmeraldas, which is the urban epicenter of the nation's Afro-Ecuadorian population. Just like Guayaquil, the wet season is hot and oppressive and the dry season is warm and muggy. My mom's mother was of African descent and her father was of European descent. I never met my grandfather as he had died. However, I did have the privilege of meeting my Grandma, Teresa, and my mom's sisters, Elsa and Marlene. They welcomed me with open arms when we went to visit them. They were extremely poor, their house built out of tin on the summit of a steep hill. Its floor was made out of metal and stood on four stakes that kept the home suspended a few feet off the ground. There was a big hole in the living room patched with another light metal to cover it. I was asked to make sure I did not step hard on it as I could fall right through, which did happen once I tried it out for myself one day. Suddenly, I felt my feet break through the metal ground and my body being sucked down forcefully through the hole and I went rolling half way down the hill as my mom ran after me. Suddenly, my body was tossed in an area with branches that brought my body to a complete stop. As always, she picked her exuberant daughter up and walked me back to the house.

My grandmother Teresa was a slim tall black lady. One of my most cherished memories was accompanying her to work. We walked down the hill in extreme heat as she was carrying an oven and two metal chairs on her arms and, at the bottom, we walked along one of Esmeralda's dirt roads where she set up her small oven and baked "maduros" (sweet plantains) for sale. Maduros look like bananas and they are soft and sweet and smell and taste like canela and candy all at once. In Ecuador, they bake them and combine the sweet flavor and cut the maduros in the middle and add cheese to it. The combination of the sweet and salt is a heavenly combination. I sat next to her on a small metal chair and felt so warm being next to this kind and loving woman. I waited patiently for her to give me my "maduros" as she knew how much I loved them. And I still do.

In Guayaquil, I slept with my mom in her bed every night when we returned to Mrs. Theresa's house. I did not want to sleep in my own bed. I was not only her child and very attached to her but also not an easy child. I was hyper, constantly getting myself in some sort of trouble. One time the school called my mom because I fell off a monkey bar, not from trying to hang from the bars, but for trying to walk on top of the bars and then landing to the ground. I remember observing the other kids trying to hold on to the bars, but that seemed a bit too easy, so I had to take it to a whole new level. Another time, I was walking, unaware that I was under a kid who was coming down the zig zag bar and he fell right on my head. I was unconscious and in the hospital for days. These are some of the most extreme examples of distress my mother had to endure because of me. I also recall going to a beach and my running towards the water and suddenly I was floating deep in the water, not able to breathe, just floating, not sure for how long, until I felt a hand grab me and pull me out of the water and there I saw, as usual, my mother's face ready to rescue her child. This is perhaps the reason why, as an adult, I never stopped being terrified of swimming and the open water.

My childlike restlessness and defiance against any kind of structure tested the limits of my mother's patience. When I was 5 years old, I was put in a classroom with a lot of children on my first day of school. I sat in the back, next to a window, as the teacher tried to teach us some basic drawing skills. I became bored, almost annoyed, and started pulling another girl's hair. The teacher brought me to the front of the classroom to teach me a lesson and she asked me some questions to test my knowledge. I was not a bit afraid- I answered her defiantly as I kept wondering, "Why are we trapped in these closed rooms just sitting, not doing anything useful?"

Then I went back to my desk and sat next to the window in the back and told the teacher, "My mom is right outside waving at me and asking me to step out." She looked at me confused, hesitated, but proceeded to dismiss me. To this day, I don't know why she believed me. I stepped out of the classroom, left the school and wandered around the streets alone, at 5 years old. To my surprise, while I was wandering around, just a few blocks away from the school and close to our home, I suddenly ran into my mom! She was on the other side of the street. Her eyes locked with mine and they were filled with the fury of a lioness, and some of that fury was based in fear and distress. She crossed the street hastily, grabbed me roughly with both of her hands and then I heard her raspy exhausted voice desperately screaming, "Stop!!! Whatever you are doing, you have to stop! DO YOU HEAR ME? STOP!!!" Although I was a child, I understood what my mom was trying to tell me. I was restless, I pushed limits and I wanted no rules, but I didn't understand why I was that way. This was the only time that I remember my mother punishing me physically. I never did anything like that again.

But even so, there are no eloquent words to describe how I loved my mother, the rituals we shared. Throughout the years, she picked me up from school every day. As the nuns lined us up in front of the big, tall wooden school door, I tried to be first in the line as I wanted to get out and run to hug my mom. My mom was always in front as well, waiting with arms wide open. She would lift me up, hug and kiss me, I was her most beloved treasure and I felt invincible because of it.

Life in Mrs. Teresa's home seemed both normal and abnormal to me as a child. Not that I intellectually understood that. But things were strange. We never had friends. We were told not to interact with anyone in the neighborhood. My only friends were Mrs. Teresa's children, mostly Anita.

Every morning we had a chauffeur drive us to school in a green Mercedez Benz. We never took a school bus. To get ready for school, Julia, the voluptuous black maid who always dressed in a white uniform, would comb my hair into a couple of super tight ponytails and either my mom or she would get me into my school uniform. The chauffeur who drove us would drop the girls and me at our different schools.

At my school, we were asked to attend mass and obey the nuns. I remember having one teacher who was not a nun, not even a Catholic, and I liked her very much. I was not fond of the nuns, so it was refreshing having someone different. I also liked school because I was good in sports. I was involved in basketball and I know this because that is one of the very few pictures I have of my childhood- playing in a girls' basketball team.

Day after day my mom would pick me up from school and, when we got home, my mom would give me some hot vegetable soup, which I disliked intensely. She made me sit in the dining room until I finished eating everything. For a Latin family, it is considered rude to leave anything on the plate. When it came to school, right after supper, I had to do my homework first. When finished, my mom would then test me sternly on the material. I remember one time we were sitting side by side on the stairs as I silently begged God to please spare my mom's disappointment and to send me the right answers.

In Mrs. Teresa's home, there was an interesting dynamic. Her silent husband was very unapproachable. All I knew was that he was supposed to be rich and powerful. One time in the middle of the night, we all got up because we heard noises on the roof, and I remember Mr. Mauricio walking around with a gun trying to gauge where the perpetrators were. It wasn't until years later that I found out why our life wasn't ordinary. After I was long gone, I found out that he was shot while entering the garage to get into his Mercedes Benz, the same Mercedes Benz that drove us each day to school. The rumor was that he was involved in some dubious business and perhaps this is where all the money came from. This is conceivably the reason why I felt we were isolated from others. But I do not know any of this for a fact.

One day I came back from school and I was sitting in the dining room trying to finish the unpleasant soup when I saw my mom approaching me. Suddenly, as she came towards me, she fell to her knees and held her head, bowing down to the floor, "I can't see...I can't see." There was something wrong. I froze. I was 9 years old and I had never seen my mom this sick. I knew she often experienced headaches and took pain killers a lot, but nothing like this. The other maids and friends of my mother, Elsa and Julia, ran towards her and helped get her into bed. I told myself, "Mrs. Teresa will come home and make it all go away." But Mrs. Teresa came home too late that night to check on my mother.

The next morning, I woke up next to my mom, her back towards me. She was sound asleep. As I was moving carefully to get out of bed and get ready for school, she woke up and turned towards me, her face close to mine and all I saw were those beautiful and sad hazel eyes that revealed something more than the words she whispered to me, "Mijita, que Dios la bendiga..." Then she immediately went back to sleep.

I went to school that day and then the bell rang for us to go home. As usual, I tried to be at the front of the line as we left. The school doors opened, and I didn't see my mom as, one by one, the kids around me ran to their parents. I anxiously kept searching for her. Then I saw her, ran towards her and I hugged her so hard. Unexpectedly, I felt her shaking me and telling me, "Little girl, I'm not your mother." I looked up at this woman's face and saw she was not my mom. I still cannot explain this event. I felt very confused, stunned.

Time went by and all the school kids had gone, and I sat on the sidewalk alone waiting for hours. I was afraid, almost paralyzed, and never moved, not even an inch, from that sidewalk and sat there silently with my arms around my legs until it must have been around 5pm. Then I saw a cab quickly driving towards me; it was my mom's sister, Marlene. I had met her before. She lived in Esmeraldas and there she was, a familiar face, someone I was fond of. But as soon as I saw her, I also saw tears in her eyes and, as I got in the cab, she asked me as if she was swallowing her pain, "Si algo le pasara a tu mama. Con quien quisieras vivir?" ("If something happened to your mom, whom would you want to live with?") I didn't answer. I had no idea what this all meant. I was only 9 years of age and I felt lost and breathless as if someone had thrown me into the middle of an overwhelming and unforgiving ocean, the waves pulsing over my young body.

Chapter 2.

Leaving it all behind

My aunt took me back to Mrs. Theresa's home. That whole week while my mom was in a coma in the hospital, I was in a daze. One day during school recess, I was sitting by myself lost in a bottomless, unmoored state of mind, when I heard a nun call my name, "Veronica, Veronica…. Veronica!!!" I didn't answer. It was as if I was listening to a voice that was coming from far away. I couldn't connect her voice to my inner reality.

Suddenly, the nun came hastily towards me and shook my body as if she was trying to wake me up from a horrible dream. She stared at me with concern and, with a softer voice, said, "It is time to go back to class." I didn't answer, but followed her anyway. I heard the other children whispering about my mother, Victoria. They must have known she was dying. They were more aware of the reality of her death than I was. I believe the nuns must have cautioned them about my state of mind. I remember feeling isolated, disconnected from myself and from everyone. I wanted to be left alone to sink into the depth of my inner world.

One afternoon as I came home from school, I was sitting by myself at the dining table eating the soup one of the maids had made for me; the same dining table my mother used to serve me soup and plead for me to eat. The environment around me was quiet, solemn. Then, unexpectedly, the phone rang loudly in the living room, a loud siren warning of danger that is to come. Elsa rushed to the phone to answer it and all I could hear from the living room was her cry, "Victoria died, Victoria died."

That was the sound of the end of something I couldn't make sense of in my head. Everyone around me started to cry and scream profusely. I began to cry because everyone else did, not because I knew what it meant, not because I felt anything. I was devoid of any emotions, but at the same time, I could feel the weight of a life that I didn't want crushing in on me.

The days after are just an impassive ambiguous memory. A couple of weeks later, my paternal grandmother, Maria, showed up. "Te recuerdas de mi mijita? Soy tu abuela. Queria llevarte a comer un helado. Te traigo luego." ("Do you remember me? I am your Grandma. I came to invite you for some ice cream. I will bring you right back.") I looked at her with suspicion and I said, "Yo no quiero ir. Yo me quiero quedar aqui!" ("No. I don't want to go...I want to stay here.") I barely remembered her, but she was part of that past in a box that I had closed since the day my mom and I left her home when I was four.

Even though I did not know why my mother decided to take me away from them, I had some warm memories of being surrounded by my father's family. We all lived in my Grandma's home as there seems to be a custom in Latin American families for sons and daughters to live with their parents even after they get married. You can have even three generations living in the same home. There can be something beautiful about this tradition as the connectedness we feel to our loved ones can make us unfamiliar with the isolation of the soul. I feel people need this. In my experience, the loneliness and lack of deep connections one experiences in the most dominant nations of this world are often replaced with technology, loveless relationships or destructive behavior.

However, because I declined my Grandma's first request to take me for an ice cream, she quickly manufactured another idea and, with an exerted effort to sound enthusiastic, she said, "Let's go and get a banana shake. You love banana shakes! I promise I will bring you right back." I remember feeling that my world was hanging on by a thread; nothing felt safe. I began to feel breathless again and I asked her one more time, "Banana shake?" I wavered because a banana shake was my favorite drink.

"But you will bring me right back, yes?"

"Yes, I will bring you right back," Grandma said.

But she never took me to get the shake, instead she took me straight to her home with only the clothes on my back. That was the last time I ever saw anyone from my past, especially Anita who was my best childhood friend or any relative on my mother's side. Later in life, I found out my Grandma didn't want me to stay connected to anyone from that past and blocked them from coming into my life. I forgave her for this because, although it is painful to remember how my past was so suddenly and painfully erased and I had to become intimately acquainted with so many deep losses, I knew that Grandma in her own mind, was just trying to protect me.

She and I returned to the same home my mom and I left when I was four. When I walked in, my two younger uncles were in the living room doing homework on the long dining table. They looked up and my eyes met theirs, but they immediately put their heads back down to continue with their school assignment. They never said a word to me.

Somehow, I resigned myself to this new chapter of my life and never looked back until 38 years later when I returned to Ecuador right after Grandma's death.

The years following my arrival at Grandma's home were full of happy moments and some erratic ones. For the most part, I was a cheerful young person. I became close to my family and Grandma was the pillar of this home. I looked up to my uncles, who studied a lot, were athletic, and handsome. Often women were after them, and I felt proud of them. I wanted to be like them. My aunt was like an older, distant sister as she was in her own world and got married very young.

My Grandma mostly reigned with an iron fist. Make no mistake, if I didn't get the grades that she expected of me, I would get a beating so hard that at times I thought there was something terribly wrong with her. As an adult, I understood that that was all she knew. She did the best she could with the difficult life that had been allotted to her. One day, I must have been around 12, she told me about herself, while she was cooking.

"When I was born," she said, "I was abandoned by my mother." I was surprised since my grandmother didn't show vulnerability very often. I could tell this story was important to her, so I listened attentively. As she sat down, I held her hand as she continued her story. "My mother was a young beautiful woman who came from a very wealthy family. They were real estate moguls in the capital, Quito. My mother got involved with my father who was from the main city, Guayaquil, a poor uneducated dark skin man. No one of that status would have wanted their daughters to get involved with someone like him. Her family gave her an ultimatum. If she stayed with that meager despicable man, as they called him, my mother would lose her family and therefore her inheritance. My mother decided to leave me behind with a resentful father and never looked back."

When she grew older, my Grandma looked for her mother with the hope that she would discover a different reason, perhaps her mother didn't really want to leave her. The truth is that her mother never looked for her. As my grandmother used to tell me in her old age, "Why would she abandon me? Why would a mother abandon her child?" I wish I could have taken some of this pain away from her; she never really got over this. Even as she was dying and I held her hand, she called out her mom's name. It was so sad to me. I don't understand why so many of us humans are deprived of that saving grace and love that we need to feel whole.

My happiest and most cherished memories were my time in school and with my classmates whom, for the most part, lived in my neighborhood. My neighbors were like my extended family. We took care of one another and this sense of community, this sense of belonging, is what I long for even now. If I was ever hungry and I felt like going to my neighbor across the street, I would just walk in and ask, "Are you about to have lunch?" and they would answer, "Yes, come and join us." Even the streets were narrow and picturesque, as if they invited a sense of closeness and connectedness. If something happened to someone in the neighborhood, it was as if it happened to all of us in the neighborhood. We took care of one another, there wasn't a lot that divided us. I had many friends and cousins I grew up with during that time who are still dear to me.

One of the most unforgettable and fun traditions of my childhood was the New Years Eve celebration or Ano Viejo. For weeks leading to this celebration, each family in the neighborhood made a big "Ano Nuevo" doll or dummy as a personification of the old year. The dummy is constructed with rags and old newspapers personifying a cartoon character, superhero or a political figure and is set on a chair for weeks outside each family home . As you walk through the neighborhood, you see all the colorful masks and monigotes lined along the sidewalk. In New Year's Eve as the clock approaches midnight, each family starts to bring their "Ano Viejo" doll to the middle of the street-all the dolls in the neighborhood are linked up as each family prepares the kerosene and fire right before midnight. Then 10 seconds before midnight, all of the community stands in the middle of the street close to each of their dummies and we start to count together out loud, "10, 9, 8, 7, 6, 5, 4, 3, 2, 1." And just like that we left the old year behind and we saw the fire take away what now belonged to the past.

"WOW. FELIZ ANO NUEVO!" Everyone in the neighbor screams with joy as we all start hugging each other. It is a full celebration, families embracing, as we watch the dummies being burnt past midnight. I loved to feel the warmth of the fire in the streets, the closeness and love among all of us and the noise of laughing voices, music and then the smell of the food. Each family prepared a special meal that we could all share with one another. There was no need to ask for permission, we all visited each other's homes to taste the delicious meals.

Playing outside with my neighbors and school friends was an exhilarating ritual. Across the street was Jessica whose father taught science at the school we all attended. Her mother was a proper and strict lady. Then, there was a handsome young guy we called 'the Martian' because his head was too big. Next was my dear cousin Patricia, whom I was closest to, and her sisters Anita and little Alexandra. There were other kids on the block we would play with on the weekends. We'd roller skate, making a line and following one another for blocks. We would hold hands and try all different kinds of maneuvers. We also cycled a lot, and this is where we got even more creative. We would put a big stone in the middle of the road and place a wooden tablet on top so that we could ride our bikes fast on top of it and jump with our bikes, our bodies suspended in the air, curious to see how far up we could go. One day I fell so hard on the pavement that the metal of my bike seat penetrated the skin on my leg. I could see I was badly hurt. I went home and hid the wound because I knew that if I told my Grandma that I did something really stupid and put myself at risk, she might be so upset at my recklessness that she would beat me some more. Quietly, I washed it with soap to get rid of any debris and saw something white inside my cut which made me nervous but, luckily, eventually it healed on its own.

When any of us crossed the line, corporal punishment seemed to be how Grandma chose to discipline us and I understand why. She was only 15 years old when she had her first child, my father. She had 6 children overall, five of them men, with whom she had to learn to use an iron fist to keep them on a straight and narrow path. Her husband died young, in his early 30s, and she had to raise all her children on her own. She was tough on me too, at first, but as the years went by, she became more affectionate and sacrificed herself in many ways so that I could achieve things she and I could be proud of. She wanted me to finish a college degree, knowing that would be the best legacy she could leave me. She fought for me and would do the unthinkable to make sure I could have it all.

Education was extremely important to her and she would not compromise on this. "Do you know I never had the opportunity to go to school?" my Grandma once told me. "After my mother abandoned me, my father didn't really want me so my Grandma, Petra, tried to take care of me. But we were very poor. My father was physically abusive, bitter and resentful about the woman who left him. I guess I looked like her and he turned against me. He put me to work at a very young age, I must have been 6, and I was selling vapor rub in the streets."

Vapor Rub is a big deal in Latin American countries. It is used to heal pretty much any illness- headaches, colds, muscle pain, and even heartbreak! Vapor Rub seemed to be the answer for anything!

"Eventually, a wealthy woman who saw me in the street selling asked my grandmother, Petra, if I could work for her and do chores around the house, that it would be a lot safer for me to work for her than be in the streets. My Grandma agreed to let me go but always visited me and watched over me."

Then my Grandma told me one of her most fascinating stories and I understood why I never wanted to take the opportunities life gave me for granted. She noticed that the young children in the house she worked for were learning reading and math. They had a teacher who showed up at their home to give them daily lessons in the living room. Grandma continued, "I wasn't allowed to participate, I was just the little maid." But she had an indomitable desire to learn, to be educated, even at a young age. "I must have been about 6 by then and I figured out the exact time this teacher came to teach the daily math and reading lessons. I made sure I finished my chores in time. I milked the cows early so that before the wealthy children would show up in the living room for their lessons, I would be hiding behind the curtains. And there behind those curtains, I would listen to the instructor teach these children how to count. 1, 2, 3, 4. I could feel myself breathing as I was trying to repeat the numbers in my head. And now the alphabet, A, B, C.D. I couldn't see, but I tried to imagine what these letters looked like and later I would look at their books when no one was watching."

My life in school became the focus and joy of my younger years. In Ecuador, you have to choose a concentration in 6th grade. Mine was math and physics. I was good at them. In fact, my classmates who lived in my neighborhood got together every evening after school to work out physics and math problems. I remember this being a fun time for us. Physics was interesting; it explained the world around me in a logical way. I had an incredible physics teacher whose energy in the class made us want to sit down and listen. Math was not about emotions, either; it was about pure logic that no one could dispute. You just had to figure out the answer to every problem. I imagined that if we looked at life this way that there would always be an answer, you would just have to simplify the question and work it out, till you got the answer.

I was also involved in sports. It gave me purpose and confidence. I was part of the pentathlon team in school and trained religiously to compete nationally. Before school started every day, I had to be up earlier to train with the team. We would run up the hill for an hour; my forte was disk and javelin. This is where I was supposed to rank number one in the nation. I was never the fastest runner but performed relatively well in relays and long jumps. I recollect the feeling I had when I was competing, and the stadium full of students cheering for us. Hearing the excitement and ovation was magical.

I trained all year to compete in the national games. Everyone knew I was up for the first place in disk and javelin. Everything seemed to be going as planned, we were a couple of weeks away from the big games. My coaches could already smell the victory. My school, Colegio Nacional Guayaquil, prided itself for its athletes. Our school running track was where we usually practiced, but as we got closer to a race, my team would practice in a huge coliseum where the games were to be held.

One day after I came back from school, my grandmother proceeded to give me the big news, "We are going to the United States." I was fourteen. I wasn't excited about the news and I asked her, "When is this supposed to happen? I have a national race soon!"

Her reply was, "We are leaving in 2 weeks!"

That was right before the major national sports competition that I had trained for all year, the one I was supposed to win! "Grandma, I don't want to leave before then. I worked so hard!"

She didn't listen and didn't seem to care. I don't think Grandma valued sports. For her it was just a past-time. The following day in school I gave the coaches the news, and they became worried, and decided to speak to Grandma. The male coach must have been in his 30s. He was big, brown and tall, and the other coach was a woman, short and brown with curly hair. I sat there listening to them as they tried to help Grandma understand the importance of this event. "Veronica is the best in this category. She is going to win the nationals. We have trained so hard to make sure she is ready! Can you postpone the trip until after the national competition?"

She looked at them uninterested in what they had to say, resistant to changing her mind. My coaches left my home very discouraged and embraced me goodbye. That was the last time I saw them. All I remember is, that a week or two after, I took a plane with Grandma to come to the United States, to live with my father.

Chapter 3.

Miami and a Foster Home

A pink flamingo and a big sign greeted us, "Welcome to Miami." I had not been prepared for anything about my father's life or what we were getting into. It turned out he had a little girl of about 4 years old with his new wife! The first time we were both having a Coca-Cola, she threw a temper tantrum because she didn't want her soda, she wanted what I was having, so our dad and her mom took away the soda I was drinking – to give it to her. She never stopped after that, whatever I was having, she just had to cry for her parents to take it away from me.

My stepmom was cold to me from the beginning, however, I learned later in life that she did not even know I existed until a few weeks before I moved in with her and my father. The only words she ever directed toward me was to give me orders. She hardly ever smiled. There seemed to be a problem about whatever I did or said, and Grandma was caught in the middle, trying to keep the peace.

At that time my father lived in a town called Opalocka, mostly inhabited by African Americans and Latinos. The community seemed isolated; a bit run down. The streets felt much wider than what I was used to. No one walked, everyone drove. I felt as if someone had transplanted me to a physical world of steel and ugliness. The neighborhood seemed to have no life, no spirit. My father had bought me a small bike as a welcome gift, and I decided to immediately take it outside. I wanted to feel normal; In Ecuador, I often rode my bike everywhere with my friends but now I was alone. I couldn't wait to feel the breeze around me and imagine myself back in my little neighborhood where I came from. Suddenly, I heard my father screaming, "What are you doing?!!! Come back NOW! You do not ride in this neighborhood whenever you want! It is dangerous!" My young spirit felt an isolation of the soul that I had not experienced before. I couldn't just go anywhere, and I had no friends.

My father worked a lot, arriving late in the evenings. He used to drive a truck and deliver goods outside of the city or even the state. One time after I came home from school, my stepmom asked the neighbor, a loud Cuban lady who came with her husband in the Mariel, if she could look out for me while she ran some errands. They had a 9 year -old son who acted too low brow for his age. My stepmom walked me to their doorstep and walked away. This neighbor and the little boy and his father were watching something on TV and, as I looked their way, the father didn't hesitate to tell me they were watching pornography and gestured for me to join them. I had no idea what pornography was; I was too young to fully understand the wrongness of the situation, but I felt it and refused to step inside. She kept asking me and finally I articulated as firmly as I could that I was not going to go inside and, if they insisted, I would tell my father and that I was going to wait for my stepmom outside their door. They let me go.

My stepmom came back pretty soon, and I shared the incident with her and my father. I believe that was the one reason why we moved out of this neighborhood soon after.

We moved to Hialeah where there was a large Latino community, particularly Cubans. Everywhere I went, it seemed that the main language spoken was Spanish, but Cubans have a different accent, a different way of speaking – at times a lot louder and rougher than what I was used to. I would often wonder if they were upset. Eventually, after making some great Cuban friends in school, I learned about their history, particularly about the Cuban exile where many left the island to escape Castro's regime, and I understood them a lot more.

As an example, the Mariel boat lift of the 1980s is a time that marked their history. The pre-Mariel group consisted of the mostly middle and upper classes of the island who fled due to fear of retaliation after the communist takeover led by Fidel Castro in the late 1950's. Their group was seeking political asylum. The second group consisted of those people who left Cuba during and after the period of the Mariel boat lift and these people were and are economic migrants. Miami became the home of this nostalgic group of people who loved their island but could no longer go back. In fact, one of my Grandma's closest and perhaps her only friend in Miami was a Cuban woman named Hilda. Hilda and her husband were two of the kindest people I met there. She often looked out for Grandma even until my Grandma's final days in Miami.

I went to a Junior high school in Hialeah. A lot of the students were Latin, there were Americans as well, but they would not make any effort to interact with us foreigners. In fact, you could see the different ethnic groups segregated. Those of us who were immigrants and didn't speak the language made an effort to stick together.

I had a wonderful ESL teacher, Mrs. Velasquez. I had to do a lot of studying on my own; every assignment I had to translate word for word. So, what would normally take someone an hour or two to study would take me twice as much time with all the translation involved, and then I had to make sense of the lecture and finally memorize the words in English so that I could answer the test questions. I became the top student in her class which I knew because she always placed the names of the top 5 students on a board in the classroom. I used to study with the same discipline that I had when I was in Ecuador. I wouldn't have done it any other way; this was all I knew.

I had been in Miami for about 4 months when the situation at home with my father and his wife became worse. We lived in a small two-bedroom apartment in an apartment complex filled with Latinos, particularly Cubans and Caribbeans. I didn't have any friends in the complex. I shared the second bedroom with my Grandma. The main bedroom was for my dad, his wife and their little daughter, who must have been five years old by then.

My father never hugged me or talked with me as I saw other fathers do with their children. I never heard the word love from my father's mouth or even a compliment. He often looked tired; all he did was work. He had a terrifying personality, and I would make mistakes because he made me feel nervous. He also treated his wife this way, as well. And when it came to school, he would often sit down to test me on the homework. He tried to teach me English with his thick Spanish accent, which I now blame as the reason why I never got rid of mine. I was utterly frozen when he taught me how to drive, God forbid I didn't follow the rules perfectly. Every time we hit a STOP sign, "You must count 5 seconds before you can move." I'd move the car and then I would hear a scream, "STOP! THOSE WERE NOT 5 SECONDS!" He reigned like a dictator.

Calling him "Daddy" was something I could not do. I called him by his name, Adolfo. A pretty despicable name. I never thought about how this would affect a father whose daughter had been taken from him at an early age and, when he finally got her again, she coldly treated him as a stranger. From what I know, he never stopped providing for me. He went to the States right after mom and I left him when I was four and worked hard to send money to Ecuador to provide for those left behind. But the child I was could not see the complex and broken father in front of me whom, I must admit, tried in some ways.

Sadly, he was also irrational. One afternoon after I had come home from school, around 2pm, I had finished having lunch and I went to the bathroom in the hall to brush my teeth. Suddenly, the door opened abruptly with an overbearing force, and immediately I felt my father grab my hair and my body and he started to hit me. I fell to the floor. I could smell alcohol on his breath as he yelled curse words. I shouted back with all my force, "Leave me alone! Don't hit me! Leave me alone!"

My father continued to hit me as he screamed, "Why do you have to be disrespectful to my wife?"

"I wasn't. I didn't do anything!!!! Stop!" But this wounded being kept hitting me and I could see the pain in his eyes, the pain of someone who doesn't know what else to do but to attack. I believe it was my Grandma who intervened while his wife just looked on, devoid of any emotions, devoid of any love.

After this incident, I felt more disconnected - to the place, to them, to the world around me, except for my school which was my only refuge. One day when I came home from school, my father started with me again – to this day I can't remember why- but this time I fought back, "This is the last time you are going to hit me! This is the last time...!" And I grabbed a table and threw it at him. I cannot explain how it feels to be beaten

38

violently, especially by someone who is supposed to love you with the tenderness of a father. In spite of the prior events in my childhood, I had always been a happy young girl, but now I felt myself withering away. I didn't want to live.

I left their home when they were not looking and turned myself into social services. I think I knew about this because I had spoken to one of my classmates about the treatment I was receiving at home and she informed me that this was a place I could go to for help. After I went to this government agency, they kept me there and took me to a foster home. All I took with me were the clothes I had on and my schoolbooks. Interestingly, running away seemed to be all I knew how to do to survive. Perhaps I learned it from my mother.

I was now under the government's jurisdiction.

The foster home was located far from where I used to live with my father. It probably took me 15 minutes by car to make it to school when I lived with him, but now, it took me three hours. I was in a different side of town and, for those who remember Miami then, public transportation was nothing like New York. You had to wait an hour or so for a bus. I had to take 2 to 3 buses to make it to my school. I didn't want to change school locations as I loved my school, particularly my teacher and my classmates, mainly those few Cuban girls I was close to. I had become close friends with some Dominican and Colombian girls, as well. We would go to lunch together, laugh, and have conversations about our lives. The foster care mom, where I was placed, treated me with respect and care, yet I remember keeping a distance from her and most people there initially.

I had to inform Mrs. Velazquez why I was arriving close to 2 to 3 hours late to school. Her eyes got teary and she made an extra effort to help me make up for lost class time and assignments. She would tell me what I missed, what pages I needed to read to catch up and, somehow, I managed to keep my grades up.

Several kids in Mrs. Velazquez's class loved to joke around a lot, wouldn't finish their assignments and just didn't seem to care as much about school so one day she stood up in front of the class and said, "Why can't you take class seriously! While some of you have so much, your parents' support, a home, there are others who have to sacrifice so much just to be here." She was emotional and looked as if she was about to cry. After class, she asked me to stay, "How are you doing?" I gave her an update on my situation and then she told me, "I have a gift for you." I didn't know what to say. I remained quiet. "It is a bible. It is for you, Veronica. I want you to have it." She wrote something on the first page, "May you always know how much God loves you. Love, Mrs. Velasquez."

I took this bible with me to the foster home and, after finishing my school assignments, I began to read it each day. I remember getting to Psalms 23: "The Lord is my shepherd; I shall not want more. He leadeth me to green pastures…." I began to feel that perhaps there was this powerful benevolent presence somewhere out there. This feeling of peace that came every time I read became my solace. So, I read dutifully each day after school and the girls at the foster home began to notice.

There were two white girls, two black girls, one Puerto Rican girl and myself at the foster home; all around my age. The two black girls, I wish I could remember their names, had their hair pulled back in a ponytail and wore these simple beautiful dresses. I remember them almost as if I were watching a movie from the 60s. I heard that one of the black girls was there for getting into a violent fight with her sister that almost took her sister's life. I don't know how much of that was true as I only experienced her as innocent and kind. The only other information I had on the rest was that the white girls, who were both tall and blonde, were there because of drug use. The Puerto Rican girl never said a word to me or interacted with anyone in the house. She was pretty, and all I heard is that she had problems with her stepmom just like me. She was the oldest of all of us, independent and confident, and hardly ever there. The ones who were the warmest and kindest to me were the two young black girls. The two white girls, attempting to have some fun, on one occasion, grabbed me and threw me on the floor. One of them held me down on the floor on my tummy as the other one took a lighter and then sprayed it with hair spray and all I saw were flames coming towards my bottom and I screamed. They seemed to take great pleasure in seeing me scared.

Mrs. Velasquez invited me to attend her Lutheran church on Sundays where her husband was a minister. The services were more animated than I was used to when I attended Catholic services as a young girl in Ecuador. Everyone was so warm, and Mrs. Velasquez made sure to introduce me to everyone. She was a sophisticated beautiful Cuban lady, with light blue eyes and the most charming personality. One day after the services, while I was waiting for her in her car as she said goodbye to people in the congregation, I had a few minutes by myself so I put my head down and attempted to say my first prayer ever, "God, if you are somewhere, please help me find you."

When I said that prayer, my young self felt this overpowering peace surrounding me. My teacher then got into the car and took me back to the foster home.

One afternoon, when I was reading the bible sitting on the bottom of a bunk bed in my bedroom which I shared with the other Hispanic girl, the black girls came in and asked, "What are you reading?" I looked at them amiably as they seemed very interested, "I am reading from the bible." They stared at me for a few seconds and then eagerly asked, "Could you read to us?" "Of course!" I was happy to have company. After that day, I would come from school and sit on the chair next to the long wooden dining table where I always did my homework and they sat on the floor and listened attentively to my oration of the bible passages. Particularly, I remember reading to them from Psalm 23. As I read, I saw them looking at me intensely with tears in their eyes, perhaps because despite the uneasy journey they'd had to travel in life, this gave them hope. In those few moments, each of us held to hope so tightly and we were no longer afraid.

"The Lord is my shepherd; I shall not want. He maketh me to lie down in green pastures: he leadeth me beside the still waters. He restoreth my soul: he leadeth me in the paths of righteousness for his name's sake. Yea, though I walk through the valley of the shadow of death, I will fear no evil: for Thou art with me…Surely goodness and mercy shall follow me all the days of my life…"

I would repeat this again and again in my head, "Surely goodness and mercy will follow me all the days of my life."

Day by day, the foster girls stood on the grass waiting anxiously for me to get home. When they saw the bus arriving at the usual time, they would start shouting, "THE PREACHER IS COMING. THE PREACHER IS COMING!!!"

Even though I was young, I felt that I had this assignment to share God. Not that I had any exclusive rights to Him, but I was eager to help them see that we could free ourselves from the illusion that we were helpless and alone. It was like when the Israelites were asked to cross the Red Sea and escape the afflictions of Egypt. We too were called to plant a seed of faith within ourselves and witness the Red Seas in our lives open miraculously so that we could leave our struggles behind. This powerful God who could open the Red Sea was all we had and that was enough.

After a month, my father showed up at the foster home. He seemed defeated and humble in a way I had not seen. He said to me, "It is time to leave this place. You don't need to be here. You have a family. Please come back home."

I was standing on the other side of the metal fence inside the property. His voice started to crack. This was one of the first times I knew my father cared about me.

The next time my father and I saw each other, we were in front of a judge stating our case. He was standing on one side and I was on the other. The judge looked at me and asked me to speak, "I just want to do well in school. I don't drink, I don't smoke. I don't want any trouble. It is hard to live with my father." I was comfortable speaking in front of people, advocating for myself. Perhaps it was because I grew up seeing my mom never be afraid of anything.

My father was on the other side standing behind the podium, tired, his spirit beaten, which a young person like me could not understand. He could barely talk. Then the judge's stern gaze turned to my father, "You should be ashamed of yourself," he uttered. "You have this daughter who is a straight A student- she doesn't drink or smoke – all she wants is to be a good student and you haven't been the father you ought to be for her."

My father was silent, an air of desolation around him. The judge then turned to me and asked, "What do you want to do, young lady? Do you want to be adopted by a family or would you like to go back to Ecuador?"

My father desperately looked my way from his wooden podium. He still had his truck driver khaki uniform on. He seemed worn out, the bags under his eyes showed the sleepless nights he must have had, and he spoke faintly, "Don't let anyone adopt you. You have a family. Go back to Ecuador."

His words touched me. I listened to him reluctantly and told the judge, "I want to go back to Ecuador."

I was reminded of a bible verse that says, "Honor your mother and father, so that you may live long in the land." Despite the chaos, the sadness and difficulties, there was a deeply rooted part in me that felt that in some ways my father might know better.

After 6 months in Miami, I was ordered by the court to go back to my country. My Grandma stayed behind for a bit so that she could work and save money to eventually bring me back to the States.

Once I returned, I was to find those few months in the US had changed me. It took me a few months to re-integrate into my old school. I was a year behind because of the transition I had gone through, so I had new teammates. It is interesting that even a few months away from my motherland left an indelible footprint that fragmented my spirit. When you are made to leave the only life you know and you are planted in a new unfamiliar environment, you are forced to become an outsider. I no longer connected with my own people in the same way because I had tried so hard to connect with others who were indifferent to me, who could not see me, to whom I was invisible because I did not look like or talk like them. But after a few months, I eventually once again felt the natural warmth of friendship of my people and fit in with my life there and made friends that would last a lifetime.

Chapter 4.

The Mormons

I returned with a determination to continue my search for God. I kept on praying, reading, and visiting several religious denominations with an inexpressible yearning to find answers. One day as I was walking back from one Evangelical church where I stood in the back and got chastised for wearing pants, I saw two tall American women on the street and it reminded me of my time in the US, so I said "hello" and they immediately came toward me. "Hi, my name is Sister Thompson and this is Sister Patten. We are Mormon missionaries and we have an important message to share with you." They had very strong American accents in Spanish. I politely listened and then, as I was about to walk away and head home, they asked me if they could share a message with my family and me. I hesitated for a second as I didn't know how my Grandma would react, but I invited them to follow me anyway. Grandma saw me walking in with them and looked a bit skeptical, but I had a way of making things seem normal by sounding confident. I explained," They'll just be here for a few minutes to share a message from God. They come from far away, so I am going to listen." She looked serious but didn't answer, which I considered a form of approval, so I invited them to sit down.

–The two Mormon missionaries were 6' feet tall blondes, Sister Thompson from Boise, Idaho and Sister Patten from Santa Monica, California. Neither of them spoke Spanish very well, but Sister Thompson was able to express herself much more than the other one. There was something beautiful about them, as if they had a magnificent air of goodness about them. These were sister Missionaries who had left their regular lives in the US to serve a full time 1 ½ year mission in a foreign country to preach the gospel they believed in. They wore long dresses and sandals, what I now call Jesus sandals, and a name tag that said Sister Thompson or Sister Patten and underneath it read, "The Church of Jesus Christ of Latter-day Saints." They emanated an air of love, virtue and devotion for this message.

At that point in my life I was 14, young, strong willed and filled with this idea that there was a meaningful path out there in life and it was my assignment to find this bigger truth. Therefore, I was eagerly looking for a way that would lead me to God.

The lady missionaries proceeded to open a pamphlet which they used as a guide to the topics they wanted to cover. "We are here to share the true gospel of Jesus Christ." The first discussion, as they called it, was about God the father, his son Jesus Christ and that we are all His children. Immediately after going over our relationship with God, the discussion turned to Joseph Smith's story.

Joseph Smith was the founder of the Church of Jesus Christ of Latter-day Saints or widely known as the Mormon church. The story describes Joseph Smith who lived in Albany, NY in the 1800's with his parents and siblings. When he was 14 years old, he was wrestling with this idea that, if there is only one God, why are there so many different religions that contradict one another, especially if God is not a God of confusion. He attended different religious organizations of the time and became concerned about finding the truth. The missionaries went on to explain that Joseph read James 1:5 from the Bible, "If any of you lack wisdom, you should ask God who gives generously to all without finding fault and it will be given to you."

At that point, I was listening attentively. Strangely I identified with this 14 year- old American boy, who came from this Yankee culture. Somehow, I felt connected to the story. I was breathless; my whole being was immersed in this story. What was going to happen next!

Then a monumental revelation occurred in the story. He decided to test this promise that if you ask God sincerely, He will answer you abundantly. Therefore, Joseph Smith went to a grove of trees, knelt down, and proceeded to ask God, "Which church is true?"

The missionaries explained, at that moment of prayer, Joseph Smith was overcome by a dark force, he couldn't talk or move. He felt that he was about to be destroyed, but he kept fighting.

I was looking at the pictures of Joseph Smith that the missionaries were showing me that went along with the story and I felt like I was watching the most exciting movie. I could almost visualize each event inside my brain. I could hear the sounds of the trees; I could feel his struggle. Then, during this moment of darkness, Joseph Smith suddenly saw a light and, in the midst of this light, two beings floating on air. One introduced the other and said, "This is my beloved son, hear him." God the Father and Jesus Christ appeared to Joseph Smith! One of the key things God told Joseph Smith was that none of those churches were true but that, through him, He was going to restore the only true church of Christ, the same church that Jesus established in the

New Testament. That all the other churches praised God with their lips, but their hearts were far away from Him.

This was it! I felt that my search for God was now over. What more proof do I need than God Himself coming down to tell this young man that this was the only true church!

After that discussion, I felt spiritually awakened as a young person. I wanted to know more. I was excited. I followed the sister missionaries outside Grandma's home and eagerly asked, "When can you come next?"

To which they responded, "How soon would you like us to come back?"

"You can come tomorrow right after I finish school! I will be ready!" I answered without hesitating.

There they were at my door the next afternoon and I welcomed them with some fresh lemonade. They were very thankful as they had been proselyting out in the hot streets all day and they must have been thirsty. Now it was time for the second discussion where they discussed the steps to be redeemed: Faith, repentance, baptism by immersion and the gift of the Holy Ghost. At the end of the second discussion they asked me if I would like to get baptized. I can't remember if I agreed with this hasty invitation to join their church, but I know I didn't resist it either. I think I had more of a desire to keep on going.

I believed it was during this visit that they introduced to me the Book of Mormon, A New Testament of Jesus Christ. The Mormon Church looks at this book as the most-pure form of scripture, particularly because it wasn't translated and altered the way the bible was. It contains the writings of prophets who lived in the American continent from 2000 BC. Mormon was the last prophet who lived in the American continent 400 AD and he kept the records of this civilization in brass or gold plates. These records were buried by his son Moroni in the geographic area of Manchester, NY 400 AD so that they could be preserved and found in the latter days by a prophet whom God would appoint to restore "the only true church of God."

In the early 1820s, after the apparition of God the Father and the Son, Joseph Smith had another heavenly visit, "Angel Moroni." The same prophet who buried these plates in the 400s AD appeared now in the form of an angel in 1823 to lead Joseph to the place where the plates were hidden.

Fascinating! I thought. God himself shows up, angels appear, hidden plates as scripture! Mormons seem to have some monumental truths!

These discussions took place in my Grandma's living room. The missionaries would visit my home around 7:30pm, but had to head back around 9pm as part of their mission rules. My Grandma surprisingly would leave the living room to give us some privacy. I would sit across from them on one of the couches, while they shared the bigger couch facing me. We always started the discussions with a prayer that had a structured format, "Heavenly Father... We Thank Thee.... We ask Thee... In the name of Jesus Christ. Amen."

Then the missionaries would proceed to open their missionary pamphlet. This time, the one they were about to discuss completely left me speechless. It was what they called, "The Plan of Salvation." It answered questions such as, "Where do we come from?" "Why are we here?" and "Where are we going?" When I heard such a detailed explanation to the biggest questions of humankind, I asked myself, How is it that they figured out the biggest mysteries for us all?!

According to the Mormon church, they were given revelation through the prophets that, before we came to this world, we all lived with God as spirits, that we are all His children. Their next concept makes other Christian religions cringe: that

God has a body of flesh and bones but in a glorified exalted state. Therefore, as spirit children, we want to be like Him. This is why God created the Plan of Salvation to send us to this earth to obtain a body, live by faith, repent of any wrongdoing and be obedient to His commandments. It is a journey to exaltation, a journey to become Gods!

Joseph Smith and one of the subsequent prophets of the Latter-day Saint (LDS) church, Lorenzo Snow, stated the following regarding the pathway of God and man, "As man now is, God once was. As God now is, man may be."

The doctrine of making Gods that will rule in other worlds one day is the concept that other Christian churches abhor and see as blasphemous. It is a mystical belief that other denominations seem to have a great level of discomfort with.

Mormons do not seem to be the only ones who have deeply contemplated or believed this idea of exaltation and, even though I was greatly uncomfortable myself with it at the beginning, it started to make more sense as I got deeper into the religion. Becoming Gods was also discussed by C.S. Lewis who is one of the greatest philosophical and religious writers of our times. "It is a serious thing to live in a society of possible gods and goddesses... there are no ordinary people. You have never talked to a mere mortal. Nations, cultures, arts, civilizations- they are mortal, and their life is to ours as the life of a gnat. But it is immortals whom we joke with, work with, marry, snub, and exploit- immortal horrors or everlasting splendors." *C.S. Lewis. The Weight of Glory.*

I personally found this concept captivating, but more so as I got older. The idea that I am immortal and that I am dealing with immortals all the time resonated not because I loved the idea of being a God, as this is a thought that is hard to hold in one's mind, but what I loved was the idea that we have so much potential for infinite goodness.

During the discussion, in regard to this notion of the Pre-existence, the Mormon missionaries taught me that Jesus Christ was anointed from the Pre-existence to atone for our sins. He was chosen to have this assignment to become our Savior because God knew we were going to mess up. This idea of the divinity of Jesus never stopped flowing through my veins.

"This life then became a probationary state, a time to prepare to meet God," as the Book of Mormon states. When we crossed from our pre-existence sphere to this planet called earth, we go through a veil of forgetfulness. We are not supposed to remember our lives before; this is the only way we can learn to live by faith. This is all part of the plan, the perfect plan as explained to me by those missionaries who held up a diagram showing how it was all going to work. My mind was fixated on this astoundingly new profound concept.

After you get baptized and live faithfully for at least a year by following the code of conduct of the church, you can receive a recommendation to enter the Temple. Temple and churches are very different things. It is never that easy to explain the temple, but that is where you perform certain rituals (masonic-like rituals) and covenants that will teach the mysteries and symbols to prepare you to obtain the highest level of the Celestial Kingdom. Here you have the promise that, if you abide by these covenants, you and your loved ones will live in the presence of God forever. Imagine what this could mean to a young person like me who had lost her mother at the age of nine.

That night in bed, I kept reflecting on the sisters' message that death is not the end, and thought "I am going to see my mother Victoria again. I wonder what she will look like. No puedo esperar para darle un abrazo muy fuerte." This idea that we never really lose those we love impressed me deeply and made me feel whole and warm inside.

This is when I learned that Mormons believe that those who follow certain rituals and covenants only found in the Mormon temple, could obtain the right to live with the Heavenly Father and Jesus Christ in the highest degree of the Celestial Kingdom, and become like God and create their own worlds and their own spirit children that they can rule upon. But in order to do this, they must be baptized in the Mormon Church because they are the only ones who possess the Priesthood authority.

"What! Only the Mormons make it to the Celestial Kingdom? What about my friends, the Catholics?" I asked. I had not heard much of Muslims, Hindus or Jews back then, but I would have felt just as badly for them as well! I had many close school friends of different faiths and I was overcome with sadness at the thought of losing them. And I felt anxious for anyone who didn't know this truth, and I now believe this led me to want to proselyte even at a young age and want to share this gospel of exaltation with everyone I knew.

Moreover, Mormons are taught that they have to be worthy to go to the temple so that they can receive endowments (special undergarments that they wear all the time) which is a symbol of the covenants made in the temple. Also, Mormons must get married or sealed for time and all eternity here as a family. This is why it is a big deal for Mormons to marry someone of their same faith. Otherwise, they are giving up on this ideal eternal outcome. Anything outside of this or walking away from these promises will lead Mormons to eternal separation from God and their loved ones. Families are only eternal if they remain rigorously faithful to the religion until the end. It is a huge burden to carry to feel that that you could be void of these promises for eternity. And this burden was to follow me for many years and miles of my life.

One hot summer day in Guayaquil, Ecuador, I was sitting on our front porch feeling the dry heat penetrating my skin, a tranquil reminder that I was in my home country. The porch was surrounded by a cement fence and to the left of the porch there was a tree with red flowers that Grandma had planted. The image is still vivid in my mind. I was waiting outside for the missionaries to come to my place to teach me another lesson. Sister Thompson and her companion approached the front porch at the usual time with their glorious smiles, "Hola! Como esta Veronica?" I was as usual happy to see them, "Good to see you hermanas. Come in!" The lesson that day was a bit different than the rest, they were coming to share about the Authorities of the LDS church and why one must obey and follow their counsel.

As Sister Thompson and her companion were showing me a pamphlet with a picture of the current Prophet of the church, Spencer W Kimball, and his twelve apostles all dressed in a white shirt, a tie, and black suits, I stared at the picture and something disturbed me. I thought, why are all these men white? Why am I to subject myself to these white Americans? But I wouldn't dare say that out loud. I think that was the first time that I was ever completely silent! They must have noticed my reaction and asked, "What's wrong?" All I could make myself say was, "They are all Americans!" Their answer was, "They are the men whom God chose to lead His church and all humanity."

I could feel my whole body resisting the idea that God would only choose a group of old white men from the US to lead all humanity! It felt like colonialism. Despite my misgivings, I forced myself to dismiss my emotions and yield to an ideology that I wasn't comfortable with so that I could continue in this path that had brought me a lot of happiness.

That day I also learned that, in order to be temple worthy, there were rules you must follow. You must pray, read the book of Mormon every day and fast once a month. You must follow the law of chastity; you can't have sex before marriage. Marriage is only and indisputably between a man and a woman. This was the central dilemma of our century and the church leadership felt an unwavering duty to protect the sanctity of families. To continue to add to the list of what you must follow: you can't drink alcohol, tea or coffee, no drugs of course and some go as far as not watching R-rated movies. You must pay 10% of your earnings to the church; this is what is called 'tithing.'

At 14 years old, I didn't object to any of this as I grew up in a rather conservative family and I was probably already living these principles in my own way. My life was rather simple and rigid. I did have to give up coffee, which is a bigger deal in South America, as we are known for our delicious coffee and it was part of my breakfast ritual. Tithing I didn't even have to think about as I was not even working.

In regard to sex, they were referring to anything that is not pure and chaste, therefore, touching yourself for your own sexual pleasure or another person out of the bounds of marriage is prohibited. You must even watch your thoughts. It is not uncommon for a Mormon member who is single to constantly carry the burden of denying themselves any pleasure, but they are promised that one day they will find the person that God has reserved for them either in this life or the next and they will be eternally happy.

To continue the explanation about what happens to Mormons after they die, the Mormons refer to the scripture in John 14:3, where Jesus says, "In my Father's house, there are many mansions." Therefore, in its simplest form, according to the LDS doctrine, after you die, you go back to your spirit form where you continue to be instructed and it is a state of waiting until your resurrection as we will all be resurrected as Christ was. After the resurrection where your bodies will be restored to their perfect form, you will be judged and inherit either the Celestial

Kingdom (highest glory or glory of the sun), Terrestrial Kingdom (glory of the moon) or Telestial Kingdom (glory of the stars).

I think it is important to explain further the Celestial Kingdom, as this is where the most fundamental belief of the organization lies. First, Only Mormons who have followed the rules of the Mormon church and have remained true to the covenants made in the Mormon temple, can obtain the highest degree of glory and obtain the right to live with God in this Celestial Kingdom. The Celestial Kingdom has 3 levels, and only in the highest will you be able to live with your family and live with Heavenly Father-Elohim, as the Mormons call him. This is the one for which you must earnestly and tirelessly deny yourself all ungodliness in this world so that you can earn the highest glory. Then, if you fall short and end up in the middle or lowest level of the Celestial Kingdom, you will end up single forever, you will not be able to procreate like the Gods, but you will be like the angels in the presence of Gods.

Last, we have the Terrestrial and the Telestial worlds. The Terrestrial is for good honorable people who never accepted the 'true gospel of Christ,' the ordinances and teachings of the Mormon church. However, they will live good lives, but without the promise of being surrounded eternally by their families. Moreover, they will not enjoy the presence of The Heavenly Father but will receive the visitation of Jesus Christ. This pretty much means any good person in the world who never knew of the Mormons or accepted joining the Mormon church.

And then comes the Telestial Kingdom: These are the people who made some significant mistakes while they were on earth, even committed crimes, but once they go through some process of penitence after they die, they will be resurrected, to this kingdom where they will be entitled only to the visitation of the Holy Spirit.

Mormons don't seem to talk much about Hell but, surprisingly, Hell is for those who had known the truth, but became enemies of it. I, at times, thought about this concept and wondered, what if I ever fall from this truth? Does that mean I would fall into an abyss of misery and condemnation? Would Hell be my reward? Then, I tried to not even think of it, especially at 14, as it was a scary thought, and at that point, my faith was burning with deep devotion and I could not even possibly imagine getting lost from this straight and narrow path.

This foundational dogma of striving all our lives to arrive at the highest level of glory is at the core of the beliefs that keep most Mormons running in a long and exhausting race to perfection. It is a grueling endurance race, where only those who deny themselves of all ungodliness survive. It is a culture of risk avoidance; keeping yourself spotless till you get to that finish line.

After a few weeks of listening to these discussions, I decided to get baptized.

"Veronica, this is your 6th discussion. How do you feel about getting baptized in a week?

"A week? I don't know. What happens during a baptism? What do I need to do?"

Sister Thompson explained, "You will be immersed in the waters of baptism fully as a sign of death and resurrection. It is a symbolism that you are willing to leave your previous life behind and follow the example of Christ.

You are already obeying the commandments and all the required rules before a baptism. So the only thing that we need is your grandma's consent. She needs to sign this form."

I was only 14 years old and at that age, I knew she may not agree to this, so they I tricked my Grandma into signing the authorization to proceed with my baptism. I showed her the paper and told her that the church needed her signature to allow me to participate in some sport events. She didn't read the paper, surprisingly, and signed it.

On the day of my baptism, the missionaries came to pick me up and I asked my little cousin Lorena who was a few years younger than me to accompany me. When we got to the luxurious modern church, I saw many small rooms where they held classes and a main open area with many chairs facing a small pool where they held the baptisms. There also was a mirror on the wall so people could watch every move as someone got baptized. Before we began, we had to wait in a room for one of the 'Elders' or a male missionary who are the only ones allowed to interview us and approve our baptism. The Elders had to ensure that we believed everything that we had been taught, that Jesus was the Christ, that Joseph Smith was a prophet, that we have a testimony that the Book of Mormon is true, that we are willing to pay tithing, avoid drugs, alcohol, coffee or tea, and no sex before marriage. In short, that we were already following all the extensive rules before our baptism. If we failed to abide by any of these requirements, we would not be allowed to be baptized.

I remember I was waiting in a small white room with Mario, an older Ecuadorian man in his late 20's, who was going to get baptized with his wife that day. She was being interviewed in another room by an Elder. "I am not sure I want to proceed with this baptism," he stated rather nervously as he started to feel the weight of the moment. "I am not sure I believe in this! We grew up Catholic…that has been our faith for generations!" He was sitting on a chair looking downward, low-spirited, and lost in thought. Even though I was only 14, I spent time listening to his doubts. I knew the sister missionaries would be disappointed if he backed out of his decision to get baptized and I recollect telling him, "I think this is a good decision for you and your family. Just because we have been taught something all our lives, it doesn't mean that it is right for our lives now." He looked up and our eyes met as he listened attentively. "What if you are being shown a new way to live that could bless you and your wife in so many ways? What if the decision you are about to make today does not only affect you but also the lives of your new child and generations to come?" He stayed silent and now he looked past me…as if he was thinking about what I said. Then, I added one more line, "At times, whenever you are about to make a good decision in your life, doubts come because there is another force that does not want you to do what is right." He then nodded, as if yielding to this unknown path. Our conversation lasted for about half an hour. Suddenly, someone opened the door, "Mario, it is your turn to talk to the Elder now." Even though I was nervous that he would change his mind again, I felt that I had convinced him enough to proceed with his baptism. That night, he and his wife got baptized. This set a precedence for how I would operate and evolve for many years of my life in the church.

It seems that for those of us who have at some point found some sort of religious faith, we often feel the need to rescue others. We feel the obligation to act like saviors in a world that is too complex and too enormous to comprehend. But even in our most sincere attempts, we fail because we try to fit 'the other' into the mold that we have created for ourselves; the mold that we've shaped ourselves into. I know I did. First, I often carried the unbearable shame of never measuring up and then, as an adult, the remorse of convincing many others of the illusion that this was the only true path, the only truth, and forced a belief on them that perhaps didn't serve their divine right or purpose. Particularly because, as a whole, this belief can be divisive, limiting and egotistical when considered in an expansive and diverse creation that consists of many paths. Those diverse beliefs allow us to interconnect deeper understandings, awareness and wholeness. But I was too young then to understand all that.

Martin Luther King's words echoed for me as I contemplated these truths throughout my life, "In a real sense all life is interrelated. All men *and women* are caught in an inescapable network of mutuality, tied in a single garment of destiny."

But when I was 14, my "single garment of destiny" came to be when I was immersed in water and baptized and I entered a religious denomination that would shape the next couple of decades of my life.

I became a devout Mormon and the church was my world. I made sure several family members listened to the missionary discussions and, as a result, some even got baptized. My uncle and his wife who lived with me were one couple. My cousins and their dad who lived close to me got baptized too. The missionaries in the area were fond of me. They used to call me the non-Yankee Joseph Smith- full of conviction for this gospel. After school and if my homework was done, I would accompany the missionaries so that I could help them teach other 'investigators' (what they called those learning about the church.) I used to love teaching and I would feel proud sitting next to the missionaries.

I often felt as if I had a broken wing, yet it turned out I enjoyed joining this race to perfection because I thought that if I tried hard enough, perhaps my wings would heal.

During my time in the church in Ecuador, I met many good wholesome members of the church who were wonderful people. And because of that, I felt that the whole world was noble and safe.

The sister missionaries who taught me the discussions spent a few months in my area. They became my role models. I behaved like them and I attempted to dress like them, even though I never liked dresses. I recall the first time I looked for a skirt to wear. I wanted to start feeling comfortable wearing one, but instead I felt rather awkward. The sister missionaries caught me walking in the streets wearing one and whistled at me as a form of compliment and I felt embarrassed.

I still remained active in my other activities. I rode my bicycle a lot with the other young kids in my neighborhood and spent a lot of time studying as well. I also used to love roller skating as did every young child in my block.

But Church was definitely my second home. Besides the Sunday services, Mormons have what they call, "Family Home Evenings." These occur every Monday and is the day where families get together and share a spiritual or ethical message, songs, and then you finish with some fun games and refreshments. For those whose families are not all in the church, the church held Family Home Evenings at the church or at someone's house. My home, or I should say Grandma's home, became very popular because it held all of these fun Mormon events and it was where missionaries would bring investigators to listen to their message. At that time, my Grandma was not living there as she had gone back to Miami to prepare the way for me to return. I was living with my uncle, his wife, and his 4-year-old daughter who were situated on the second floor of my Grandma's home and had become my guardians while I was in Ecuador. Because they eventually got baptized in the church, we shared this Mormon experience together.

I remember around that time, I had a crush on a very handsome boy. This was my very first time of being attracted to a boy. His name was Edison Javier Macias Vera; he was athletic, well-mannered and kind. He gave me my first kiss. We were both nervous. It felt innocent, my heart was beating fast. I thought at that age that this felt like nothing I ever experienced, and we wrote a letter to each other that we would love each other forever. He was not from my city, so after a few months, his family moved back to the area where he was from in Ecuador. I was sad to see him go, but I forced myself to stop thinking about him.

Then one day, Sister Lewis, the missionary who taught me the gospel, left my area. Another missionary came with whom I became good friends. Then her companion left a month after, and next came this new Sister missionary who would turn my young life upside down. I will call her Sister Joy. She was one of the most beautiful people inside and out I had ever encountered. She was for sure very attractive, slim, blonde, with bright blue eyes, but also had an affectionate and extremely sweet personality. Everyone in the ward (this is what they called the meeting places) seemed to adore her.

Every time Sister Joy was in my presence or if the thought of her came to my mind, my heart would swell with inexplicable emotions. Sometimes I felt that I could barely manage being in her presence. On one occasion, during a Family Home Evening gathering at my home, she and her companion showed a church movie to all those attending and, while everyone was watching the movie with the lights off, I was standing next to her and she hugged me. She kept her arms around me and, suddenly, I felt my body shaking. I didn't know what to do. I had never experienced my body reacting this way before. I thought about pulling myself away from her, but the thought of pulling away from her was not by any means an option. My desire to be close to her was much greater than the embarrassment of being found out. Her embrace produced a swirl of the sweetest and most powerful torrential waters flowing in and out of my soul. Nobody else mattered. Everything around me disappeared. Every sense in my body just wanted to feel her touch.

Suddenly she asked me, "Is everything ok? You are shaking!" The only words that I could utter were, "I don't know..." She looked me right in the eyes, smiled and kept her arms around me. It wasn't completely a lie; I didn't know what was happening to me. These were all new emotions for me. It was the first time I felt this indescribable and confusing attraction.

I remember having a friend in school whom everyone knew was different. Calixta was a bit boyish. She was black, had very short hair and male energy. I was one of her few friends in school as I think most girls probably couldn't relate to her. I would visit her in her home from time to time. I felt that we were very different in many ways yet, somehow, she was the only person whom I could suddenly speak to about these newly found emotions for Sister Joy. She listened to me without judgement, without imposing any thoughts on what this could mean or how this defined me. She did enjoy listening to what became obvious to her was my first love for a woman. Calixta became that safe haven whom I could lie next to in her home and just talk openly, guiltlessly and without shame. But in spite of this revelation, I never saw myself like her. I saw her as "the other," the same as others looked at her. In my mind, I was different; I was not whatever she was.

Sister Joy and her companions taught a few investigators at my home, so I got to see her often. All I wanted was to see her face and be in her presence almost every day. What bliss this brought to my young years. As an adult, I have been known to love hard, to love profoundly and this was the first experience that taught me that I had the capacity for such emotions.

I would daydream about her and do anything I could to help her with what she was there to do as a missionary. My upbringing was too innocent to even think of anything else to dishonor her calling. As a matter of fact, although these emotions were strong and beyond what I could grasp, my devotion for God and this church was even more powerful.

There were times, however, when my young mind would wonder if this missionary had feelings for me as well. I felt that she would go out of her way to look for me. At one point, she told me one evening that she wanted to speak to me alone. She asked me if we could go somewhere else to talk. What does she want to talk to me about alone? I wondered, fearful there was a chance we were going to speak about these confusing emotions. I knew I wasn't ready to meet the enormity of that kind of a conversation.

"I don't think I can go." It took everything I had for me to say this.

She looked at me, "Why not?"

"Because I don't think Heavenly Father will be happy with me if I do." I was frightened of myself, not her, and of facing my emotions. She just looked at me and kept silent and we stayed with everyone else.

There was a guy member of the church whom I knew was in love with her and it was obvious to everyone else, also. I had never felt so jealous in my life. I even talked to her about it and let my emotions show and she assured me that she was not interested in this member's attention. Missionaries are not supposed to date during their mission, but even so, this member looked like he was mesmerized by her presence.

Not too long after this incident, she stopped coming to my home the way she used to. I would see her pass by on the streets of my neighborhood looking for people to teach, but things weren't the same. The next thing I heard was that she was going to be transferred to another area and so she left. As a young person, you tend to feel things deeply and I cannot deny that I suffered greatly with the loss, with the void, the isolation that these feelings caused because I did not understand them.

I knocked at Calixta's door many times during this time and lay down next to her in complete silence. I often didn't need to say anything for her to understand my fragile and confused young heart.

Many years later, when I was in my early 40s, I learned that Calixta became more isolated and drank herself to death. I know what killed Calixta and this gave me a sense of regret for not having stayed in touch with her, for not having understood myself a lot sooner so that I could have also been there for her. But her loss also gave me a sense of liberation, courage and purpose. I cried when I heard about what happened to her, and it helped me to realize I was no longer willing to hide, to live ashamed, to live in agony, even though I was to learn that to commit to live this way- which is accepting, loving and embracing all of who you are – is a process, sometimes a long arduous process.

One day I decided to write a letter of the intensity of my love for this missionary, to put it all in ink and confess the darkest matter in the universe, the enormity of my love. I sat on the sidewalk right outside my home where all the young men in the neighborhood liked to play soccer in the streets. As I was almost finished writing this letter, a strong wind made the letter fly away and I wasn't sure where it landed. I felt chills at the possibility of anyone finding this letter. A few minutes later, a young man in my neighborhood started to walk towards me as he was reading it. He looked at me for a few minutes, paused, and with a smirk on his face, looking straight into my eyes, handed it to me. I looked back at him almost defiantly, demanding silence from him. After all, I was the niece of the badass good-looking uncles who were only a few years older than me and well respected in the community.

Sometime after Sister Joy left, I replaced the intensity of my sadness with the busyness that comes when you get really involved with 'church callings.' Every member who is considered worthy can serve in the church in a variety of positions: women normally can teach, help with children in the nursery and serve in leadership positions caring for other women. They are not allowed to preside over men. On the contrary, men can preside over men or women as they are the only ones who possess the 'priesthood," which is the authority to act in the name of God. However, I often gave talks in the church, held positions of leadership where I had to teach and continued helping the missionaries to some degree.

I was now 16 years old and I received the news that I had to go back to the United States. My Grandma had sent for me; she had saved whatever money my father gave her to babysit his daughter, my half-sister, and bought me a ticket so that I could return to her.

It turned out my Grandma had rented an apartment for she and I to live together in the States. She received some assistance from the government to be able to afford some of it. At that time, I didn't realize all the trouble she must have gone through to provide us a home, where I would not be exposed to the problems I'd had with my father and his wife. When you are young, you can be blind to your parents' sacrifices and I became purposefully oblivious to Grandma's. Instead, I couldn't wait to leave her and be on my own. I hated that we received help from the government. I felt a sense of false pride, maybe because the church had taught me that LDS people should not rely on the government.

My Grandma was a hard worker and sold Avon so that we didn't lack anything. Selling was her passion and she received awards for being the best salesperson. Even until her last days when she was in a wheelchair and could barely walk, she would tell me, "I wish I could walk again so that I could go out there and sell my Avon Products. I wonder if my clients are still around." She felt a sense of pride in being useful and independent. But some people, due to their circumstances, even with their hard work, cannot earn enough to live a dignified life.

IRONMAN PART 1.

I decided to listen to that man in South Africa, learned more about an Ironman, and finally, at 42 years of age, decided to take on the race. It was a big undertaking. I ended up training rigorously for a year, in every kind of climate, condition and terrain, both in running, biking and, the hardest for me, swimming. I had pushed myself psychologically, physically and emotionally, all to break fears and limits that held me back. It consumed all of me.

I had my reasons for that.

After hundreds of practice sessions, the day had now come to actually do the race. The first part, swimming, which I had put most of my attention on learning, since I had to start from barely knowing how to swim, was always the most strenuous and scary for me. I hated the water and was frightened of it, but I had prepared rigorously. To begin, I needed to be on the Jersey side by Palisades Park at 6am. To do that, we had to be at the NY ferry at 4 am. Daniella and I woke up at 3am; she helped me set out all my race nutrition: energy gels, energy drinks and transition clothes in the order of each race. She separated each item and packed them nicely inside my Ironman backpack ready for the transition area. She got everything ready for me and, before we took off, she told me she had cut a sticker with the shape of a heart which she placed on my left arm and said, "I want this to remind you during the race how much I deeply and truly love you and anytime you may feel like giving up, just remember that I will be waiting for you at the finish line."

We got to the NY Ferry in midtown and there were hundreds of athletes, everyone looking majestic, but I knew, like me, that underneath their confidence, we each had a multitude of fears, doubts, and uncertainty. We were about to do what some consider impossible: we were to race for 140 Miles, which includes a 2.4 mile swim, 112 mile bike ride and a 26.2 mile run.

Daniella was able to sneak onto the NY ferry that was supposed to carry only the athletes to Palisades Park and she accompanied me all the way to the starting point of the race. I put on my wetsuit & goggles and joined the rest of the athletes waiting for their big ship to carry hundreds of athletes per category. There were quite a few ships to ensure that over 2,300 men and women could be taken to the middle of the Hudson River so that we could jump at the sound of the start whistle and swim the distance.

While waiting for the alert to start, I began to feel the weight of the immensity of the moment. I looked at one of my teammates who was standing close to me with a somber look on his face. We remained silent. I started trembling inside. It hit me like a ton of bricks that, in a matter of minutes, I was going to have to jump into the Hudson river.

Suddenly, it was my time to go. I jumped in at the deep end and so did so many other athletes. The Hudson River water can feel as if you are throwing your body into a washing machine. As I began to move my arms in an attempt to swim, unexpectedly, I suffered a panic attack. After all, I had taken months to learn how to swim and face my private terror, which is water. The pressure in my chest felt unbearable, I was gasping for air. Unpredictably, as I was struggling to survive, stuck in one place, doing enough to stay afloat, other athletes started to swim around me and, not surprisingly, on top of me, sinking me deeper into the water underneath them. I was fighting a sea of fast swimmers around me and over me. Everyone was competing for seconds to make it to the end, while at this point, I was just trying to stay alive. I turned on my back and all I could see was the sky, the sun through my goggles and felt a horde of swimmers rushing around me. I made an incredible effort to calm myself down despite all the madness around me. I had to access an unbelievable mental focus and have a dialogue with myself to stay calm and tell my chest to open up so that I could start breathing. I stayed on my back for probably five minutes as everyone continued to rush around me then, with small progress, my chest started to open up slightly. I was not able to breathe well yet, but still I turned my body over to get on my stomach so that I could attempt to swim free style. I took a few strokes, but I was barely moving forward; my form was off. I still struggled to breathe. I reminded myself that I had gone through this before and that I could get through this again. Suddenly, I started to breathe and found myself moving forward, slowly, stroke by stroke. I swam for over an hour until I started to see the end.

Once I was a few feet away from my first finish line, I told myself, "I have gone through the worst, nothing will stop me from finishing this race now."

It was much like what I went through in the early years of my life, losing my mother, being taken away from everything I knew, coming to the States and beginning my growing up years facing great adversity. Most of the time, I felt as if I had been thrown uncontrollably into the midst of a hostile ocean. But all of this, unbeknownst to me then, was also teaching me the invaluable meaning of grit and resilience. Just like the race, I ended up going stroke after stroke through it.

Chapter 5.

Back in the USA

My first day at a new high school in Hialeah, Florida, I showed up at the office and they assigned me a student who showed me the way to my ESOL class, English for Students of Other Languages. I opened the door carefully and heard the blasting sound of salsa music. Everyone around me was dancing. I proceeded to walk quietly to an open seat that didn't have any books on top of the desk and sat there and waited for the festivities to end.

After some time, I asked one of the students, "What are you celebrating and who is the teacher here?" She pointed to a Caribbean lady who was dancing in the front of the classroom with the other students. I observed what was going on with annoyance as I felt I was wasting my time. Class was over and I didn't know what to think. The next day of school, the same episode repeated itself; there was dancing, speaking Spanish, and everyone seemed to be having so much fun. I proceeded to ask the teacher in front of everyone, "When are we going to have class? I didn't come here to learn how to dance. I came here to learn English!" She gave me a sarcastic look, and within days, I received a C in conduct. After I got that C, I went to the school office and pleaded for them to change my ESOL English class and also my math class as they had put me in a very low -level grade. It wasn't even Algebra.

The school officer insisted, "You don't speak English! What English class do you think you can go to? You are not going to understand what is going on!"

I pleaded, "You have an introductory English class for students who are not as advanced and you have Americans there, can you put me in that class? I will learn! I know some English! And in regards to math," I told him, "I don't need to speak English to understand numbers!" I explained that I had already completed advanced algebra classes in my country and that I was even doing physics before I came to the States. I grew impatient and raised my voice, "How dare you put me in a basic math class? This is not even algebra. Please don't set me back like this!"

The school administrator looked at me and hesitantly agreed to put me in the less advanced English course for 11th graders with native English speakers. He didn't want to put me in an advanced math level class, but we reached a compromise and he finally said, "Alright, I will let you switch to Algebra with an American Professor. But just remember, he doesn't speak any Spanish."

I walked into my first native speakers' English class where I would eventually learn about Shakespeare's "Hamlet" and John Milton's "Paradise Lost." The only other book that I remember at that time that made a huge impression on me was "The Scarlet Letter" by Nathaniel Hawthorne where I could feel the degradation and shame of the adulteress woman who was forced to wear a scarlet letter "A" on her dress. I used to wonder, "What if I had to wear a letter to show my biggest sin? Would I be able to bear such humiliation!" I could feel her agony.

I visited a local Mormon church and started attending a Spanish ward. There were many Cubans and people from different places from Latin America and they became my second family. Since I was still 16, I had to attend seminary. Seminary is for young people in the church who go through advanced scriptural studies, each year covering one of the Latter- day Saint's scriptures including the Bible. Some of the other scriptures, besides the Bible and the Book of Mormon, that the LDS church upholds as sacred text are the Doctrine & Covenants and the Pearl of Great Price. The Doctrine & Covenant, simply explained, is the modern-day revelation that was given to the modern Prophet Joseph Smith for the members of the LDS church. The Pearl of Great Price, written on Egyptian papyri, is a book of great controversy that claims to have ancient revelations from the Book of Moses and the Book of Abraham and was given to Joseph Smith in 1835 after he purchased it from a traveling mummy exhibition. According to Joseph Smith, the book was a translation of some ancient records where members could learn deep mysteries, including details of Abraham's early life, Moses' revelations of the fall of men and a vision of the cosmos.

These writings were canonized by the LDS church in 1880 as part of what they call "The Pearl of Great Price" and it became a doctrinal foundation for the church. The Book of Abraham Papyri was lost in 1871. However, fragments were found in 1966 in the archive of the Metropolitan Museum in New York and in the LDS Church archives. "Upon examination by professional Mormon and non-Mormon Egyptologists, these fragments were found to have no resemblance to Smith's interpretation and were identified as common Egyptian funeral texts, dating to about the first century BC." (Wikipedia) As a result, the book has been the source of significant controversy. I found out about all this information when I was in my late 30s. Before that, I refused to listen to anyone who would say anything negative about the doctrine of the church. I had friends in the church who started to dig into this part of the Mormon history but I avoided getting into these types of conversations as the church had conditioned me to believe that entertaining these conversations would lead me to apostasy ending in the loss of my soul.

My first year in this ward, I immersed myself in the studies of the Book of Mormon. There were about 7 students around my age in the class. Our teacher was a beautiful woman with Ecuadorian roots but born here in the US. I felt motivated by the way she taught the classes. We had to memorize and master many verses from the Book of Mormon and got tested and competed with each another to see who came up with the fastest answers. I became obsessed with memorizing every assigned scripture and soon I was expert at reciting them by heart and knowing exactly where they were found in the book. My competitive nature seemed to annoy some of the other young people in the seminary class. They couldn't care less about my intensity and I couldn't care less about being accepted by them. I had acquired such devotion for this book that I would do anything to attend the seminary classes. I went to school, went to seminary and worked.

My father was still part of my life as he visited Grandma and me on a weekly basis. Nevertheless, I had residual resentment for what I went through with him and his wife when I came to the States the first time. I avoided interacting with him as much as I could, but I still needed his help. I am sure he retained some anger at my reporting him to social services when he started to hit me. The disconnect between us was deep and this was to haunt me for most of my life. I have tried as an adult to understand this person who gave me life. Despite all the things that I resented my father for, I have always known that he brought us to this country. He went through the arduous and expensive process of applying for the US residency for each member of the family and then the US citizenship. His father died when he was 14 years old and he had to give up school and work a lot to help Grandma financially and support his four brothers and sister. Since he was the oldest son, he became the father figure for everyone else. He made sure all his brothers could finish school and eventually go to college. In fact, all of them eventually became engineers. Being a provider and a ruthless disciplinarian was the only thing he knew. As an adult, I learned that he had a profound inability to demonstrate any affection, after all he himself had never experienced any.

When I came back to the States, my father once again taught me how to drive and lent me one of his cars, a very old blue Buick 1970s. It was nothing to be proud of, but it took me to school. My family didn't know that after school, I went to the Mormon church for seminary classes. I also worked in a fast food restaurant called, "Taco Bell." My legal first name is Maria, but I never liked my first name. Since I was little, I have only responded to Veronica. However, the manager was a kindhearted Puerto Rican guy who used to call me Maria and he was the only person I ever allowed to call me that.

My first day on the job I was asked to work helping the clients in the front and did it with a big smile on my face. I have no idea why I have been like that most of my life, either I wore a frown when I was in deep thought or mostly I beamed a big grin, no matter what was happening in my life. I remember being around 10 years old and one of my schoolmates' relatives died and a few of her classmates were invited to the funeral. I was standing by myself not thinking about anything in particular, and she approached me somberly to tell me that it was really rude of me to have a big smile on my face at her relative's funeral, to which I quick replied, "But I am not smiling!!"

After taking a break from the cash register, I wiped tables and would walk around and talk enthusiastically to customers. One day the manager told me he wanted me to do the dishes in the back. At the end of the shift, it must have been 9pm, he walked me to the kitchen area, and I saw these huge pots and pans as he started walking away. It smelled so much like left over food and I despised the smell. I stared at the huge pots in despair. After a while, this Puerto Rican manager came back to find out why I was taking so long and found me crying. "Maria, what's wrong?!"

I answered, still with tears in my eyes, "I have never done dishes like this before in my life!" and I proceeded to cry even more. He looked at me for a moment without saying a word as a brother would look at his little sister and then said in that beautiful Puerto Rican accent, "Ven aca Maria, you don't have to do this. From now on, I will put you at the cash register." I am not sure why he let me get away from this unpleasant task, but he did. Neither my mother nor my grandmother ever allowed me to do kitchen chores. They wanted me to go to school and kept me away from anything they thought might distract me.

One time my father came home and asked, "What was my car doing at that church around 3pm?!"

I kept quiet. I was stunned and afraid of his anger, even though I should have been used to his intimidating ways. My body would often tremble at the sound of his voice.

"You are only allowed to use the car for school and work! If I ever see my car parked by that church, I will take it away from you and you will have to walk everywhere!"

The following times I went to seminary, I tried to park behind the church where it would be harder to see the car. But my father eventually found out and took the car away from me, "You will figure out how you are going to get to school and work." I ended up having to walk everywhere after school on those melting 90 degrees' summer days. I walked about 30 long blocks to church to attend seminary. At times the seminary teacher would give me a ride back, but not always. The other girls would get into one car and never ask me if I needed a ride. And so I walked to school, seminary and work.

At school, I would hardly say a word in any of my classes. I was lucky to sit next to a Cuban boy who was born in the States in my English class. He was rather handsome and kind, so I enjoyed his company and he helped me when I got lost in the reading. I tried not to bother him, but there were many times I needed help. This was now Shakespeare and literature. I tried to catch up by reading the same material again and again when I got home.

In math class, I understood a lot, but I still wouldn't say a word, even though I had already spent over a few months in the classroom. I was very self-conscious of my English because I could not quickly formulate a sentence and I had a very thick accent. Some kids in the classroom started to make fun of me. My Grandma didn't have a sense of fashion so she bought me the ugliest, biggest glasses and some of the boys called me "Garfield," and everyone would laugh. The teacher just observed. On another occasion, one of the Cuban American boys said out loud, "Hey… HEY YOU! I AM TALKING TO YOU! WHY CAN'T YOU TALK? DID ANYONE BITE YOUR TONGUE?" Other kids looked my way, but I stayed still, looking forward as if they were not even there. I pretended that he wasn't talking to me. He wouldn't stop and said next, "WHY CAN'T YOU SPEAK ENGLISH, MAN! YOU HAVE BEEN HERE FOR MONTHS!!!!" When I wouldn't answer, he said, "WHAT'S WRONG WITH YOU!" The laughter in the room became louder, and I became smaller. I just couldn't understand why there were those who felt so falsely superior for just being born in this country, as if their language gave them some misconstrued illusion of greatness.

Back at home, no one made fun of anyone for being different. Instead we embraced a foreigner as our own, as our friend, and would share with them even what we didn't have.

The professor rushed towards me; he was a very kind white American man in his 50s, I think. As he approached me, he made a sign with his finger to follow him to the front of the class. He wrote a difficult and long Algebra equation on the board and told the rest of the students that they needed to solve the equation and he was going to time how quickly we got the answers. He then proceeded to hand me the chalk and said, "Ven Aqui." Pointing to the board, he wanted me to resolve the problem in front of everyone. I looked for a second and then started working on it while the rest of the kids were looking down at their papers tackling the same problem. I started to write on the board. I felt free. This was the first time I could speak without words. It was as if this teacher allowed me to unbury a part of me that no-one could see and, suddenly, I was no longer invisible. I started simplifying one equation after the other as fast as I could until I got the answer in a matter of minutes.

The teacher looked at me with a warm smile of approval and then we looked at everyone in the classroom. They were still looking down at their papers.

The teacher then said, "Put your pencils down." No one else had finished the exercise. The kids looked at me and looked at the exercise on the board and they were stunned, and the teacher said, "You see! This is the person you are laughing at!" After that day, none of those kids ever made fun of me again. My young self will forever be thankful to this American teacher.

He knew I had mastered the material since I had done very well in the assignments and tests. But what he did in that moment was give me back some peace and dignity which I didn't know, as a foreigner in this land, how to fight for on my own.

Everyone in High School seemed to become more cool and respected if they had a boyfriend. So, I started to date this strange but handsome young man in my church. He was 6'4, athletic, dark haired with olive skin. He was the oldest son of a second-generation Colombian family. His family was considered an honorable Mormon family, but their son turned out not to have anything honorable about him. He would try to push boundaries when we got together, and I wouldn't have been surprised if he had already slept with other girls. Having sex before marriage is one of the biggest sins for Mormons, after murder and homosexuality, so I wouldn't go there. Also, he was boring; it was difficult to have any meaningful conversation with him and I couldn't believe how someone so handsome could be so unattractive and dumb. However, I was insecure at that time and thought if I kept him around, it would give me some sort of status and normalcy, even if he was a shell of a man.

We had gone out for a few months, but when he showed up at my house to pick me up, my Grandma and father prohibited me from seeing him. They told me that they didn't trust him and would not allow him in the house. Maybe they had a point!

My last year of high school, I wanted to have more friends. In order to feel accepted, I started to act out in class. I would arrive a little late because I thought that would make me look cool. At this point, I could already communicate in English well so, from time to time, I would make jokes that annoyed one of my teachers. My grades went down that year but, but in spite of my lack of dedication, I still managed to graduate with honors because of my high grades the previous year.

The day of my graduation came, and I only invited my Grandma, but she proceeded to invite my father and his wife. My father didn't seem to want to be there. He was still resentful that this second time in the States, I had chosen to live with Grandma, and I had limited communication with him.

Those who graduated with honors got to wear a yellow tassel and sat in the front of the graduation class. The parents were not sitting too far off from where we were. I could see my Grandma if I looked just a few rows back, but I also saw my father and his wife next to her. My father and his wife looked serious. My Grandma had bought one of those cheap $5 dollar disposable cameras that existed during that time and tried to take pictures of me during the ceremony. I saw her getting up and trying hard to capture me. I don't even think she knew how to take one. My father and his wife never got up from their seats.

Once the ceremony was over, some parents approached some of my classmates who had graduated with honors and, as I was being introduced to them, we were interrupted by my father, "Hurry up! Let's get out of here." Because I didn't move right away and kept on talking to my other classmates and their parents, all I heard was my deranged father say, "Hijo de puta, move it." That was my father's default expression to anyone or anything that infuriated him. I was deeply embarrassed. My Grandma looked stressed, but she hardly ever dared stand up to my father. The heavy silence of that moment was interrupted by one of the mothers who turned towards my father to say, "You should be ashamed of yourself!" and stared at him intently. My father kept on walking away, his wife followed and then Grandma and I began walking slowly behind them. I still have that one blurry picture my Grandma took of me during graduation day.

Chapter 6.

On My Own with 87 Cents

A few weeks after my graduation, I got a job at a gym in North Miami Beach. This would give me enough money to pay for a small room, so I decided to leave my Grandma and live on my own. I think I wanted to walk away from all of it, even if it meant that I was walking away from Grandma too. I even took a break from the Mormon church. Even though religion had always been a refuge, even that had now become an empty shell. I felt disconnected from it- The routine of the same church services, same church songs, the same conversations, the same people who only knew how to comply, who were programmed to succumb and never question, the never ending guilt of never feeling good enough for that fleeting destination to perfection, all of it made me walk away for a period.

I spent a lot of time in the gym and that became my life. I took a training that the gym offered to become an aerobics instructor and a weight trainer. I thought at that time that aerobics instructors were fun and cool. I worked hard at the gym, so I was asked to become an assistant manager in charge of sales.

I rented a small room in Hialeah for $400. Even though there was a gym right across the street from me, they didn't want an amateur like me as that was the most popular location of the franchise so, if I wanted a chance, I had to work in their newer location in North Miami. This was about a 40-minute drive.

I also started attending college; I picked Miami Dade Community College because I happened to receive a letter right before I graduated from high school letting me know that they were giving me a full 2-year tuition free scholarship. I never took the time to think about what college I could go to, so I took whatever came as a default. With my income from the gym, I would be able to pay for books, rent and food. I had not figured out gas or other additional expenses. This was my first experience of living on my own, so I underestimated how much money I needed to support myself.

I worked every day and went to school. Suddenly I needed a graphing calculator, $100 back then, for my calculus class. I also couldn't manage to pay for the gas that old big Buick needed every week. There were times I was driving to school and I could see the gas meter almost to the last line and I would press the pedal so lightly, sweating, as I prayed, "God please don't let me get stuck in the middle of this road! Please help me make it to school."

I ended up not having enough money to buy a book or graphic calculator for my calculus class. I made copies from someone else's book to read the assigned chapters. I did well on the assignments and quizzes but, at the end of the semester, the professor informed us on how we were going to be graded. "All the work you have done till now will be worth 40% and the final exam will be worth 60%. The final is important for you to pass this class and don't forget to bring your graphing calculator, you will need it for most of the exam." The day of the final exam came, and I told myself that I was going to answer whatever I could, but I would wait for someone in the classroom to finish early and ask them to lend me their graphing calculator. We had about an hour or so to do this exam. I finished answering the only question that didn't need a calculator. I held the pencil tightly in my fingers and looked around, just waiting anxiously for someone to finish so I could have a few minutes to do the exam. Thirty minutes went by, then forty-five minutes, and everyone was still working on the problems. I could feel my heart pounding and then I heard the professor say, "Time is up." Everyone started turning in their papers. I waited till the end, sitting in a daze, for everyone to leave and I followed the professor on his way out, "Professor, Professor! WAIT! I didn't have money to buy the book! And the graphing calculator was way too expensive for me! I thought I could wait for someone to finish so that I could borrow it! I have a scholarship! I can't flunk this class."

He paused and said, "Why didn't you talk to me before? I had an extra book in my office." He looked at me again, didn't say anything for a few seconds and then said, "The best I can do is withdraw you from my class so that it won't affect your GPA."

I realized I needed to make more money or cut some expenses. So, I decided to talk to the manager of the gym across the street from my house and asked her if there was a way I could transfer to her location. I had already built a good reputation in the location where I worked. I was her number one salesperson and I could do almost anything they needed me to do: teach aerobics, weight training or manage the business. She told me she would be happy to have me as she always needed people. But when I went back the next day to speak to my manager where I worked, she got mad, "I am friends with the general manager. You know I need you. If you leave, I will make sure your life is a living hell and you will not be able to transfer to any other gym location." She was taking advantage of my circumstances. This triggered something in me, and I could feel my blood boiling. I found myself raising my voice, "Don't you ever threaten me again. I am not coming back. I quit."

Sadly, she was true to her word. When I went back to the manager of the location across the street the next day, I was immediately woken up to the politics of this business. She already knew what had happened and, before I could say anything, she said, "I can't have you work here. Your manager went to our US Manager and I am not allowed to hire you." The same week, I went to the competitor gym in the neighborhood and, to my surprise, my ex-boss was friends with that manager there, so they wouldn't let me even apply.

I now had spent a couple of weeks without a job and I had little savings. The crazy woman manager from North Miami called me to tell me, "I know you need the money. I know you are alone. So, I am giving you another chance to come back and work for me or you will continue to suffer since I made sure no one will hire you." I hung up on her. But I had no idea how I was going to survive.

I had enough money saved to pay for rent, but I had no money left over for food. I came home from school and I started looking through the dirty laundry to find any change so that I could buy something to eat. I found some quarters and pennies which added up to exactly 87 cents. I had enough to possibly buy something at McDonalds. Because I had a healthy lifestyle, I never went to fast food restaurants, but this time, I was grateful for McDonalds. I looked at the signs, "Hamburgers less than a dollar." I still needed to see how much they were with tax. I took a deep breath and I apprehensively approached the cashier. "How much is the cheapest hamburger you have?"

"87 cents," she replied.

It was serendipity. I was so grateful to be able to eat that day. The fact that it was exactly the change I had made me feel that someone out there was aware of my existence. I didn't have to go to bed hungry. The next day, I went to school.

After school, I went to my apartment. I had no idea what I was going to do for food that day. I lived in a small room with only a mattress on the floor, my clothes in the closet and there was a small kitchen and a fridge. I heard a knock on the door, "Who is it?"

"Betty."

She was a friend from college. I was surprised she would just show up; she had never been to my apartment.

"I just came to say hi."

When she came in, she didn't sit down, she just stood there in silence, looked around and then went to my fridge and opened it and saw it was completely empty. She then looked at me and said, "Why don't you come and live with me?"

My initial response was to tell her, "I am fine."

She looked at me again and said, "Veronica, why don't you come and live with me?"

I was lying on my mattress looking at her in silence and then said, "I don't have money to pay you rent. I don't have a job."

To which she replied, "You don't have to pay anything until you find a job. You can live with my parents and me, we have an extra room."

I got up from my mattress and we both proceeded to pack my few belongings and we left the apartment and I moved to her home.

They were very religious, and even though her mother and the rest of the family welcomed me with open arms, her father would look at me as if I was by default a sinner. They were

Evangelicals and anyone who has not accepted Jesus in the way of the born-again Christians is not saved. In retrospect, I realize that many of these religious organizations suffer from this psychological frenzy and enormous illusory complex of believing they are the only chosen ones.

In addition, he thought I spent too much time on my physical appearance, and this was frowned upon. In spite of this, I was deeply grateful to my friend Betty, her mother, sister in law and one of her brothers as they offered me a home, a safe haven and their friendship but, as soon as I found a job, I paid them and, within a year, I left.

During this period, away from the Mormon church and obsessed with fitness, I partied a lot with a few friends from college, including Betty. At that time, I often attracted guys and I started going out with a few of them because I enjoyed the attention and how they would cater to me. I didn't fall in love with any of them.

It is not that I did not find men attractive, I did. I believe there are a lot of good men out there and they are less complicated than women at times. But something did not allow me to feel deeply close to them. And even though I have always been a passionate human being, I did not allow myself to get too intimate with them either, particularly because of the church rules. But I went far enough physically that, according to the Mormon rules, my actions would be considered sinful.

Even though my life was filled with parties and guys, I started to feel empty, the emptiness that you experience when you don't have people to share God with. This time, I missed the church community, the spiritual experiences I'd had and connection, so I went back. Initially, I was put on probation for a few months for deviating from the church rules.

I was not allowed to take the sacrament. The sacrament is a small cup of water and a piece of bread that all members partake of during a special ceremony on Sundays. It symbolizes the body and blood of Christ to acknowledge Christ's atonement or the sacrifice he made to cleanse us of our sins. Therefore, partaking of this holy sacrament unworthily becomes a condemnation to your soul and you must confess to the bishop any sin that is keeping you from participating in this redeeming ordinance.

Being on probation was hard and uncomfortable since taking the bread and cup of water when they pass it around on Sunday is what everyone does. Mind you, for Mormons, the rules are even more strict than in most Christian churches. If you watched an R rated movie or drank coffee during that week, this could be a reason to not take the sacrament. On one occasion, a friend of mine who was single told me that he didn't take the sacrament because he was having impure thoughts about a girl.

The humiliating part is that everyone around you knows something must be wrong as you have to signal to the priesthood passing the sacrament in your row that you cannot partake. Even though you are sitting less than an inch apart from other members, the best thing to do is to keep your head down so you don't make eye contact with anyone who could perceive the shame in your eyes.

The passing of the sacrament takes a while as they have several young and older men of the priesthood pass a silver container holding the small cups of water and another one the bread. They go row by row until each member has partaken. There is complete silence, only a somber Mormon hymn plays in the background. It is a very ceremonious and sacred ritual each Sunday. So, if only the worthy can participate, then those who are not members of the church cannot participate of the sacrament either as you have not repented of your sins and have not been baptized in the only true church of Christ.

After a couple of months of being punished, and after the bishop told me I was now forgiven, I was able to take the sacrament again. I dedicated myself fully to church callings and my life revolved once more around this community of faith.

At this time, I was working as an Assistant Manager at a health spa in an area called Coral Gables. The manager, Andrea, was an upbeat and thoughtful woman from Ohio. I was her right hand and she frequently left me in charge. We sold a lot of memberships and I remember one occasion where I oversold more than our daily quota by $4000 and she told me, "Let's leave those contracts for a rainy day."

I was puzzled and confused as to why. A couple of months passed, and it started raining intensely. I looked at her joyfully, opened the desk bottom drawer and took the contracts out and said, "Andrea we can count the money now!"

She looked at me and laughed so hard, she almost fell to the floor. "Veronica, that is an American expression! When I told you to leave the contracts for a rainy day, I meant for a day that we couldn't sell as much. I can't believe you had those contracts in your desk for that long. Thank God it rained."

Chapter 7.

Mission Call

After a year of working for Andrea, I made a decision that I wanted to serve a Mormon mission and take a break from school. Besides, that is what most young Mormons in the church do, we go on missions. For men, it's a 2-year mission and for women 1 ½ years. For young men as soon as they turn 18, they must get ready to go since it is expected of them. There is a lot of shame for those young men who decide not to go.

It is a big deal for young people in the church to serve a mission. Those who are born into the church are taught, before they can even speak, that, outside of marriage, a Mormon mission is the greatest and most honorable thing they must do. There is a funny hymn for little boys that goes, "I hope they call me on a mission…I hope they call me on a mission…I hope they call me on a mission" and it goes on and on as if they want to make sure the boys never forgets this.

On the contrary, girls are taught that their most honorable calling is to get married to an honorable returned missionary. Returned male missionaries are a hot commodity - every available single woman goes after them with a fierce determination to marry them.

I was not done with my Associates degree and had one semester left, but so strong was my excitement that I didn't care that I wasn't done with that part of my education. I took all my savings, all the money that I made working as an assistant manager and gave it to the bishop so that I could pay for my mission. He sent it to the church headquarters.

When you apply to go on a mission, the paperwork goes to Salt Lake City where the top leaders of the church – Prophets and Apostles- work and live. What we are told is that the current prophet of the church and his leadership get everyone's applications from around the world and that they pray and receive revelation as to which part of the world you are supposed to be sent to. Therefore, your destination is an inspiration. You must consent.

Once you send in the mission application, you must wait a few weeks until an envelope from the church headquarters arrives in the mail. Inside is the answer to where you will be sent. The suspense, the excitement, the glory seemed unparallel to any other feeling I had ever experienced before.

Usually Mormon families get together and make this a special big gathering where the young man or woman opens the envelope in front of everyone. Because my family was not Mormon, I remember sitting on my bed and opening the letter by myself, "You have been called to serve a Mission in Chile, Vina del Mar." I paused. "Chile! I have never been to Chile! Since it is in South America, it must be a beautiful country." A lot of thoughts were going through my head at that moment. "I would have loved to have gone to France but, hey, at least it is not Minnesota." That is how I consoled myself and I also rectified myself quickly. "This is where the Lord wants me. I am going to save so many souls who are waiting for me in Chile!" That is what we had been ingrained to think, that as missionaries we become saviors to a world full of gentiles!

I immediately phoned a few of my most beloved Mormon friends, "Guess what? I got my mission call." I could hear their excitement, "Oh my Gosh! (Famous Mormon phrase as we are taught not to use the Lord's name in vain) Where? Where are you going?" I would then give them the big news, "I am going on a Mission to Chile, Vina del Mar!" I would hear the excitement on the other line, "Oh my Gosh Oh my Gosh!!…Congratulations!!! You are going to be an awesome missionary!" These are the typical reactions to just about anyone who opens their mission call.

One of my close Mormon friends, Ruth, a strong, attractive, and confident woman from El Salvador in Central America, told me that she would buy me all the clothes that I would need as a missionary, such as the long dresses that are appropriate for this calling, the shoes that I needed to walk in for long hours of proselytizing. She was a returned missionary and had all sorts of Mormon guys dying to go out with her. But she was hard to please and therefore "unmarriageable."

Her mission had been in Spain, which she often referred to as very hard work and she didn't seem to have had a great time. "The Spaniards are difficult. They do not care to listen to these teachings. I went a whole year and a half without baptizing anyone!" Then she looked at me and said, "Don't worry that will not happen to you. You are going to South America; people are a lot more receptive there and the church seems to convert hundreds every month! You are going to baptize people all the time."

Before I left, Ruth and I had a conversation about something that I couldn't make myself talk about to anyone. But I was about to go on a mission, a calling that I considered very sacred and I could not leave with such a disturbing secret.

"Ruth, I have been carrying a big burden for some time, but I have never given into it." I looked down and I felt as if my face was crumbling. I paused and couldn't make myself say another word.

Ruth looked at me with the honesty and composure that was unique to her and said, "I think I know."

I reacted, "What do you mean you know?"

Ruth continued, "Just say it Veronica."

My lips felt as if someone had glued them tightly together and it required great strength to utter anything. I finally said, "I have this other side of me that is not good…" My face tensed and my chest constricted as if I was about to die of suffocation. I continued, "I am attracted to women. I pray all the time Ruth. I read the scriptures every day probably longer than most people. I am doing everything I can Ruth to get rid of these thoughts and attraction." I started to cry.

She was sitting a couple of feet from me and did not move or reach out to hold me, was almost emotionless and then said, "I know you do. I already knew."

I looked at her and asked, "How did you know?"

She said, "I know…I have had some similar feelings in the past, but I have never given in to them either."

I felt as if someone had lifted from me, if only for a moment, a little bit of this insurmountable weight that I had been painfully carrying alone. I did not want to ask her any questions about her own revelation. Then she said, "You are going to be a wonderful missionary." And we never talked about this again. I wasn't equipped to go any further on this subject, maybe neither was she.

My Grandma wasn't happy I had to go to a foreign country for almost 2 years to serve a Mormon mission, especially for a faith she didn't share and did not know anything about as she always kept her distance but, strangely, until then, let me live it. She also didn't know my bishop or any of my Mormon friends so I can imagine her distress. I didn't see this back then; all I saw was a thoughtless grandmother who had little regard for what I felt was my duty to serve God. I was so determined to serve a mission that her opinion had little validity for me. Before I left, we got into a heated discussion as I didn't have luggage and I asked her to lend me hers, but she refused. I got so upset that I stormed out of her apartment in the middle of a torrential rainstorm. I was driving on the Palmetto expressway leaving Hialeah, the city where Grandma lived, and it was raining hard, as if the rain could feel the intensity of my fury. I had zero visibility. I drove at a high speed with my heart racing with anger and disappointment and suddenly I saw the shadow of a car in front of me and I pressed on the brakes abruptly. My car started spinning. If I was about to hit any cars around me, I wouldn't have known it. All I could see was a dense and vicious rain through my windshield as my body tossed around in all directions until my car came to a complete stop. My hands were still holding tight to the steering wheel. I looked at the rain falling hard through the windshield. I was uninjured, alive, and I thought, God must want me to go on this mission.

The next day, I headed to the airport. Andrea, my manager, and Ruth were my closest and most supportive friends and wanted to be there to bid me goodbye. Even though Andrea wasn't religious and was losing her business partner, she demonstrated that I meant more to her than money, and she was a true friend. Ruth was, of course, someone I trusted with all my heart. I went through the gate as I waved goodbye and made my way to the airplane. As I was sitting in my assigned seat close to the front of the airplane, suddenly I heard a commotion at the door and a desperate voice crying, "You have to let me see her! Mijita Mijita…where is she?!"

Suddenly, I saw her with the desperation of a mother, "I am so sorry Mijita." It was my Grandma! She came towards me escorted by the agent and flight attendant and rushed to embrace me goodbye, tears coming down her face. I can still feel her heart pounding against mine as she tried to breathe through her tender lioness heart. We hugged for a minute, and then she proceeded to put her hands on my forehead then towards my chest and then from one shoulder to the other- "En el nombre del Padre, del Hijo y del Espirito Santo. Amen." The sign of the cross, the ancestral familiar loving blessing that reminds you where you are from and the surrendering of all of who you are to God, "Que Dios te bendiga mija." Then the flight attendant and agent escorted her out.

As I saw her walking away, I observed her back filled with sorrow, her head looking down and a heaviness in her steps, crying till I could no longer see her, and then she disappeared through the door of the airplane. Oh, how I wish I could bring this moment back and tell her that I love her that much too.

Chapter 8.

Temple Experience

Before I went to Chile, I had to go to Utah. I was 21 and, of all people, Philene was to be my guide at this stage, the missionary who had taught me the LDS gospel when I was 14. She offered to be the one to take me to the temple to experience my first temple ceremony where I was to get my endowments. There I would make special promises to the Lord.

No one wanted to tell me what would happen at the ceremony. Back in Miami, Ruth said to me, "I am not supposed to discuss what happens inside the temple. To be honest, I had a hard time with it, but just go with an open mind."

I looked at her and thought, "Why is it such a secret?"

Philene did not discuss any details either, but she had traveled from Idaho to Utah to assist me.

My temple experience started first with 'the washing and anointing." At this ceremony, I was going to be given the garments or the Mormon under wear. As explained to me, I was to do this alone, but I couldn't understand why. I was taken to an arca with a few small rooms covered with thick white curtains.

There I met an old lady dressed in white whom they called a Temple Worker. Each room had someone who was going through the same experience, and even though only curtains separated us, I could hear whispering since whispering is a symbol of holiness.

There, in that room, I divested all my clothing, including my underwear, and put on a white robe that was open on both sides. Respectfully and ceremoniously, the Temple Worker touched certain parts of my body to sanctify me, and each area of my naked body received its unique blessing. As she touched my body, I chuckled a bit out of nervousness. The experience felt surreal, I tried to bite my lips so I wouldn't laugh. I felt myself breathing intensely, but somehow, as she bestowed these blessings on my body, unaffected by my reactions, I surrendered.

The temple worker finished this part and then she whispered in my ear, "You are going to be given a new name. This is your real name in heaven."

When she said that, I secretly prayed that God would reveal that my real name was really a boy's name. I thought, "My life would be so much easier if I were a guy."

I hoped God knew what the world didn't.

After she told me my new name, she continued to whisper more instructions with a solemnity that I had never experienced before in my life, "You should always remember it and must keep it sacred and never reveal it to anyone, except at a certain place..." I was now bound by this oath. Hence, my celestial name is not Veronica...it is something else; a name I must never repeat. A name that will only be used the day the angels will play the trumpet and Jesus will come for the second time and say, "Secret name...Rise!"

After I received the endowments, I was ready to start the actual Temple ceremony. This is a 3-hour ritual where we watch a movie about the creation and our first parents, Adam and

Eve. We also learn the mystical secret signs and tokens that are needed to be admitted into the celestial kingdom. These are hand-shakes, signs and words that we must memorize so that when we meet the angels after this veil of existence, we demonstrate with our knowledge of these signs that we are the chosen people. These heavenly beings then will know we are worthy to be admitted into the highest degree of heaven.

Later in life, I learned that these were masonic rituals introduced by Joseph Smith when he was a prophet in the 1800s as he was a freemason himself. The similarities of symbols, signs, robes, aprons, handshakes, ritualistic raising of the arms, and narratives between Masonry and Mormonism is almost never discussed in the church. I didn't learn about this until my late 30s. The church's formal explanation about this subject is that these Masonry rituals date back to the times of King Solomon in the Old Testament and Joseph Smith recognized that the Masons had preserved some of the same rituals that were part of those times.

During the ritual, all you can see is white – curtains are white, chairs are white and all of us are dressed in white. Women wear a white robe and men white pants and a white shirt. Men sit on one side of the room and women sit on another side and we have to follow the instructions that are given to us very closely. I felt as if someone had asked me to go for a car ride to the store and, suddenly, I found myself on another planet. I had no idea what was happening around me.

As I sat there watching the film about creation, and it got to the part where Adam and Eve disobey God by eating of the tree of knowledge of good and evil, I saw how they realized they were naked and covered their nakedness out of shame.

They paused the film at this point and we were asked to take a green apron out of a white purse made of cloth, which had been given to us at the beginning of the session. We put the green apron around our waists to symbolize the covering of our own nakedness. I thought, "I now have an apron around me. Things are becoming more strange by the second." But I was also thinking, Surrender.

Then, the temple worker standing in front of the room showed us the proper signs and meanings and then other temple workers went around the pew testing our knowledge and doing the sign with each person to make sure we were doing it exactly as it was shown to us. (I still hold respect for or fear about this ritual and I cannot make myself describe the signs.)

At some point, towards the end of the ceremony, they asked a few volunteers to come to the front of the room, men and women, to be part of the prayer circle. Women are supposed to cover their faces with a veil; men are not asked to cover their faces. All of us formed a circle, put our hands up as we repeated at the same time, "Oh God hear the words of my mouth" and then we would lower our hands and we repeated these words three times. "Oh God hear the words of my mouth, Oh God, hear the words of my mouth." Before this experience was over, we were told that if we ever revealed to anyone any of what happened inside the temple, that we would be destroyed.

I thought, since when have I been ok with covering my face in submission? Why is all of this a secret? And why do I need all of this to be with God one day? Is God really this complicated? What had I got myself into?

Then came the time that we had to simulate entering the Celestial Kingdom. The front of the room had a thick white curtain with several holes across the middle where you could only see the hands of each temple worker waiting on the other side of the curtain to welcome you. These temple workers' job is to test us again on our accuracy with all the rituals, hand signals and narratives verbatim, then only after, they would pull our hand and say, "You may come in."

When you go in, that room is the final stop. It is supposed to symbolize the Celestial room where there is complete meditation and silence. If you are there with friends, your friends or significant others can approach you, but again only in whispers. This is the moment where you may spend a few minutes in meditation with God and then leave to change back into your regular clothing but always being sure to wear the temple garments or Mormon underwear.

After my initial temple ceremony, I was never to take those garments off. It is supposed to be a reminder of all the covenants I made with God in the Temple that day. Philene, who is a generational Mormon and this lifestyle was all she knew, asked me, "How do you feel?"

I forced myself to say, "Good…I don't understand everything, but it is ok."

I felt a bit restricted wearing the under garments. They were made of white cotton and the upper garment looks like a thin T-Shirt that covers your shoulders. The bottom undergarment is similar to long shorts that go down to your knees. The only thing that is unique about them is that they have special symbols in certain areas of the undergarments as a reminder of their spiritual meaning. You are not allowed to wear anything underneath the Mormon undergarments as they are supposed to be a blessing and protection. There are superhero stories of Mormons who have gone through accidents, either a car crash or a fire, but were protected because of the power of this divine clothing. It surely felt like Kryptonite could not get to us if we wore this special clothing. I was someone who was used to wearing exercise clothes and felt very comfortable showing my physique. Now, this was a new me, being somewhat restricted, but I was willing to go through all of it because my faith and my desire to serve a mission was bigger than any of these incomprehensible requirements.

Chapter 9.

My Mission

I was now blessed, cleansed and ready to go to the Missionary Training Center (MTC). The MTC looks like a prestigious University with several buildings that were divided at that time by where you were going on a mission and what language you were going to be learning. There was a huge auditorium where the general authorities, top Church Officials like the Prophet and Apostles, came and lectured the missionaries. As soon as I arrived at the MTC, I was introduced to my mission companion, Sister Nuttall. As missionaries, we were not allowed to call each other by our first names. She looked more like a Jewish girl, white with green eyes with wild dark brown hair. Her hair had really thick curls which enhanced her personality and charisma. Her face and demeanor revealed the natural love she has for people. She was slim and full of energy. Before the MTC, she'd attended Brigham Young University, a Mormon University, where she sang and danced professionally, while pursuing a medical degree. She, too, had put her studies on hold to serve the Lord.

As companions, we were supposed to be together at all times, except when we had to go to the bathroom and, even then, we had to wait for each other right outside the door. This is to protect each other or to avoid any sort of temptation. We were often told that the devil was after God's most devoted servants. Since we had a special calling to transform people's lives and bring them salvation, we were his most fierce target. Consequently, we had to be on guard and protect each other.

When I was first introduced to her, I didn't understand her. I wasn't used to the constant affection and attention from someone I just met. I was uncomfortable to hear her express love for me when we had only known each other a few days. My family was not very affectionate, and love was a word that was used carefully, only said when one really meant it. So, I was a bit skeptical of her instant adoration and kept an emotional distance from her. But the more time I spent with her, the more I understood that she was sincere, genuine, pure; therefore, I learned to love her back the same way. We would talk all the time, and I learned that she was raised by an affluent Mormon family who had ties to the general authorities, but I soon learned that even the elite Mormons have their shadows and struggles. And perhaps it was those tormenting shadows that allowed her to have such deep compassion, while carrying her inescapable scars.

She spoke Spanish and French as her father had a senior position at GM and she had lived in different places in the world, like Mexico and France. I can still hear her warm voice, "Hermana Carrera, Te voy a tocar esta cancion en el piano." ("Let me play this song for you on the piano.") We would lie on her side of the bunk bed at night, comfortable with each other, so much so that she would hold me in her arms and sing some of the most beautiful spiritual songs I have ever heard. I would just surrender to this enveloping sisterly love that filled my being. One of her favorites songs that she sang to me over and over was,

"Consider the lilies of the field how they grow, how they grow…Consider the birds in the sky how they fly, how they fly. He clothes the lilies of the field; He feeds the birds in the sky and He will feed those who trust him and guide them with His light."

She was sharing, in her own way, that God will always provide and that He would never let me walk this path alone.

When our time at the MTC was up, we were both going to Chile. We knew we would separate since, when you serve a Mormon mission, you don't get to keep the same companion for too long. Every few weeks or few months, you get what they call "a transfer," either a new area or a new companion. One didn't really question why it was this way. The few unofficial theories I heard was that every place we go is inspired by God and that there are places and people waiting for us in different areas and that they do not want the missionaries to get too comfortable in one place. However, Sister Nuttall and I were happy that at least we were going to the same part of the world, the same mission and that we would do everything possible to see each other.

When we caught the plane to Chile, it was filled with at least 20 missionaries. The young men, dressed in white shirts and dark pants, had black name tags on the pocket of their shirts with white letters that read, "Elder Smith…Or Elder John, The Church of Jesus Chris of Latter-day Saints." We, the sisters, wore our long skirts or dresses with the same type of name tag that said, "Sister Carrera" and right underneath, "The Church of Jesus Christ of Latter-day Saints." It was a long flight, but it was comforting to see many other missionaries on the plane. We felt that we were part of the same family.

Sister Teski was my first mission companion. She was supposed to be my trainer, but she showed little interest for anything that had to do with missionary work. Maybe she was burnt out. She was from the US and had already been in the mission for over a year, so she was not too far from graduating from her mission experience.

We were supposed to follow a rigid schedule: get up at 7am, study the book of Mormon for an hour, then the following hour study as companions and then go out and proselytize all day. Sister Teski hardly followed any of these rules. She would make appointments to see members who would entertain us and feed us, then show up at a sports practice for young men in the church and play soccer with them. I would refuse to do any of it. I would just sit and wait until she was finished.

I didn't directly express my annoyance, but I would ask Teski, "Why are we not proselytizing?"

To which she answered, "Hermana, why don't you relax? I am telling you it is impossible in this area of Limache to find people to teach and baptize. Missionaries have tried for the last couple of years and they have not been able to. The Chileans are flaky and this ward is a mess. The bishop drinks alcohol, but there is no one else that can lead the ward, so they picked the only flawed individual who would do the job. The people in this area may agree to let you teach them because they are polite, but when it comes to following the commitments they need to be baptized, they don't. Relajate! There is really nothing to do here."

I refused to believe Sister Teski. I decided to follow the rules as much as I could until I had the power to follow them completely once she was gone. I had sacrificed so much to be there. I had given up all my savings to pay for the mission, I had left my family and my life behind. I was not willing to waste my time. This was my time to serve God. I would pray that I didn't have to be with her for much longer.

After two months, Sister Teski was transferred to another area to finish her mission and I received a new companion, Sister Rich. She was relatively new to the mission, as well. She was blonde, tall, had blue eyes and barely spoke Spanish.

I am not sure if her heart was in it. She was pleasant to be around, but I resented having someone else who did not want to follow the rules. She would wake up in the mornings sometimes around 9am or even 10am instead of 7am. It was too late to have her personal scriptures study time and, most definitely, too late to study as companions, which needed to happen around 8am and, even worse, we were supposed to be out proselytizing by 10am.

I tried to compensate. I would wake up at 6am instead of 7am and study the Book of Mormon for two hours, high-lighting each verse that impacted me and writing notes on the side on what insight I gained from that scripture. Then, when it came time to study with my companion, I would sit by the small table on the chair and open our missionary manual. The chair across was empty since Sister Rich was still sleeping, so I would ask questions as if she were there so that I would feel that I was following our companionship study time.

During the winter, Chile gets really cold and there were definitely no heating systems in the homes we visited, particularly because Limache is considered more like a country area. I have always hated the cold weather, but I was so determined to follow the mission reading rules that I would motivate myself to get up at 6am whispering to myself, "Obedience Hermana! Obedience"! and I would go under my blankets, turn on a small flashlight and read the book of Mormon attentively. Many months later, after Sister Rich and I were no longer companions, she mentioned that she never forgot my diligence and that she actually heard me talk to myself and asked me to forgive her as she was having a difficult time in the mission when we were there.

However, she was there when I experienced the worst humiliation of my mission. We often visited one of the top Mormon leaders in that area whose wife was wonderful, but he himself would never look at me. When it was time to pray, he would ask Sister Rich or his wife to pray, but I was not allowed to pray in his house. Why? Because according to the Book of Mormon, "I am a disgusting wicked Lamanite."

The book of Mormon talks about a group of people who migrated to the American continent 600 years before Christ from Jerusalem. Lehi, a prophet at that time, his wife, his son Nephite and Laman & Lemuel and their wives arrived in the American continent to start a new civilization. They kept records of their history and, according to the book of Mormon, Nephite was the righteous son, who was always obedient and followed his father's counsel. On the other hand, Laman was the rebellious son, always disobedient who battled continuously with his brother Nephite and father Lehi. God then punished Laman, his brother Lemuel and all those who followed Laman with a "Dark Skin." A dark skin was supposed to be the sign that separated the wicked from the righteous, Good vs Evil. The Lamanites, who are despised in the Book of Mormon, are what Mormons today consider to be the ancestors of the Indigenous people of the American Continent. "Nephite, being the righteous one, had white and delightful skin." Later on, at some point in the Book of Mormon, the story describes that when the Lamanites repented of their sins, their skins became white, precious and pure just as their brethren, the Nephites. I never knew what to make of these scriptures. I loved many parts of the Book of Mormon, but this one was unbelievably humiliating. I still cannot believe that I stood silent and condoned these teachings. As some Mormon friends used to tell me, "Just put it in a box until one day God will reveal more to us so that it can make more sense." I learnt throughout the years that if I wanted to continue in this church, I had to learn to put a lot of things in a box and seal them tightly.

The most grievous and deplorable belief Mormons have been taught about the concept of race are about people of African descent. I happened to read during my mission the writings of Bruce R McConkie, particularly the one titled, "Mormon Doctrine." Bruce R McConkie was a member of the First Council of the Seventy, a general authority highly respected and regarded in the church, who explained that in the pre-existence, the spirits who were not righteous and not willing to follow God's plan for us were born with a dark skin and are the descendants of the African race.

(For a long time, the church taught that the restriction on black people not being able to be baptized came from God and many leaders gave several race-based explanations for the ban, including a curse on Cain and his descendants, Ham's marriage to Egypt, a curse on the descendants of Canaan, and that black people were less valiant in their pre-mortal life).

This brother in Chile treated me as if I was cursed. I took the humiliation, the mortification, the horror and pretended it wasn't happening. Looking back what upset me the most for sometime was my inability to stand up for myself in those moments of betrayal and humiliation. At that time in my life, I believed that I was in God's only true church, so I couldn't even process the ugliness of these beliefs. Many people had been kind to me in the Church. This attitude was horrible, but at that moment, I stayed with the spirituality I believed in. And with time, and as I got older, I would come to stand up against what I believed was wrong.

We did have one more interaction. "Your people, the cursed kind, should stick to your own. When you finish your mission, will you be marrying a black man?" I was dumbfounded and did not respond, excused myself and left his home. Shortly after this, I was transferred out of this area. I was glad I never had to see this man again. It was a moment in my life that I never wanted to look back to. Perhaps because the greatest betrayal was mine for not standing up for myself.

My companion never said anything, nor stood up for me; maybe she wasn't supposed to. I was just happy when I finally left that area and I never had to experience anything like that from another Church member in Chile. Conversely, most of the Chileans I encountered gave me an incredible amount of love.

Sister Rich and I didn't last long as companions, maybe about a month or so. Soon after, I was made the senior missionary and given a newbie, a new sister missionary from Chile who was all heart for this calling. Together, we found many people that we committed to baptism. As her trainer, I wanted to make sure she understood that we were first there to obey all the rules without exception and only then God would bless us in this work. But she didn't even need me to explain this, she was truly there for the right reasons. We baptized more people in three months than other missionaries had baptized in years.

My nickname in the mission was "the machine." That was for the most part flattering, but not completely. That nickname was given to me not only because I wanted to follow the rules with exactitude but also, from my companions' perspective, I was all about work that often I lacked emotions. In other words, to some of the missionaries in the field, I did not come across as very warm or affectionate. I wasn't fun! I was mostly programmed to do what I was supposed to do.

Furthermore, I did not believe that we had the luxury of feeling tired or depressed. In my mind, there was no reason to have either of those emotions when we were too busy doing the Lord's work. How could we have time to feel sad if we are constantly working, knocking on doors, talking to people in the streets about the gospel? I wouldn't chat much about personal stuff either with most of my trainees; most of our conversations were about missionary work. If my companions would spend too much time talking about their personal lives, past boyfriends, I would find it trivial. In fact, our mission President had discouraged us from talking about our personal lives as it was a distraction from our spiritual calling. I had not learned the meaning of grace yet because I did not have it for myself.

But when I look back, I had some very special powerful spiritual experiences that I will never forget. My investigators, as we called those receiving the missionary discussions, most of them loved me back ten-fold. I hold their memory tightly in the most sacred space of my soul. How could I ever forget this part of my life? How could I ever turn my back on any of it?

One of my first spiritual experiences as a Missionary was in Limache. The main streets there are paved, but most streets are dirt roads. The houses in the main areas are medium size and built out of cement as opposed to the poorest areas where most houses are the size of a bedroom in Manhattan. A lot of them are built on a hill.

The church in this area was disorganized in a way that I had never experienced. The bishop would show up extremely late to open the building and there would be a line of members, maybe around fifteen, waiting. The leadership was almost nonexistent.

On my first Sunday, a few of the members, my companion and I were waiting impatiently outside the church for the bishop to open the premises. After over thirty minutes, he showed up nonchalantly and let us in. As I was walking in with my companion, a member approached me with urgency, "Sister, Sister! We don't have anyone to teach the primary children. Can you do it?"

I was speechless. I had never taught children or had been around children much, so I asked, "How old are they?"

I could sense the need in his voice, "They are the children that I bring every Sunday from the orphanage. I grew up in that same orphanage and they are 5 to 7 years old, around that age! Follow me to the primary room…They are waiting, sister!"

I hesitantly followed. The children were sitting down at their desks. The room looked like a school room. Those little faces were attentively looking at me waiting for me to speak and I had no idea what to do. There was only the silence of my thoughts, how do I even start? What do I say? What if I lose complete control of the room?

Suddenly I had an idea, what if I just teach them how to pray? Yes, that is easy. We Mormons follow the same format every time.

Our Dear Heavenly Father…

We give Thee thanks…

We ask Thee…

In the name of Jesus Christ.

Amen.

I tried to become animated. "CHILDREN, WE ARE GOING TO GO OVER OUR PRAYERS TODAY!"

They all cheered! "YAY!!!"

"So, we start our prayers directing them to our Heavenly Father and then we give Him thanks for all of our blessings. But, let me ask you, what do you give thanks for?"

They raised their hands and each of them gave me an answer.

"I am thankful for the bread that we get each day."

"I am thankful for the air we breathe."

"I am thankful that I had breakfast this morning." And the answers were those simple and pure answers that had a wisdom that we adults seem to forget.

Then I asked, "What would you want to ask God for?'

One of them quickly answered, "I want a doll!"

Then they all started raising their hand, "Me, me, I want to share!"

"Ok. Your turn," I said to one of the children raising his hand.

"I want to see the beach."

And the answers kept on coming enthusiastically.

Then Mariela, a 5-year old tiny precious Chilean girl, raised her hand and, with a sad look on her face, said, "I pray for all those children in Africa who don't have anything to eat." She put her head face-down on the desk and all I could see was her tiny little head as I felt all her emotions.

How could a 5-year orphan girl feel so much tenderness and sadness for the misfortune of other children? Mariela deeply touched my heart and, although many years have passed, I have never forgotten her little innocent angelic face.

On another occasion, my new companion and I were proselytizing in the middle of a torrential cold rain when the spirit, as we used to say when we were inspired to do something, led us to the top of a hill. In the midst of the heavy rain, I saw a home and we knocked on the door. I was feeling sick at that point, cold and shivering.

A woman opened the door and she immediately asked us to come in. She said, "Oh Dios, you must be cold! Please come close to the oven. You need to dry up a bit." Once in, I felt comfortable and serene inside her home, but I noticed that she looked at me rather intensely and then she asked me to follow her. My companion stayed in the living room and then the woman said, "Yesterday I had a dream that God was going to send an angel to my house and that I must let you in."

Her beautiful words made me ponder if I had indeed been divinely assigned to do this work. I felt this special human connection with her and a great affection for her children. Not too long after this first encounter, she and her two sons got baptized. I remember particularly, Cesar, her first one, a serious young boy who felt passionate about politics would eagerly share the Chilean history with us. Through him I learned about the oppressive dictator Pinochet and what the people of Chile went through at that time, how they were liberated, and the sense of pride they felt for this beautiful country. There is a level of maturity, depth and at the same time naturalness that I have experienced in the young people of our Latin American countries that is endearing which I miss.

I was given another companion after a couple of months and I became her trainer or senior companion. We worked hard, we baptized many, but we never became close friends as I treated her more like a missionary companion assigned to me. Since we are all mirrors of each other, I think my distance was more of a reflection of the distance to my own heart.

Nevertheless, there was one person I couldn't wait to see, Sister Nuttall. Every time we had a regional meeting with our Mission President, all of the missionaries got together, and Sister Nuttall and I couldn't wait to update each other on what had transpired so far in our missions. She would write me letters sharing her experiences and struggles, she also had a hard time with her trainer. We longed to be with each other as family would. Our Mission President became aware of our devotion and made it a point for us to never serve together as companions in Chile.

We never figured out why he was so resistant to having us serve together, but Sister Nuttall was the one who requested it a few times and her hypothesis was that he was afraid we would be too crazy together.

On one occasion in one of our P-days (Partial days off), which were Monday half days, we were allowed to be regular human beings and have some play time. All of the missionaries got together but the activities were limited to approved missionary activities. No TV, no music, and we still had to abide by the strict mission rules. We were allowed to watch an approved movie like Star Wars, which I had very little interest in. My apathy to Star Wars did not probably win me many friends and I can see their point!. But this time, we were in some beach area that had some high dunes. Sister Nuttall and I climbed to the top and then she told me, "Do you want to lock together like a ball and we just roll down the dune?" I didn't hesitate, she put her head inside my two legs and I did the same until we curled into a ball and rolled down this dune. On the way down, as we were coming down with such a force, Sister Nuttall ejected in one direction and I on the other. When we arrived at the end of the hill, all roughed up, the rest of the missionaries found it amusing, but not our mission President who shook his head. I could hear his thoughts, "There they go again!"

I really took my mission calling seriously. I had chosen to give all to it and I could not afford to not be the type of missionary that God would want me to be.

And, because I was aware of my own internal struggles, I had profound empathy for anyone struggling with what seemed to be an insurmountable "sin." My companion and I found an older man in the town of Belloto who was an alcoholic. He must have been in his 50s, with weathered skin, and a warm smile. I will call him Pedro. The whole town knew him as he had not been sober for many years. When I approached him to talk about God, although I was a few feet away from him, I was distracted by the strong smell of alcohol coming out of his pores. My companion seemed initially a bit uncomfortable about our going up to him, but I swiftly made my argument, "God loves Pedro as much as He loves you and me and nothing should stop us from teaching him the missionary discussions. We preach all the time that God is a God of miracles, then why would this be any different?" She nodded in agreement.

Pedro was a kind, loving, humble man, who listened to everything we had to say attentively, and I believe he truly made an effort to stop drinking. Being raised a Mormon, I never experienced the chains and shackles of addiction to any substance or drug, in fact, as a Mormon, I didn't even drink coffee. However, I did understand the pain and the affliction of trying hard to get rid of something that you just can't control.

When we took Pedro to the church services, the bishop of the ward asked to speak to me privately, "How dare you bring this alcoholic man to our ward? Everyone thinks he is a lost cause and he makes everyone here uncomfortable!" My companion sat next to me and remained quiet, but I knew she was on my side.

I told the bishop, "Is this a church just for perfect people? If that is the case, then there is no place for Christ here. If we teach that Jesus came to redeem us all, then that includes Pedro. You have no right to tell me I cannot bring him to this Church."

"That is insolence," he replied angrily. "As a missionary you are supposed to be obedient to what your leaders tell you. I am going to report this incident to the Stake President and your Mission President."

I calmly, said, "Go ahead and report me. I hope they have better sense than you do." I wanted so desperately to believe that we didn't worship a God who only favored the Latter-day Saints and who saw everyone else as 'the other,' to be rejected by the hollowness of men.

Jesus himself was misunderstood, rejected and crucified by men. Why are we any different? Maybe everything repeats itself and that gave me hope, hope that after Gethsemane and the crucifixion, there is also a resurrection for all of us. And, the truth was, when it came to the shadows of mankind, I saw myself more like Pedro than any other "Latter-day Saint."

There were many days of proselytizing, working with the community, and trying to do good. Until one day, the Mission President's niece, Laura, was sent from Utah as she was attending BYU and had come to spend some time with her uncle and family at the request of her parents.

The mission president thought that she should spend time with Sister Carrera as I was his top baptizing missionary and an example to the other sister missionaries. In fact, women are not supposed to lead in the big mission conferences, but he often made me one of the key speakers in the major missionary conferences and he even had me serve for some time as a traveling sister, teaching struggling missionaries how to teach and baptize.

When Laura arrived at our apartment, her smile just lit the whole place. Laura was from Argentina but grew up in Utah. She had thick long black hair, and a beautiful face. As I stared into her deep black eyes, I fell into an endless night where I didn't long even for the stars. We became inseparable. In fact, we would often try to get a member to accompany my regular companion to proselytize so that Laura and I could spend more time together proselytizing as well. After a few weeks, I started to feel a bit out of control with my emotions. Even on our half days off when we got together with other missionaries, I couldn't stomach seeing her around other elders. She was magnetic and, therefore, I always thought the elders would make an extra effort to be around her. I would go back to my own room to read but, being the thoughtful person she was, she would come and check on me.

At this point, I was praying so hard, "God, what is going on with me? Why do I have this attraction?!" I started to fast more often, no food or water for a day almost on a weekly basis so that God would give me the strength to resist whatever was going on inside of me. "I am a missionary. I am supposed to be an example!" I would say that to myself as I struggled with the emotions of being deeply attracted to this girl. How can one feel such overwhelming prohibited emotions and have no one to talk to!

I am not sure our Mission President noticed anything unusual, but he called Laura to our apartment and told her that she had to go and live with them in the mission home and that her time with me and my companion was over. I felt as if he was putting an end to my happiness and there was nothing I could do about it. Laura begged him not to leave, but she had to obey her uncle's orders. After all, he was the mission president.

I had taught myself through the years to put my duty for God above my own heart. After a couple of weeks of not seeing Laura, I was surprised when she unexpectedly showed up at our apartment since her uncle had given her orders not to return. She said, "I left my uncle's house because I'd rather be here. I wanted to see you."

I believe she only saw me as a friend and for some reason she was intensely drawn to me. But me, I was in love. The pain of being in love with a friend is so difficult because you have to keep those feelings inside. I knew I had to take her back to her uncle.

We got on a bus and held hands as we traveled back to the mission home. She put her head on my shoulder as we took that long bus ride. Nothing else was real, only she filled the space of my existence and I needed nothing more. As we arrived at our destination, we said goodbye.

The following weeks, I was a little sick and lonely until the next mission conference where all the missionaries came together to listen to our mission president. I knew Laura was going to be there. But I was not prepared for what she had to say.

I saw her walk into the room where all the missionaries were sitting and then she came up to me and said, "My uncle is sending me back to Utah. I wrote you this letter. I want you to read it when I go away." I was sitting next to Sister Nuttall. I excused myself as I followed Laura to a black car that was waiting for her at the entrance of the building. Her uncle was there. She looked at me with those deep black eyes that melted the most hidden icy corners of my soul. She gave me a hug and said, "Thank you for changing my life." She got inside the car and drove off and waved goodbye until I could see her no more.

I stood there for a moment. I could not possibly run after her…I could not possibly tell her that I had strong romantic feelings for her. I went back inside the conference and sat next to Sister Nuttall. For some reason, I felt that she understood; that there was no need to explain. I put my head on her shoulder, she hugged me and we were completely silent. I had the broken heart of a soul in shackles, not free to express the depth of one's love.

I read Laura's letter. She expressed the depth of her own love and how I had impacted her life. But it was clear by the way she wrote that she only saw me as a friend. This is the hard part of being gay. You fall in love many times with people who can't love you back the same way.

After some time, I put Laura in a box that I never opened again. I was getting really good at putting people and things in boxes. I was to learn that this was the only way I could survive in this church. Whatever I had been taught that was not supposed to fit into my life, I had to lock it in a box.

Strangely, even though I was considered a devoted missionary at this point of my mission, I was also known to be intense and a rule enforcer. Isn't this ironic? The rule enforcer who was trying mercilessly not to break the tiniest mission rule, was holding onto a spiritual and psychological invisible thread for her own life. And, at that time, I would rather shatter myself than shatter my faith.

Our mission president gave us monthly targets of the number of people we were supposed to baptize, and I fell into the numbers trap. There were times that my ambition to hit the goal overpowered my underlying pure motive to change people's lives. The ones who baptized the most were praised and rewarded publicly and that can be addictive. This pride makes missionaries lose sight of their real calling, which is the calling to minister, the calling to heal, the calling to serve and love. And I had many wonderful experiences of exactly this. My favorite people were in the city of Limache and Belloto, especially the church members in Belloto.

Maria Luisa Poblete, the daughter of the bishop, was a vibrant happy funny lady. Her short hair and slim body went along with her personality. She talked really fast like a true Chilean. She treated me as if I was a celebrity. Every time she would see me approaching the church, she would animatedly rush quickly toward me with open arms and say, "Hermana Carrera Po! Como estais? So happy to see you!!! Come here, let me introduce you to some people!" And she would proudly introduce me to anyone she could think of. I adored Ana Luisa and, even now, we stay connected.

At this point I was close to the final months of my mission. Although I had spent most of my mission giving my full heart and strength, at this point, I did what I had to do mechanically. Maybe I was growing tired. It had been over a year of countless days and months of proselytizing, walking for hours in all kinds of weather, knocking on doors, approaching people in the streets to see if we could capture their interest to hear our message. Then there was immersing myself in people's stories, their challenges, and taking them along the journey of teachings and discussions till we convinced them to get baptized. There was an inner pressure to perform and I know most of the missionaries felt it and, if they didn't, there was a sense of failure. I know because I had to help a few of the missionary companions overcome this sense of inadequacy and failure.

During this time, I received a new companion, Sister Noboa. She was a slim girl, who had green eyes and shiny dark brown hair, high cheek bones and very easy to get along with. Anything I did made her laugh, so it was pleasant to spend so much time with her. We spent a few months as companions, and she became one of my favorite companions.

One night I was sound sleep and unexpectedly woke up feeling someone next to me. It was Sister Noboa. She put her hands gently on my head and guided my face towards her chest. My senses awakened intensely, and I didn't pull away. Our lips touched and our bodies were close to each other. A few minutes after, I saw myself standing at the edge of a precipice to what I did not know. I abruptly pulled away and Sister Noboa just looked at me for a few seconds and then went back to her bed.

The next day, I wouldn't even look at her. I didn't want to get out of bed either. I barely wanted to eat; I became depressed. In my mind, I had committed a grave sin right in my own mission! What a disgrace! All the sacrifices I had made were for nothing! I am just a failure, I thought.

I spent the next few days not wanting to talk or see anyone. I was agitated at night and would wake up feeling desperate. Why can't God make me disappear! Why can't He at least do me that favor?

Even though hardly anything happened, I felt like I betrayed my calling and that I was no longer worthy to teach anyone about God. Sister Noboa grew worried and she tried to console me, but I treated her with disgust. It was as if I blamed her for bringing out these unwanted emotions in me. I pretended she didn't exist.

Looking back, she wouldn't have felt that way, unless she sensed I was different. I felt I could no longer bear to live in that world where I was a fraud, where what I had to deal with deep inside made me a criminal by the church's standards. The words of the Prophet Spencer W Kimball would ring again in my mind, "Homosexuality is a sin next to murder.' I was glad my mission was coming to an end.

I asked to see my mission president. After I finished confessing "my sin," President Michalek looked at me and said, "You are too hard on yourself, Sister Carrera. Nothing really happened. But for whatever thoughts came to your mind, just go and sin no more."

His words gave me some comfort, but I was not fully convinced of my innocence. I recognized that there was something deeper than that moment and my turmoil and despair indicated to me that I was broken.

My mission was up, and I didn't have any money, nor did I know where I was going to live after Chile. The bishop of the ward I attended before my mission contacted me to inform me that he and his family would welcome me into their home. I didn't have a relationship with him or his family, but I didn't think I had any other options as I had been disconnected from my family, so I gladly accepted.

I came back to the United States after being gone for almost two years, but It really felt like I had been gone for a decade. I had lived a completely different identity as a missionary and now I did not know who I was anymore. I felt as if someone had sent me to Mars and then abruptly placed me back on Earth. After experiencing what I had in Chile, I did not know how to integrate this newly formed person I was with my post mission life. I had heard many stories of returned missionaries who became depressed and had a hard time adjusting to their lives after coming back. However, most take on fiercely the next thing expected of them as returned missionaries, which is to find someone worthy of them to marry.

Andrea, the health spa manager, hired me again even though I had gained about 15 pounds from eating the amazingly delicious homemade Chilean food like 'Completos,' the Chilean hot dog. Completos are more elaborate than American hot dogs, made with bread fresh out of the oven, grass-fed meat, avocado, fresh cheese and a variety of other delicious ingredients that makes this hot dog a hidden treasure. Completos was just one among many other wonderful homemade meals that the generous people in Chile so graciously shared with us.

On one occasion while I was proselytizing in a poor area up in the mountains, we visited this older woman who lived in a small house where the living room was only big enough to fit a small table and two chairs. My companion and I sat on the chairs, and with the usual hospitality of the Chilean people, the old woman immediately asked us if we were hungry and we were, as we usually spent hours walking. Then she said, "What about some chicken soup?"

"That sounds delicious," I answered hastily. As missionaries, we did not have the luxury of spending much money on food so we relied on the hospitality of the people. Then the woman crossed through a small plastic worn out curtain which divided the living room from the kitchen and brought back a live chicken, twisting its neck while the chicken squawked loudly and feathers flew all over us. This was our first slaughtering of a chicken right in front of our eyes and so closely that, if I extended my arm, I could have touched the dying chicken. I was amused by the face of my American mission companion from Arizona whose face was pallid and seconds away from passing out. The whole horror scene was over in a matter of minutes and, in less than an hour, we were having a warm delicious chicken soup. I forgot the incident we had just witnessed and devoured the food. On the contrary, my companion looked disturbed and was having a hard time swallowing.

After such a different life in another country, here I was back in Miami where glamour, money and image mattered. What helped me was having the same church community and the friendship of a few returned missionaries, particularly my friend Ruth. Ruth listened to me endlessly and I eventually started to return to this old way of life, but not entirely. I felt deep within me that my life would never be the same and, in unexpected ways, it never was.

I started teaching aerobics again and, in a matter of months, I lost most of the weight I had gained back in my mission. However, I knew that there was more to life than what I was doing. It was as if someone had taken away from me my personality, my identity and I had lost my capacity to connect with the world.

After a few weeks, my favorite mission companion and friend, Amie Nuttall, called me from Europe as she was travelling with her family. "Sister Carrera, it is Sister Nuttall." My heart beat with joy.

"How are you?" I asked.

She didn't waste time as she was calling long distance, "I think you should go back to college, but I want you to come to

Brigham Young University (BYU). I do not think Miami is for you anymore. I am going to Medical school and perhaps you and I can do this together. Please, Sister Carrera, you were an outstanding missionary. You are meant to do great things. I will help you with the paperwork, we can ask our mission president to endorse you for a scholarship."

I was silent as I listened to her plea. How could I say no to such grace and love?

After a long pause, I said, "Let's go for it."

She cried on the phone and told me how much she cared for me. She didn't need to say it, I knew that gift of wonderful care that God places in people's hearts so that we can make it through this long journey of life. Within a couple of weeks, I received the application to apply for BYU Provo, but I still had not finished my Associates of Arts in my local college so there were a couple of classes that I needed to take to be a more competitive candidate, raise my GPA and qualify for BYU Provo. The strategy was to then apply to BYU Idaho as it was not as difficult to get into as BYU Provo. I would finish those two courses there and transfer to BYU Provo.

I was determined to go to BYU and, not too long after, I received an acceptance letter for BYU Idaho and my whole life shifted, transformed, and awoke to new truths, but not the kind of truths that one might expect.

When I arrived at Rexburg, Idaho, I met my lovely white young Mormon roommates. I truly felt that I was in a cowboy town. The racial makeup of the city is approximately 95.20% white, less than 1% African American and Hispanic and minorities added up to 4.04% of the population. At BYU Idaho, the Blacks and Latinos were almost non-existent.

Everyone in the dorm looked like typical joyful and wholesome Mormon young women, whose main taste in music seemed to be country music. I put my luggage down and the first thing I did was go to the school office. All that was required for me to finish was an English class with at least a B before I could transfer to BYU Provo. When I arrived at the office, the administrator told me that the class was full, but that since this was a required course for me to transfer, the professor was obliged to let me in. She suggested I go to his office right away. I walked in and saw an older white man in his late 50s, sitting in a black leather chair behind his desk. I was so happy to be at BYU that I greeted him cheerfully, "Professor, my name is Veronica Carrera and I am here just for one semester to complete a couple of required courses, and then transfer to BYU Provo. I need to take your class and, apparently, I need your approval to get in."

He started to smile, which turned into a quick laugh. I laughed with him since I thought he was just happy to meet me. Then he said, "You, Spanish people. You think you can come here and compete with the Americans, you will be lucky if you get a D in my class."

My heart sank at that moment, but I kept the smile on my face. I guess this was not the Holy Promised land I expected. I answered politely, "Well, that is not an option."

I walked away with a rude awakening that I was an outsider. For this white man, I was a person of color who did not belong there and did not deserve the same opportunities he and others who look like him did. This dilemma and injustice have followed many people of color throughout history.

During classes, I would raise my hand to participate and he ignored me all semester. I wanted to prove this professor wrong. I got a tutor, I worked diligently in my assignments and I ended up getting an A– in his class. When I received my final writing assignment, which was worth 40% of our grade, I saw the A- written on the paper with a note, "Well done." I smiled at this since it was the only time he ever said anything to me. Up to that point I had been invisible. I hoped that those two words came with some drop of respect for what I had overcome with him, and some respect for who I am.

My time at BYU Ricks College in Rexburg, Idaho was short, but significant. The girls I lived with were mostly from the West Coast and were as white as could be. I did not feel any rejection from them, if anything, I felt embraced by many, accepted by others or at least tolerated. I actually have some wonderful memories of some of the friendships I built. Everyone in our student housing attended church together and we all had the same bishop. The bishop was one of the kindest and most compassionate ministers I have encountered in the Mormon church.

During my first month at BYU Idaho, I met a Mexican girl who lived right across from my apartment in our on-campus student housing. The way she looked at me was different, not the way a girl looks at another girl. Her intense gaze spoke to me of danger. This felt all too familiar, I could sense now when a girl liked me. I experienced again this anxiety rushing through my body, as if there was something sinful within me. I couldn't fathom paying attention to her. But she visited me often and, even though I tried to discourage her a few times, she was persistent. On one occasion, when I was in the apartment alone, she came in and sat closely next to me on the couch in the living room. As she spoke to me, she came even closer and, although I was trying not to look at her directly, I could sense the closeness of her face to mine and then she whispered in my ear, "I like you." She suddenly pressed her lips lightly on mine and I didn't react or resist. It wasn't about her; it was about that physical sensation of someone touching me, a sensation that I could not allow myself to feel. All of this made me feel physically and emotionally exhausted.

A series of thoughts flashed through my mind, "Why am I always dealing with this! Will this never go away?" I started to feel like a wounded soldier who has been asked to fight one senseless battle after the other, and who just has to fight until he/she dies.

I saw Teresa a few more times and, even though our interactions were not sexual, we got close enough to know that what we had was not a friendship. She would grab my hand when we walked off campus, or she would visit me in my bedroom so that we could have opportunities to be alone. All this made me run to the bishop for help and guidance.

There is nothing more terrifying than walking into a bishop's office to confess that you are an immoral ticking bomb because you have detestable homosexual tendencies or, worse, that you have acted on them. All that rang through my head were the words of one of the beloved church prophets, Spencer W Kimball, "Homosexuality is the most abominable above all sins save it be the shedding of innocent blood..." How can someone live with the possibility of committing a sin that is in the same category as murder? I had to confess.

All bishops are available for one-on-one interviews with church members after services. Frequently, these interviews are for those who find themselves in situations they need guidance about or forgiveness, for we are taught that to be washed clean from sin, we must confess our sins to a church authority. Depending on the gravity, such as a violation of the law of chastity (including homosexuality), the process will be escalated to a Stake President, a higher authority who oversees several wards or churches. The stake president decides whether you need to be suspended or excommunicated. Excommunication is the most devastating punishment one can receive as a member of the church.

As soon as I walked in, before I could speak, I started bawling.

"Bishop, I have homosexual tendencies. Teresa showed interest in me and I allowed her to get close to me. I do not know what to do with this thing I have inside of me." I wept inconsolably.

He looked at me compassionately and without judgement. His eyes swelled with tears as I explained in detail the agony, my guilt and terrible distress.

"If you have not had any intimate interaction with Teresa, you have done the right thing. Just know that the Lord loves you, I love you and as a representative of God, I forgive you. Go and sin no more."

I left his office feeling more at peace. At least for the rest of my time in Idaho, I stopped feeling like this horrible person who couldn't control her immoral tendencies. This was the first and one of those rare occasions in the Mormon church that a bishop didn't make me feel that I was some sort of dishonorable, repulsive being. I wasn't punished, I was allowed to continue participating in my church calling and never talked about this Teresa incident again. Teresa and I saw each other from time to time but I made all efforts to avoid her.

During this time while I was walking to a class on campus, I ran into Michael. Michael had been in my Missionary Training class in Provo, Utah, and we'd spent two months sharing the same classroom to prepare to go on our missions. He was back from his mission in the Dominican Republic, so we were happy to see each other and he enjoyed chatting with me with his new Dominican accent. He was a 6'5, white American, slim, sensitive and smart. I had happy memories of Michael during our time at the MTC (Missionary Training Center); he was a good, sensitive elder. After we met, we started spending a lot of time together and I developed a strong emotional and spiritual connection to him. He was one of the most thoughtful men I had ever met in my life. He expressed his desire to see me often, so we started dating. Dating for Mormons is not like dating in the regular world, there is no French kissing or touching. Church leaders recommend that type of passion should be reserved for marriage. Hence, the most Michael and I did was give each other a peck kiss.

After having come back from a mission, marriage is the next thing to do and I was open to this idea of following the path that was expected of me. Maybe this would be my chance to have a normal life and I envisioned this with Michael. But as time passed, and as we got a little more serious, he started to withdraw and I felt an aching distance from him. Although we shared a close friendship and we could talk about anything, I couldn't get him to reveal his doubts and hesitation to move forward.

I alleged that perhaps his distance had to do with the church's stand on marrying someone of a different race. One time we were sitting together at a devotional where Elder Russell Nelson, one of the twelve Apostles of the church then, gave a talk on marriage. As I was paying close attention to this Lord's mouthpiece, suddenly the flow of this inspirational talk took an appalling tack when this man whom we all revered as an Apostle of God said, "Marriage is hard enough as it is, so make it easier. Marry your own race. Do not mix." I was deeply embarrassed as I looked around and it seemed that we were the only mixed couple in the auditorium. I wanted to disappear, and I did not even want to ask Michael how he felt. No one in this church goes against the prophet or apostles. I often ask myself now, "How did this ever make sense to me? What made me not rise with indignation against this atrocious, humiliating and harmful belief system?" It was an insult to my soul again and again and again and I just took it because there was so much good in the church as well.

Eventually Michael and I broke up. I had so many questions and I also lost a dear friend when we separated. A year later, it all made sense and it all unveiled with an unexpected twist. Michael was gay. Sometimes in life things make sense later, and for now, we just have to accept life as it comes.

One afternoon before I graduated from BYU Idaho, I received a letter from BYU Provo with truly exciting news: I had been accepted to Brigham Young University in Provo, UT. Everything I had dreamed of accomplishing within the Mormon faith, I had done. I had gone on a mission and now I was about to go to the most desired school for Mormons. Only the elite Mormons go there. When I was 14 and I had just joined the Mormon church, I read an article in the Ensign, a popular LDS magazine that all members read as scripture since it is filled with the prophet and apostles' discourses. In this article, a young woman who was a church convert dreamt of making it to Utah and being accepted at BYU. She ultimately was and I remember reading this article while I was still a young girl in Ecuador and I felt inspired and I thought, "I want to do that. I want to go to BYU someday."

My next goal was to become a teacher at the Missionary Training Center. This was one of the most honorable and prestigious jobs you could have while being a student at BYU. Only the best returned missionaries were given a chance to apply and only a very few were accepted.

I had enough money to pay for school and living expenses while at BYU Idaho, but I had not planned at all for my move to Utah. I think I had an innocent optimism then. Underneath any fear, I had an unwavering faith that somehow God would always open the way. I sure hoped so because, by the time I was about to graduate from BYU Idaho, I had only $60 to my name. This was not enough money to travel to Utah, find a place to live and pay the first month's rent or eat for the next month or so until I could find a job. I had no idea what the future held, but I was comfortable in this place of uncertainty.

The graduation ceremony came while at BYU Idaho, and I was wearing my tassel and gown standing in line heading to the ceremony. As we were walking in a straight line, one of the few Spanish girls that I'd met on campus, Rosa, was right behind me. She was a pretty light skin Mexican girl with beautiful long curly light brown hair. She had the thickest Spanish accent I had ever heard including mine and a very light cheerful personality. Enthusiastically she called out, "Veronica! Felicitaciones! We are graduating! I am going to BYU Provo! What about you?"

"Me too!' I answered.

She seemed excited for me, "Where are you going to live?"

I had no answer. It had only been two weeks since I received my acceptance letter and I was surprisingly calm given my situation. I was supposed to leave BYU Idaho in 2 days.

I told her with a peaceful smile, "I don't know Rosa. I still don't have a place to live."

Without any hesitation in her voice, I heard the unbelievable, "Come and live with me. My mom owns a home in Provo close to campus and we already have 4 people there. We have space for one more roommate!"

This truly felt like a miracle. I was grateful for the offer, but I told her, "Rosa, I have no money to pay you for now."

Without a pause, she said, "Don't worry…You pay me when you start working."

My biggest problem was solved. Now I needed a way to get from Rexburg, Idaho to Provo, Utah- $60 was not going to do that. I had one black friend on Campus, Brooks. I think she was the only black girl I had seen in the whole school. She was from Jamaica and had been adopted by an upper middle-class white family. We became like sisters. The day of my graduation, she contacted me to tell me that she had asked her adopted parents to drive me to Provo, Utah. "You are my sister and I want to be the one who takes you to Utah."

I have never forgotten these blessings. As much as I have experienced some significant trials in my life, I have also experienced a lot of goodness and it was with goodness that I made it to Provo, Utah.

IRONMAN PART 2.

I had completed the swimming part of the Ironman. Now I would face the next part of the journey.

I stepped out of the Hudson river and ran with my wet suit still on towards the bike transition area. I took my wet suit off, my shorts and sports bra underneath, so all I needed was to put my cycling shorts on top and my cycling shoes on. I also quickly put on my helmet, gloves and sunglasses. All of this happens fast, you want to gain as much time as possible, ideally in less than 3 minutes. The transition area had everything organized for me: what I was going to change into when I got out of the water and what I was going to change into when I got off of my bike.

I made it out of the water and now I had 112 miles to go on the bike. I did not start either too slow or too hard, I gave it my best, knowing as well that I had about 6 hours to cover the distance. I paced myself well. I set an alert on the Garmin watch attached to the front of my bike, which reminded me to drink my nutrition. Most of us do not, especially if we are trying to race competitively, eat anything solid. So, the alarm reminded me to drink my electrolyte drink from my water bottle every 15 minutes. For the next 6 hours I did just that. My bike held 5 water bottles. One big one in the middle of my handlebars, two bottles from the bottom tubes and two bottles on the back of my seat. This gave me enough water and electrolyte drinks to last for the first half of the ride. But with all the water or liquids one has to intake, there is a point that one has to go to the bathroom, but when to do it? The answer is most Triathletes who are racing against time, especially if they want to qualify for Kona (Kona is the most popular Ironman race where only the top athletes under each age category can race), they just don't stop to pee. You learn how to pee on the bike. So, as for me, when it was time to go, at a high speed, I lifted myself slightly from my saddle and off I went. I think I peed twice on my bike that day!

The first 56 miles, I felt strong, but as I reached mile 40, I had finished most of my electrolyte drinks and water. I only had one bottle left. As I was peddling fast to not lose momentum, I took one hand off the handlebar and reached towards the back of my seat where the other bottle with my electrolyte was located. My hand grabbed the bottle, but as I was moving my arm forward, I lost the bottle and it flew backwards, "Oops, I lost it!" There was nothing left to do, but keep on going. Because I had heard tips from other athletes that it was a good idea to save an empty bottle just with the electrolyte powder in case this happened, I actually had done that and it was in one of the few bottle holders on my bike. I made a quick stop to refuel and added water to the bottle with the electrolyte powder so it would last me for the end of the ride.

The last 56 miles, I was definitely feeling it. Make no mistake, the bike part of the race is tough. You have to peddle fast nonstop for 112 miles after having swam for 2.4 miles and I got to the end feeling a bit sick. But I didn't feel sick because I was tired, I felt sick in my stomach. The only explanation I could have was that I must have gotten sick when I swam in the Hudson. The week before the race, there was a sewage spill in the Hudson and the race was almost canceled. But a day before the race, we were told that the swim was on.

So, as I always did, not matter what I was facing, I just kept on. This is what I had conditioned myself to do all my life. I was determined to go the long distance in the Mormon Church, excelling, only to have to eventually, just as in the Ironman race, run.

Chapter 10.

The Long Road to Questioning the Unquestionable

As soon as I arrived at Rosa's house, I lay down on the carpeted living room floor exhausted and hungry. Suddenly a tiny 4'7 Asian girl came out of one of the bedrooms, "Are you the new roommate?"

"Yes, I am. Nice to meet you."

She looked at me with those wonderful serious Asian eyes and, after studying me for a few seconds, she proceeded to speak, "My name is Mai. Are you hungry? I am about to make some Chinese food. Would you like some?"

I immediately reacted with a huge, but weary smile on my face, "I love Asian food!!!"

She then smiled at me, perhaps because I showed appreciation for her culture. With that, we had become friends.

The first week I was there I applied to teach at the Missionary Training Center. To my surprise, they called me within a week and asked me to audition right away and, within two weeks, I was hired.

It turned out Mai never stopped cooking for me during our time at BYU. She loved doing it and I thoroughly enjoyed her home cooked Chinese food. Eating together every day after we came home from school became one of our rituals. Also, she and I used to pray and read the scriptures together before we went to bed. We shared many spiritual moments that created a sisterhood, an unbreakable bond and trust.

Mai had lived in Australia with her parents before coming to Provo. Her parents owned a Chinese restaurant there and Mai used to help them run it. She had met the Mormon missionaries in Australia and took to the discussions. Her parents never knew about her interest in the missionary or the Mormon church or that she had secretly got baptized, but when she told them that she wanted to move to Utah to pursue her education, her parents immediately opposed it. Ultimately, they let her go and agreed to support her financially. Mai would say often, "If my parents ever find out that I became a Mormon, they will disinherit me and stop paying for school." That was exactly what happened. Her parents found out and Mai, who was in the States with a student visa, now struggled to pay for school and living expenses.

Mai had become like family to me so I told her that I would help her in any way I could financially. I got paid fairly well at the MTC. But I thought of another plan. On my way to school, I always passed a Chinese restaurant, I think it was the only one in that area. One afternoon as I was coming back from school, I decided to walk in. The restaurant was small, with about 6 small tables with a couple of chairs next to them. I sat down to look at their menu; it was hard to read, not really organized. I asked the waitress who the owner was and, as she walked away to the kitchen, a Chinese man in his 50s and his wife introduced themselves in their broken English, "Hi, we are owners. How can we help you?'

I looked them in the eyes and spoke from my heart, "I have a friend who is Chinese. She is here on a visa going to school and she needs a job! Her parents own a Chinese restaurant in Australia, and she used to run the restaurant. Look at your menu, it is not well put together! I think you could use her help! She can help you with anything you need."

Without saying a word, they both looked at each other and I waited eagerly for their answer, not taking my eyes off them. Then the man said, "Bring her here." The next day we went, and Mai started to work for them, and they became like her second parents. As for me, every time I stopped to say hello, the owners welcomed me enthusiastically with the Chinese expressions for someone who had gained their trust and respect, "Aaahhh! Sit down and eat with us." They never let me pay.

Initially I had the intention to go for a medical degree and follow in Sister Nuttall's footsteps. But I soon found out that even though I loved biology, chemistry didn't seem to be my strong suit. During class I seemed to understand the material well, I even explained it to others, but when it came to passing the tests, my grades were not good enough. I was frustrated, even though I studied hard, but my efforts didn't match my grades. So, I decided to take business classes, and took French classes on the side as I have always been in love with the language. Business was not as interesting to me as French. I did respect some professors who were great at their craft, but I couldn't get excited about studying something like business so that I could make a lot of money one day. I even didn't seem to have an affinity with the students in my business classes.

Conversely, almost every time I sat in on my French classes, I wanted more of it. I had an incredible French professor, Madame Chantal Peron Thompson. She was married to an American, voila, her last name Thompson. She was strict and severe with the language so that if I mispronounced anything, she would make a grimace of disgust, "Mais, c'est quoi ca? Qu'est-ce que tu as dit? C'est vraiment degoutant!" But that very professor helped me become passionate about French literature. When she taught Moliere, Balzac, Stendhal, Chateaubriand, Jean Anouilh who wrote the French version of Antigone, I felt like I was experiencing a psychological, intellectual and historical puzzle. Moreover, when it came to the francophone Senegalese literature, the professor helped us extract the most profound meanings from our readings and lecture. I discovered the astounding beauty of the Senegalese people through their powerful, honest and rhythmic literary masterpieces. I read books like, "L'enfant Noir" by Camara Laye, "Une si longue lettre" by Mariama Ba and I became fascinated by the role of men and the struggles of women in the society, and the melancholy of losing one's cultural identity due to immigration, such as when the Senegalese left their homeland to move to Paris. They also wrote about the importance of education and the spiritual practice of Islam among many other central themes.

It took me about a year to admit to myself, "I've got to do what I love." I had never been a person to follow the money, but I had been told by my family and others that 'you go to school to get a degree that will bring wealth and prestige.' Yet I needed to follow what made me feel alive, so I chose to major in French literature, yet still pursue a degree in Business.

I had to choose a topic for my final paper in my Business communications class which would be 40% of my grade. I decided to pick one which I knew would stir up some resistance. I chose to research and write about, "Homosexuality in the Mormon Church." When I informed the professor, he looked down and said, "I don't think that is a good topic to write about. You need to come up with a different topic."

"But Professor, you said to choose a topic that we feel passionate about and I think this is an important matter, and one we can't continue to ignore."

He did not speak for a few seconds and then he said ambivalently, "Okay. Put a proposal together for me as to why you think this should be the subject of your final paper. Remember your class grade depends on this paper."

I did not want to fail the class, but I did not want to back down either. I wrote the most appealing one page proposal explaining that we were losing so many people in the church due to this issue. I explained that I wanted the opportunity to do the research and bring to light a critical hidden issue in the church to perhaps save many people's souls.

I read the note on my proposal, "Very appealing presentation! You may proceed."

As a first step, I went to the BYU library to see how much information I could find on the topic. It was almost non-existent. Then I went to meet with a Spanish Professor whom everyone seemed to know was gay. I sent him an email and requested an interview. He agreed.

"Professor Velazquez (this is how I will call him), I am writing a paper on homosexuality in the Mormon church. I was told that you are openly gay." He seemed to be in his late 40s, with light skin and dark hair. He carried himself with an assertive, unfriendly demeanor.

"Yes, I am," he answered suspiciously.

I was now ready to start excavating carefully and intently the hidden skeletons in the Mormon closet.

"How did you get to teach at BYU being openly gay? "

"Because you can be gay and teach as long as you are not practicing. As you know, we have to be completely celibate. I think I am the only openly gay Professor," he said with sarcasm.

I could tell he wanted to question me before he would open up any further. "Why are you writing this paper?"

"I just want to reveal the struggles that homosexuals have in this church as it is a subject that we do not seem to touch upon. The fact that it is so hidden is the motivation for me to dig in. "

Then I asked him the next question, but the answer I so desperately needed was not for my paper, it was for me. It was the question that I feared to ask myself.

"What place do you have in this church as a gay person? You know we have the Celestial Kingdom, the Terrestrial and Telestial. We know that the goal of every Latter-day Saint is to get to the Celestial Kingdom where we will live with God, with our families and become like Gods ourselves, procreate and rule upon our own worlds. Where does a gay person fit into this plan? I don't see it!"

He looked at me thoughtfully and said, "Well, I believe that God has not revealed to the Prophet everything there is to reveal yet and that gay people will have a place in the Celestial Kingdom, but we will not be at the highest degree of the kingdom. Maybe the middle level. No one has ever talked about the Middle level of the Celestial Kingdom, have you noticed that?"

I felt annoyed. His answer didn't satisfy me. I followed up by pushing a bit harder, "But those are hypotheses. If you look at the church doctrine, it doesn't seem that gays have any place in His Plan of Salvation at all. The church states clearly that marriage is between a man and a woman and that anything else is an abomination. President Kimball, the Prophet, clearly stated that homosexuality is a crime right underneath murder. Then, if this is where the church stands, how could we have a designated place in some Celestial Kingdom?"

I'd said "we," but he let it slide. I realized I got out of the character I was playing, and I had to go back into character.

The professor seemed a bit irritated. He looked at me for a few moments and told me he had to get back to work and then added, "There is an underground gay community at BYU. Their sponsor is Dr White, a Science Professor. I think he can help you with a lot more information."

As soon as I left Professor Velazquez's office, I sent an email to Dr White asking for a meeting to discuss the subject. He answered me right away and we made an appointment for the following day.

The next day during lunch, I walked over to the Science building and arrived at Dr White's office. As I stood outside the door, I took a few seconds to reflect; I felt as if something bigger than me was directing every step I took. Finally, I knocked and opened his office door.

The professor was an older white man probably close to 60 years of age, with grey hair, dressed in a white shirt and dark gray pants. His office looked like a regular college professor's office, but BYU has a modern architectural structure so even the professors' offices are impressive. He was sitting in a lovely black leather chair behind a very tidy desk. The walls were covered by a multitude of books overflowing the bookshelves and the BYU logo in the background.

"Dr White, I am Veronica. Thank you for taking the time to meet with me. As I explained, I am writing a paper on Homosexuality in the Mormon Church and I was informed there is an underground gay community at BYU and that you are their mentor. I would love to ask you some questions."

Before I had an opportunity to begin, Dr White studied me and then asked, "Why are you interested in writing about this subject?"

I had become a master at masquerading or so I thought. I began by creating some distance from myself and the subject.

"Well, Dr White, I think this is a subject that causes a lot of pain and confusion and a lot of us do not understand enough about it. I think that there are real people out there who are suffering due to this incredible struggle and we need to find a way to address this dilemma as a church. As for me, I am a journalist at heart, and I am interested in talking about the real issues that most people find uncomfortable."

I felt like the biggest actor on the grand closet stage. He sized me up a bit and then said, "I believe that gay people are born that way. Science has evidence of this…" As he continued, I was no longer listening to his scientific explanation, my head couldn't process anything else, but time had stood still for me on this thought: "Gay people are born this way." I had never ever heard anyone in the church dare to make this statement; it was contrary to anything the prophets had said. This thought gave me some comfort, but it also troubled me.

I waited for Dr. White to finish and I followed up with my most important question at that time, "But Dr. White, if the Prophets of the church view homosexuality as an abomination, the Bible itself condemns the behavior, then why would God create gay people? Why would God want to create broken people? That would be so unfair!" I could barely hold back my tears.

I think at this point Dr White must have figured out that I was more deeply involved than I initially pretended to be. "Because I believe God created gay people just like he created anyone else and I don't believe it is a mistake…"

He went on to explain more about why homosexuality is part of nature. But my mind was fixated on his words, "being gay is not a mistake." I am not a mistake? Then, he explained that the bible was written by men and that a lot can be left to interpretation and manipulation.

He got up from his chair and started to pace back and forth as he went on with his argument. "The Bible also says that whomever divorces his wife and marries commits adultery and whomever marries a divorced woman commits adultery as well. I guess we have a bunch of adulterers walking around even in this church! The bible also says that women should not preach but should learn in silence or that we shouldn't perform any work on the Sabbath. And the list goes on. Does any of this make sense to you?"

Our conversation lasted for about an hour and then he said, "The reason why you can't find much information in the BYU library on this topic is because they only make books accessible that agree with the church doctrine. However, I could grant you access to a black box section at the BYU library that will allow you to check out books that are not normally available to students. You will find a lot more information on this subject for your research."

I walked away feeling the impact of a plane crash. This experience had shaken the very foundation of my spiritual beliefs, what I believed about myself, whom I had chosen up to that point to follow blindly. Could I even dare challenge the incontestable holy text or the revelation from the mouthpiece of God, our Prophet?

I went straight to the library and checked out 6 books. I sat in the library and started reading the first book. It was the story of a bishop who came out as gay. I couldn't stop reading and I went to the next book and the next book. I found many stories of gay Mormons and the disturbing statistics of suicide among the gay community in the church. In particular, I read the story of a young man who shot himself in the mouth outside of a Mormon temple.

With each weary step I took on my way home, I carried a heavy sorrow within my soul. The emotional burden from reading these stories felt unbearable. I could not hold back my tears from what I felt was a mirror image of my life. I did not want to end up dead. Yet, something was redemptive about this whole experience. There was another reality out there that I had not dared to see before and it was both liberating and terrifying at the same time. It required a lot of courage for me to question the unquestionable.

The next day, I couldn't wait to head to the library after class. I walked out of the humanities building where I was taking French classes and, as I was heading towards the library, I felt someone following me. I cautiously turned my head to spot who was behind me and I saw a young white man. But this was no surprise! They are all white, but this one, in particular, was right behind me and there was something different about his presence. I tried to take a right turn and he also took a right turn. I cut through a building and he cut through the same building. I was now a short distance from the library. I rushed to get in, and instead of walking forward, I quickly turned to the right of the entrance to see if this young man was still following me. And he was.

He walked in hastily and, when he did not see me, he stood still by the entrance and looked around and, when he looked to his right, our eyes met.

"Why are you following me?" I asked.

He immediately asked, "Are you Veronica Carrera?"

"Yes, why are you looking for me?" I replied.

"I am the President of the Gay club at BYU. I heard you are writing a paper on homosexuals in the Mormon church. I do not want you to write something that could be more damaging to us. We are operating with no support from the University or the church. We cannot have any type of negative attention."

He looked very concerned, a concern I did not share as I was not out and I had never been part of any club, particularly a clandestine underground club.

I assured him that my purpose was not to damage anyone in the Mormon gay community, but I wanted to bring up this controversial issue because we need to talk about homosexuality in the church and not be silent anymore. I told him that I intended to send the paper to the Prophet of the church when I finished.

Our conversation was short, but he told me that he was going to reach out to me in case he had more questions. We never talked again. After weeks of research and being deeply invested in the topic, I wrote a paper titled, "Wanderers on Strange Roads."

I got an A on the paper, but I withheld sending it to the Prophet then for fear that they would find me out and affect my standing in the university. I held on to my paper for many years, waiting for the right time to make my case all the way to the Mormon Prophet, the mouthpiece of God. Perhaps I thought one day my paper would be the voice that would engender compassion and understanding for all homosexuals or anyone who would not fit into the Mormon Church's perfectly designed plan of salvation.

Chapter 11.

My First Real Kiss with a Woman

After I wrote my controversial school paper on homosexuality in the Mormon church, I felt as if my mind and spirit had changed, and I was no longer afraid to look at my misgivings and question the unquestionable in the Mormon church.

My roommates and I used to attend regular church services every Sunday together. There, I became fascinated by Angie – an American girl from Arizona. She had dirty blonde hair, light eyes, slim, but she really reminded one of a librarian. During Sunday school, she would ask the most analytical and challenging questions. She was pursuing a master's degree in psychology and I was fascinated by her liberal mind, her quest for knowledge, love of people and the deep conversations we had at church. After a few weeks of meeting her, I told her about the paper I wrote and that took a lot of trust on my side, but it opened a conversation about sex, homosexuality, and race. Angie was not uncomfortable wrestling with any topic and found the church rules exhausting. Although she was a believer, she did not subscribe to all of what the church taught.

Angie was truly one of the few American girls at BYU who had a sincere interest and curiosity about people from different backgrounds and thought systems. One of her closest friends was a non-Mormon, beautiful intelligent Indian girl whom I will call Aditi who was doing her PhD Psych degree at BYU. Although you could hear a slight Indian pitch in her voice, Aditi's English was impeccable, and it seemed that she came from a highly educated family. After talking to her a few times, I felt comfortable enough to ask, "How do you feel about being a Hindu in a Mormon University?"

Aditi proceeded to explain that a few non-Mormons, Hindus or Muslims for example, decide to attend BYU not only because it is a good school, but just as importantly because it is somehow similar to their own cultural values and that it is very affordable compared to other universities. Then she added, "But I didn't have a good experience when I first arrived. Once I received the acceptance letter from BYU, I arranged housing from India." She paused as if she was getting ready to tell me something difficult. "I called a place in Provo that advertised that they had space for one more roommate. I talked to the main roommate who, after speaking, emailed me a contract and I sent her my deposit."

Angie interrupted, "Wait until you hear what happened next!"

Aditi continued with the story, "The first day I arrived, I was wearing my Indian attire. I knocked on the door and these two white Mormon girls opened the door and they looked me up and down and then looked at each other quite surprised and, after a moment of silence, with an uncomfortable nervous tone in their voices said that they were very sorry, but that they didn't need a roommate anymore. One of them went inside and came back with a check to give me back my deposit."

Aditi exclaimed, "I had nowhere to go and I found myself on my first day in Provo, Utah in the streets carrying my luggage. I ended up going to a hotel that night and stayed there until I could find a place to live."

We talked that day of this peculiar society's intolerance and how difficult it was to truly fit in if you were not the stereotype of the white holy Mormon.

Whenever Angie and I had some free time, we would make the effort to either talk or see each other. The desire to see her was unquenchable. There were times where she would bluntly stare in my eyes for a long time and breathe deeply. I consciously told myself that she just adored me as a friend. One day one of the roommates at my place moved out and Angie asked Rosa if she could take her place. She was to share a room with Maggie, an African American conservative older woman, and I stayed with Mai in the same room. Rosa, who was the daughter of the owner of the house, shared a room with her sister. There were six of us, two Mexicans, one African American, White American Angie, Chinese Mai and me- the Ecuadorian. I really think our house contained all of BYU's diversity numbers.

Although we now lived together and were able to spend even more time together, I made sure to spend quality time with Mai as well, as she was like my little sister. After a couple of months of all of us living together, our other roommates acted slightly uncomfortable. I imagine they found Angie's and my connection a bit unusual.

One evening, I decided to sleep on the living room couch. I wanted to be alone with my thoughts and I slowly felt my body relax as I fell into a deep sleep. I must have been unconscious for about a couple of hours when I woke up to the touch of Angie's lips, softly touching mine and licking them sensually. She then started to French kiss me and I had never been French

147

kissed by a girl before. She lay on top of me and the weight of her body on mine arose in me the most torrential emotions and we kissed even more. It was my first real kiss with a woman. All of it felt too good to pull away. I realized I had it in me to be passionate- I wanted more and more, and then…

We heard a noise and, as I looked up, I saw Maggie, the African American womanl who was Angie's roommate. She had got up to go to the bathroom and saw us kissing. It must have been around 3am. Maggie looked madly disturbed and then furious. She shouted to all the other roommates, "I found them kissing and that goes against the university honor code and church rules! We need to turn them into the bishop!"

Everyone woke up and gathered in the living room. Rosa and her sister Alma looked disappointed, uncomfortable and sad. Rosa then tried to calm Maggie down, "I do not think we need to tell the bishop, but maybe you need to look for another place to live, Veronica." Then she looked at Angie and asked her to find a place to move to, as well. Angie wasn't as close to the other girls as I was, and she couldn't bear being in the middle of all the commotion, so she called Adita and went to stay with her that night. We didn't say a word to each other. I stayed on the couch motionless as if the weight of the moment didn't allow me to move.

Mai looked at me from the door of our bedroom and didn't say a word either, but her delicate Asian eyes spoke their sadness, as she listened to the roommates' reproach and censure of me. As I sat on the couch, all I wanted to do was cry. How did I go from experiencing so much pleasure to deep distress in a matter of minutes?! But in that moment, I also faced a bigger threat. I could be expelled from BYU after all the sacrifices I'd made to get there. I thought, I may not be able to graduate!

Mai came to sit next to me and said, "I will not let you go through this alone. I will go with you wherever you go. We can move together wherever you want." Just like the story of Ruth, I thought.

Looking back, friendships have always been my saving grace. Although I have walked through the darkest valleys or have sunk in troubled waters, either God's light has guided me or the angels in my life, whom I am honored to call my friends. Mai was one of those angels.

Mai, however, had started dating a returned missionary from Logan, UT who traveled often to Provo to see her on weekends. Their relationship had started to blossom and become serious. So, I saw less of her and I knew there would be no 'us' rooming together.

That week, I decided to speak to the bishop. It is doctrinally entrenched in you as a Mormon that the moment you do something wrong, you must confess; otherwise, you are being dishonest with God, his servants on this earth and the consequences could be dire. Also, I wanted to feel that I was worthy as a human being and, especially now, worthy to continue teaching at the Missionary Training Center after kissing a girl. I was walking around the school feeling that everyone knew, that everyone could see my "scarlet letter." When I saw the bishop, he told me my kiss was not a grievous sin and that I could use some time fasting and praying to cleanse myself of sinful desires.

I moved out that week. At the same time, Mai's Mormon boyfriend from Logan proposed to her and most Mormons get married immediately so there is less of an opportunity to sin. I attended Mai's wedding as the only person there representing her as family. Everyone at the wedding was from this small town in Utah and one lady who was related to the groom approached me, looking at me as if I was a unique piece of Art from some African museum and she asked, "Are there more of you at BYU?" I was a bit confused for a moment and I repeated, "More of me?" and I realized, 'Oh Yes, she means my dark skin.' I forced a smiled and nodded, "Yes." She looked a bit shocked and went off.

There was a vacancy in the International Language housing, an on-campus student complex for students who were majoring in different languages. I was accepted in the French house. On the same floor, we had the Italian house and on another floor, was the German and Portuguese house where I made some great friends; particularly, I became close friends with Camilla, a German girl from Sao Paulo who became the teacher's assistant for my Intro level Portuguese class, which I decided to take after we became friends.

Soon after moving to the International Language housing, all I spoke at home was French. I became more engrossed in my literature classes and I was learning to analyze different pieces of literature. Madame Thompson, whom I had great admiration for, asked me one day, "Would you be interested in studying abroad in Paris and Aix-en-Province? We will be leaving in a couple of months." I didn't hesitate and found a way to cover the finances of the trip.

Through this opportunity, I became closer to some of the BYU students in my class. I had the opportunity to see my West Coast Mormon friends in a new country, outside of their comfort zone and realized, even more, how they carry their unique culture everywhere they go. One of my closest friends from the class was a girl who was originally from Idaho nicknamed "la Moyenne." This nickname came about because she was the middle child and therefore a complete introvert. Moyenne had unfashionable curly blonde hair to her shoulders, and she dressed in the typical long Mormon flowery dresses and hardly wore any make up. She looked and acted very Idaho Mormon, but one day after class, we wanted to discover Paris, but not the normal touristy things. Thus, as we walked around through a regular suburban neighborhood, I saw a sign, "L'eglise Evangelique."

"Hey Moyenne, let's go and see what that church is about? Have you ever been in an Evangelist church?"

I wasn't surprised to hear that she had never stepped into any other church besides the Mormon church. It was a rather small ordinary church; it did not compare to the big and expensive Mormon church buildings. When we walked in, we saw people holding hands in a circle about to pray, and one of them said, "Bonjour! Bienvenue! Venez et priez avec nous!"

Moyenne hesitated, but we had just been invited to join a circle of prayer with our new Evangelist friends. Moyenne and I stayed next to each other and held hands with the rest of the group. Prayers in the Mormon church are very solemn, reverent and monotone, but here suddenly, people started raising their voices, speaking in tongues and I was trying hard not to burst out laughing. I would open my eyes from time to time to see Moyenne's face and her white face looked as red as a beet. She was making a monumental effort not to laugh as well. However, one could hear the snorting noises from the tremendous efforts we made to not embarrass ourselves. While the circle kept on screaming while being possessed by the Holy Ghost, "Mon DIEU ETERNEL! SAUVE NOUS DU PECHE… SAINT ESPRIT VIENT A NOUS!", suddenly some of them started shaking and I could no longer control myself. I laughed so hard that I broke off the circle and ran to the front door and left the building. La Moyenne ran right after me. As soon we got outside the church, we laughed until we couldn't laugh anymore.

My time in France was magical – learning the literature, eating croissants and drinking hot chocolate in the mornings, visiting Musee de Louvre, La Tour Effeil, Notre Dame, Sacre Coeur, Versailles, and meeting the local French people.

One day, when I went to speak to the concierge of our hotel in Paris, I heard a melodic French voice behind me. "Bonjour, tu reste ici aussi? Je m'appelle Elena. Enchantee." From the moment I saw Elena, I thought that Russian women must be some of the most beautiful women in the world. They have an air of elegance, finesse and sophistication that I was instantly drawn to. I took a couple of seconds to compose myself, "Enchantee. Je suis venue en France avec ce groupe des Americains pour faire des etudes de literature."

Elena was like those women you see in one of those refined portraits in the Musee de Louvre. She was not tall, she was about 5'4. Her body and eyes seemed like those of a ballerina who moves with finesse and melody. Back in Russia she was a pianist and obsessed with the arts. She did not understand much about religion as that is not something that Russians obsess about, but here in Paris, she was about to spend her time with a Mormon.

From that moment on, we were inseparable, spending time together at breakfast and evenings. My French improved significantly with Elena. She didn't speak any English and didn't want to. She helped me with my assignments as well, since she was doing her Masters in French literature. She made my time in Paris feel like a fairy-tale.

My nights were filled with the excitement and anticipation that, every morning, I would wake up and get to see her again. I loved walking next to Elena. I loved the way she looked at me. I felt that I was the center of her world and she was my Paris. It is fascinating how one person's existence can fill your whole world with such exquisite joy.

The day came that I had to leave Paris with the group of Americans to study in Aix-en-Provence. Elena and I swore that we would never lose touch. I had never kissed her, I was too shy to try anything, but there were moments we lay down in bed together where she allowed me to caress her face. I remember her asking me if I had ever had sex before and I told her in a shy manner, "No. The religion doesn't allow it." She looked at me, hugged me and we stayed close to each other most of the night. The night before my departure, Elena asked me to call her to make sure she came down to say goodbye, but for some reason she didn't answer her phone. My BYU lively French Professor was in the hotel lobby and exclaimed to all 15 of us, "It is time to go. Vite! We have a long drive. S'il te plait! Head towards the bus now."

As I was walking away, I kept looking back towards the hotel to see any sign of Elena, but sadly I didn't.

When we were all in the bus ready to leave, suddenly I saw Elena running towards the bus and stopping in front of the closed door. I saw her face, sad and concerned. All the Mormon Students and my BYU professors had their eyes on us. The bus driver opened the door, I had no idea what to do.... I stepped down to look at her and, without being able to say much to each other, she gave me a hug and a kiss on each cheek and spoke softly close to my ears, "Appel moi quand tu arrive en Aix-en-Province. J'irai te visiter." Despite our efforts to see each other, she couldn't come due to my rigorous class schedule and hers. We talked about me going to Russia to see her, she wrote me a long letter from Moscow telling me about her studies and her family there. But that was the last time I ever saw her. I often wonder why life brings these magical people into our lives to then just have them dissipate like a dream, causing a death and awakening of the soul.

After a few months in France, I went back to Utah and lived again in the International Language Housing. My time there was one of the finest times at BYU. I was surrounded by very talented people who spoke multiple languages. We all went to the same church services on Sundays, we got to know each other really well. At that time, I held a calling as a Sunday school teacher and I have always been passionate about teaching spiritual subjects. One day after class, a Swiss girl whom I will call Valentina walked toward me and handed me a note, "Thank you for such a wonderful lesson. You blessed me today with your words."

Valentina was studying Classical studies at BYU and worked at the university as an Italian Teacher's assistant. Her class was right next to my French class and I used to see her on my way out every time class was over. I was smitten by her overall elegance, only adding a well draped scarf to whatever she wore, and her intelligence. I couldn't express it, though, since I was so used to repressing my emotions which felt like I was constantly holding the lid down on a boiling pot. The difficulty of me expressing any romantic attractions was heightened not only by my constant fear of the church's punishment but also because I have always been a bit shy when it comes to my romantic life. Not because I am severely shy, but because I fear insulting anyone as I anticipate that most women would find another woman liking them as insulting. Consequently, I veer away from the rejection and embarrassment.

Valentina and I started to chat a few times after class. I made sure I waited for her when I came out of my French class and we left together at times. I looked for every opportunity to connect and talk with her. In church on Sundays, she would wait for me after I finished teaching my usual Sunday school class. We would walk somewhere in the premises to tell each other more about ourselves.

"I love Switzerland," she would often say," It is hard to be here in America."

"Why is it hard Valentina?"

"I don't know. I think Americans are a bit narrow minded or maybe it is because I live here in Utah with the Mormons. I know I am a Mormon, but I have a hard time with the church culture and some of the beliefs."

"You mean like the story about Joseph Smith and the book of Mormon?"

She made a face to say, Yes, like that.

"Do you actually believe the Joseph Smith story, Veronica?"

"I really do, Valentina. I mean, I taught this for almost two years while I was a missionary in Chile. It would be too hard to not believe. Almost impossible! But I struggle, too."

"Have you ever tried challenging your beliefs?" she asked. "Have you ever wondered if any of this is not true?" She looked seriously at me.

I was not ready to tackle that subject. I of course had challenged the Church's view on homosexuality, but I was not ready to discuss that either.

I noticed that, after a couple of months, we had more of a need to be alone together. We didn't make any effort to invite our other friends to come along with us. In spite of the amount of time we spent together, I tried to convince myself, "This is only a friendship." Anyway, why would she be interested in me! I told myself. She is straight, beautiful and a Mormon! And so many guys must be after her!

My life was pretty busy then – exercise in the morning, school all day and then I taught each evening at the Missionary Training Center. Weekends were filled with going out with friends I'd made in the language housing and Sundays were all about church. There was not a lot you could do on Sundays. You cannot shop for anything; you can't watch television or do any sports; you cannot do anything that isn't church related. So, all there was to do that day was attend church services, read the scriptures, fast, pray and get together with Mormon friends to discuss topics that were appropriate for this holy day.

I was already experiencing a deep attraction for Valentina. Her almond shaped eyes, long shiny black hair, thick black eyelashes and brown eyes made me want to look at her all the time. But most intriguing was her introspection and thoughtful mind. Like most Europeans, she spoke several languages and was so well read that I was enchanted by how much I learned every time I spent time with her.

Then one afternoon after school, I decided to do laundry and went to the common laundry area. No one was around and, as I was folding my clothes, Valentina came in. "I want to talk to you," she said. "There is something that I can no longer wait to tell you." I sensed what was coming and I wanted to avoid a conversation that could be dangerous for both of us.

"I can't talk right now Valentina. I have to get back. Maybe another time?"

She nodded, as if saying yes.

That night as I was getting ready to go to bed, I suddenly heard small rocks being thrown against my bedroom window. I wasn't sure what it could be, so I opened the blinds and there I saw outside, Valentina. She waved me down and I immediately left the bedroom to meet her.

It must have been past 11pm. I opened the front door and she stood there just looking at me. "Valentina, what is it?" I smiled and she just stared at me with the look of an adolescent in love. I gave her a hug and softly said, "Come in."

Valentina and I sat in the living room, the lights were off, and it was just her and me on the couch. We communicated by whispering so as not to wake anyone else up. In that moment, everyone else disappeared. She looked at me with the intensity that is particular to those deep Swiss Italian eyesand said, "I like you. But not like a friend."

Sin or not, I couldn't think. Her words pierced my very being and, at that moment, any guilt or shame that I could have had, became non-existent. "I like you too Valentina. I have liked you for a few months. I think about you all the time. I look for you after classes just to get a glance of you." My mouth moved close to hers as if there was an inevitable force pulling me toward her and I kissed her first softly. I was her first kiss with a woman, and she responded as if she had never been more at home. We stayed on the living room couch lying next to each other all night kissing, and I lost myself in the tenderness of her passionate embrace.

Valentina became my first love and I became hers. We had a relationship that lasted for many years – it was loving, passionate, traumatic, and sad. Her love for me was loyal, stable and solid. I, on the contrary, had many years of demons to fight.

The day after I kissed Valentina, out of respect, I called the Missionary Training Center to quit my job as a teacher. I thought that would be the most honorable thing to do as I couldn't face the trainee missionaries since my attraction for a woman didn't honor the church's standards. I think this is the first time that I allowed myself to really challenge the church's views on homosexuality. I was so in love with Valentina that nothing we felt or did could feel as wrong as the church wanted us to believe. That was my last semester at BYU, so I lived off my savings and there wasn't that much time left before finishing school. However, Valentina had one more year to go but we were determined to make it work even long distance.

I had no idea what I wanted to do with my life after school. I contemplated joining the FBI. I had heard that some top FBI Officials were Mormons and that they were very fond of recruiting Mormons. I went to see them. I was told I would be the perfect candidate, "A Latina who speaks four languages and has never drunk alcohol or done drugs." They told me that I would be assigned to the intelligence unit. But as I was signing papers, I realized I never wanted to be in a position where I would have to hurt anyone physically, so I backed out of it at the last minute.

Then came the easiest option for the interim. American Airlines showed up at BYU to try to hire since it is well known that Mormons, for the most part, speak several languages as they serve missions all over the world. One of the girls from the Italian house signed up to work as a flight attendant so Valentina and I talked about it and I thought that it might be a great way to see the world and find out where we wanted to settle down.

American Airlines gave me two options: to be based out of Texas or New York. My goal was be a flight attendant for less than a year then try to apply to work for the corporate office in Texas.

Valentina would not even consider living in Texas., "Do you think that after living in Provo, Utah for this long with narrow-minded Americans," she said, "I am going to want to live in Texas! We have to go to New York!"

New York seemed to be a big dream for a lot of people, but it wasn't my dream at all. Nevertheless, it was important for me to listen to her as our goal was to find a way to build our lives together. Therefore, I went through the flight attendant training in Dallas, Texas for two months. There I learned a lot of respect for flight attendants. The training is very military, so strict that every day if someone from our training class didn't pass a test or didn't remember verbatim what one was supposed to say during evacuation simulations, that person was fired on the spot. All we knew was that when the next part of the class session was supposed to start, a seat would be empty and then the same lead instructor, a tall blonde woman, would grab a student's name tag from the desk in the morning, so we knew the person was gone. Fired! That happened a few times a week. We were all terrified.

They took us all to a big airplane that was there for training purposes. We were being trained to jump. They asked a few of us to take a jump seat station and the rest of the students were supposed to pretend they were the passengers. I sat in the jump seat in the middle of the plane. Depending on which jump seat you are seated in, the commands are different. Our knowledge and nerves were being put to the test. The plane started to light on fire. I heard the flight attendants in the front start their commands, screaming, "OUT OF MY WAY, OUT MY WAY…" most commands had some language like this. I, on the contrary, froze; my usual anxiety and panic attacks kicked in. I could not scream and all I saw was the fire, so I opened the emergency window and exited on my own, leaving everyone inside, and I started to cry. There were two lead instructors, and one of them came after me, but instead of firing me, he started to console me. I think some people were shocked that I wasn't let go. The tall American woman instructor was scary for a lot of people, but I think she was fond of me, so I didn't feel unsafe. Perhaps, she believed I had it in me to do well in the program and I did. I did finish performing well for the rest of the program.

I made a few wonderful friends during this intense training. I remember a girl from Japan who told me that she had recently divorced and, without any friends or family in this country, this opportunity was all she had to rebuild her life. She had no savings in the bank and no one to rely on. I felt so much love for her as a human being, she was gentle and thoughtful and

I'll never forget her saying, "I have hit rock bottom in my life so all there is left to do now is go up from here." I helped her study a little bit for the exams as she needed a little help with her English. I made sure she passed all her tests as I wanted her to succeed and she did. She graduated and later on she came to NY to visit me.

I would never admit to anyone during training that I liked women. In fact, because my hair was still shoulder length at that time and I made an effort to discuss girl stuff, I don't think I gave people a lot of clues that I was gay. There was a guy in training who had a crush on me, and I welcomed his attention. I just wanted to appear normal.

Strangely, there were two girls in training whom I became friends with who got involved romantically. They would not sleep in their assigned rooms but shared the same bed so they could sleep together. It was with one of them, Althea, that I first had conversations about gay sex. Up to that point, Valentina and I had just experienced the only things that came to us naturally given that we both did not know much about sex. In fact, we really had not had sex up to that point. But Althea explained to me what I needed to do to have sex with a girl. She really didn't teach me much, she probably didn't want to shock me and thought if I learned one thing that would be good enough. I wonder if she and her partner were stunned that, in my twenties, I was still kind of clueless when it came to sex.

Training was over and I flew to New York for the first time. I remember the plane descending; I was sitting wearing the impeccable white shirt and blue American Airlines business suit. I looked out the window as the plane began to land and I saw the Statue of Liberty, all the majestic NY buildings surrounded by the Hudson River and, for the first time, I became excited about this new chapter of my life.

I was given the international routes, mostly France and I would be the one to translate the announcements into French. I traveled to Brazil, Venezuela, Scotland, Haiti and other places in the Caribbean.

I didn't realize until that point that the airline industry attracts a lot of gay people, particularly men. Every time we landed in some country, they would enthusiastically shout, "Let's go to a gay bar! It is going to be so much fun!!!"

"But I am not gay. What am I going to do there?" I would say assertively, as a good Mormon girl.

They would say, "Oh honey, the music is so great. Everyone is going. What are you going to do in your room alone?"

The guys were wonderful and friendly but every bar I went to with them, the guys would hook up with someone. I couldn't fathom the idea of hooking up with strangers.

On one of the flights we landed in Caracas, Venezuela, so I accompanied the guys to a gay bar. The flight attendant was about 40 years old and was hitting on a guy who was barely 20. As we decided to go back to the hotel, I got into a taxi and my flight attendant colleague followed and came in with the young guy he had just met at the bar. I asked the young boy in Spanish, "Estas bien? Tu no conocez a este hombre. Ten mucho cuidado por favor." He looked at me as a brother would look at an older sister and whispered, "No te preocupes, estare bien." I for some reason felt that I wanted to protect him. We got to the hotel and they went to the flight attendant's room together.

My first exposure to a gay lifestyle was this free for all, sleep with whomever you want, but I couldn't see myself in that world. I didn't know how to process this way of being so, when it came to my homosexual feelings, I felt that I didn't belong anywhere, as if I was floating in the outside sphere of this complex and confusing reality. "How can I ever think of leaving this Mormon life for this No-limits lifestyle where anything goes! This isn't me either. Is it even possible to be me and still hold the values that I grew up in?" I questioned myself constantly. Valentina visited me in NY any chance she had, even if it was just for a long weekend and, since I had a more flexible schedule, I would visit her more often. We would book a motel far enough from BYU so we could spend time alone away from the Mormons. We could barely keep our hands off each other, but my visits to BYU got more dangerous each time.

There were already rumors at her dorm that there was something strange going on between us. The distance and time in between visits made us go crazy and the chemistry between us was undeniable. It became more and more difficult to hide that we were wildly in love. Every time I would drop her off at the dorms, someone would recognize Valentina and me and I am sure we started to become a topic of conversation. On our end, we just spent time discovering how to be intimate with each other. A lot was new to us, but we only needed to start kissing and all of our senses worked harmoniously together to experience one of the greatest delights in life, being physically close with someone you are deeply in love with. I had never experienced something more beautiful, more glorious and at the same time more desolate, knowing that we might never be fully free to love this way.

One of Valentina's roommates, Glenda, the perfect Mormon, a rule enforcer, a pharisee as I thought of her, confronted us when I dropped Valentina off at the dorms one day. "I think there is something wrong going on between you two and YOU, Valentina, you don't even sleep here when she comes and visits." She looked at us with such repulsion that I knew something was about to explode.

I told her, "You are crazy, Glenda. You better stop."

Later that day, my phone rang. "Ciao, it is me! Valentina!" She sounded agitated, and her voice was frantic. "The bishop called me and said that he wants to see you and me in his office after school today. I think Glenda told on us. I am about to graduate and, if they know about us, they will kick me out. I will lose my visa and I can lose it all!" Then she started to cry.

I listened to her crying as I tried to think quickly what needed to be done.

"I love you Valentina. I will never let anything happen to you. And whatever happens, I will always be with you." That seemed to calm her down a bit. But I never needed to promise her anything; she had an unwavering faith and confidence in us. And when I was around her, I knew, I would always be loved.

We both entered the bishop's office and, as we went in, I took a quick look at Valentina and she looked pale, as if she was about to faint. My heart was pounding as if I was hearing the sounds of those drums when you are about to be executed.

The bishop was sitting in the black leather chair behind his desk. Behind him was a picture of the second coming of Christ, the judgement day. This was the same small room where all of the students went to confess their sins or to discuss any church affairs. The bishop was not alone, he had his counselor standing right next to him who was tall and heavier set and had an intimidating manner. I felt as if we were in the FBI interrogation room. These two white men, dressed in white shirts and ties, were looking at us sternly as if they were about to start a crime scene cross-examination.

The bishop started, "So you both know that we represent God in this office and lying to us is like lying to God. Do you understand?!!!" His tone progressively got louder as he spoke.

I was determined to save Valentina no matter what these men would say to us. Valentina was speechless and I could sense that she was trembling. In my mind, I just kept telling myself, Breathe and stay calm.

The bishop continued, "There are rumors that you two have a homosexual relationship! Let me make this clear to you," he said looking at me directly, "being gay is an ABOMINA-TION – A CRIME in the eyes of God and you must confess!"

His counselor stood there, completely still, staring at us as a sniper does his victim and his main sights were on me. I always believed that I looked more suspicious to these white men than Valentina did. If anything, I thought that maybe they thought that Valentina was just a victim of my evil homosexual self. Valentina was white, she fit in more with the Mormon stereotype than me.

I kept surprisingly calm and, when they gave me a chance to speak, I asked, "So you have brought us here because you said there are rumors about us. May I ask, who is spreading these rumors?"

My lack of emotion and questioning threw the bishop off. He proceeded, "It doesn't matter. Students here are saying that you two are committing a sin and your behavior is repulsive." The bishop went on to narrate scriptures that condemn our behavior, but I could barely hear what he was saying, since I was searching hastily in my mind how I could get us out of this pit with the lions.

"You can't bring us to your office and accuse us of some crime based on rumors and then tell us that you can't even say who? I feel offended. I feel offended by the accusations and how we are being treated!" I said.

There was silence in the room. I could tell that I was in control now. They looked furious at this point. The bishop turned red out of wrath and then pierced his eyes on me and said in a raspy voice, "I demand to know."

My brain was racing. I had to think quickly, "Are these rumors based on one person? Possibly Glenda? You know Glenda roomed with Valentina one semester and she never liked her. She was always finding something wrong. I think she finds something wrong with most people around her."

There was just silence.

I broke the silence and exclaimed confidently, "I think we deserve an apology."

The bishop and his counselor remained not knowing what to do.

"Whatever you are accusing us of, you have no proof and we are offended," I repeated.

Then, he uttered the only words he could at that moment of madness, "It is your damnation."

Valentina never said a word. Without looking at any of them or saying anything else, I got up from the interrogation chair and headed toward the door. Valentina followed. We left the bishop's office, Valentina looked relieved and I felt invincible. Maybe this was one of those few times in my life when I didn't believe that such hatred could come from God and maybe this was one of the few moments in my life when I stood up to them for who they were, just men. I realized that they were not God as they claimed themselves to be. The only thing I cared for was to keep Valentina safe for whatever time she had left at BYU.

I did not return after that incident and Valentina graduated shortly after that. I couldn't attend her graduation; I wanted to make sure nothing went wrong.

While Valentina finished her schooling, I was living with three other flight attendants to save money so that I could eventually have enough to rent an apartment for us. One of the flight attendants suspected I was gay as she had met Valentina a couple of times when she visited, but I never introduced her as my girlfriend. I still felt that being gay was probably unacceptable not only to Mormons but to everyone. That feeling of shame in anyone finding me out haunted me for many years, I would say for most of my life. Even worse, after years of being taught in the Mormon religion that having romantic feelings for someone of the same sex was abhorrent and sinful, I had developed subconsciously a devastating self-hate that made it impossible for me to believe that I deserved love. I would always welcome it, but I couldn't hold it, and I kept constantly running away from it.

One of my flight attendant roommates was chatting with me in the open kitchen as she was making herself some tea. She seemed tired as she had just come from one of her Caribbean trips. I was lying on the couch also exhausted from flying internationally every week. I was in the air constantly and most flights were overnight. I had to deal with continual jetlag, especially going back and forth from Paris, which was my usual route.

"So, I heard you are moving. Are you going to live with that pretty girlfriend of yours who visited you last time?" she asked.

I nervously answered, "Ah yes, my friend, she also got a job in NY so we decided to room together. She will be here in a few weeks."

When you are not out to the world, the easiest escape is to call your lover "your friend."

She gave me a disbelieving look and said, "So this friend, is she the reason why you are flying so much these days? I heard you are getting an apartment across the street so I guess we will get to see you and your friend at some point."

"Yeah, I like the area and that apartment across the street opened up for a reasonable price," I answered, a bit annoyed. I wasn't really friends with any of my roommates and I knew my life with Valentina had to stay private, so I had no intention of inviting them into our lives.

My phone rang, it was Valentina and the roommate left the room. "My love!" she said, "I will be there in a couple of days! After everything we have been through, I can't believe we will be together soon. I love you so much."

"Valentina, I love you too! But wait, let me tell you about the apartment I got for us. It is a small two-bedroom in Forest Hills, Queens. The area has great boutique stores, cafes, restaurants and is close to the subway so we will be able to get to the city easily."

In my excitement, I went on, "I bought a great mattress, some covers and curtains that match. I think you will like it. I even bought a stereo." That was all I could afford for the moment. We didn't have a bed frame, just a mattress, and that was our beginning. Valentina never cared about material things. She was just happy to be with me and, although we were in our twenties, I was sure she was my forever love.

Valentina came to NY without a job, but she had a discipline and determination that I always admired. She applied incessantly to different companies, but after a couple of months without an offer and the need for a company to sponsor her visa, she started to worry.

"Don't stress about it, I can take care of everything until you find something. We don't need anything now," I assured her. But this was no consolation for her.

"I can't have you support me all the time; I need to find a job. I need to help just as much. As soon as I find a job, I will pay everything back." Eventually, she got a job at a high fashion firm where she got a big promotion in PR after a year on the job. Valentina was very smart, an incredibly hard worker and everything she did, she did it with such precision, as a good Swiss. That is the way she treated our relationship as well; she was committed, attentive and devoted.

I wasn't aware that people learn what it is really like to be in a relationship through their parents. If that is truly the case, I thought, then I have an incredible deficit. But with the little I knew about love, I tried to make Valentina happy. Whenever we were not at work, we explored the city if I wasn't too tired from flying. Valentina loved museums, trying new restaurants and reading. She was passionate about books and I was fascinated by all that we talked about.

We were like a newlywed couple who would only dare to show affection in private. Life was no longer simple, with our work lives, our having to hide who we were in the real world, our not yet having intimate friends, and we failed to admit to each other that we were having a hard time adjusting to our new life, completely alone. We didn't talk about it as we didn't want to make the other person worry.

All we had was each other. When we left the church, we lost all our friends and we had no support system. I was used to the Sunday rituals. When you are a Mormon everything revolves around the community. I did not know how to create strong friendships or connections with anyone outside of the church. I believe this happens to a lot of the members as we are taught it is important to surround yourself with people that uphold your values and support your beliefs. It wasn't unusual to hear a Mormon leader say something akin to, "If you spend enough time with someone who drinks, you will eventually end up drinking. Remember, you are the chosen people. You cannot mix with the gentiles. Unless you are trying to save them."

The church has many events and activities during the week that allow you to stay connected. The Mormons are extremely organized when it comes to creating a tight exclusive community and they take good care of one another. They have what they call, "Visiting Teachers" and "Home Teachers." For Visiting Teachers, they assign two women of the church to visit you once a month to share a spiritual lesson and report on your welfare to the bishop. Home teachers are the same concept, but instead these are two men who visit you every month as well. The difference is that the men hold the priesthood or authority of God to bless, heal the sick, and preside over the church. There are many stories of miracles with these healing priesthood powers, but only the men possess this power. To question why women do not have the same authority and power is sacrilegious, you run the risk of falling into apostasy. We couldn't question this patriarchal structure, or we could be excommunicated. But in spite of all this, there was still a sense of comfort in being in the community, knowing that you are cared for and protected in many ways. It is as if you want the good, you must take the bad and you must somehow make sense of the whole, even when it doesn't make sense at all.

Valentina and I were out of the only religious community we knew, but at times, it seemed to me that I was more willing to deal with the irrational so as not to feel so isolated.

After a year of adjusting to our lives in New York and for the first time out of the church since I'd been baptized, I was lying on our bed quietly feeling the void. Valentina was sitting in the office chair in our small bedroom reading one of her favorite books, Dante's Divine Comedy, which was not surprising since, as an allegory the *Divine Comedy* represents the journey of the soul toward God.

I felt that persistent pressure in my chest…that pressure you feel when you can no longer remain quiet because you are going insane.

"I feel empty. I miss the church," I said.

She looked at me as if she had been afraid this moment would come. But she didn't say a word.

Then she said, a bit bothered and nervous, ''You want to go back?"

I avoided looking her way, "I think so… I don't know what to do."

'Why are you doing this, Veronica? Why can't we just be happy? Why can't you be happy?'

"Valentina, why can't we love each other and have God! Why do I have to choose you or God?" The immensity of my love for her did not overshadow my need to feel accepted by God and by the Mormon faith. At that time, I could not make distinctions between religion and God. In fact, it is only with time that I have come to understand that they are not the same. Religion for the most part is good until it starts to explain God through limited and divisive views and dogmas that makes anyone who doesn't subscribe or agree, the 'Other.' God is ultimately 'Oneness, God is ultimately 'Love." There is no "Other."

"But we can't go back…" She paused, then said, "I sense your sadness and I have been worried that you would say something like this! If we go back, we are going to lose each other… Besides, I don't believe in all of this the way you do, I don't believe in this Joseph Smith story or the book of Mormon. How do you know this is all true, Veronica?!!!"

I realized that we were struggling with our new life in very different ways. "Because it is true, Valentina! What if this church is true?" I was trying really hard to not let her see the intensity of my sorrow at being severed from it.

She then raised her voice and broke down in tears, "For me, it is a no brainer… I choose us and I will choose us again and again. What do you want to do!!! Go back? How? After everything we have gone through! What is going to happen to us?"

Her questions were a premonition of the dangers in my dilemma.

Valentina often questioned the church. She'd been a convert in her early 20s, but she had a natural disposition to dissect and question whether the dogmas, doctrine and all of those stories were based on actual facts. She had never served a mission. I, on the contrary, had come to the church in my younger years. I was more conditioned to believe, and particularly after serving a mission, it was incredibly hard to just walk away from something I'd taught for almost two years of my life.

At this point, Valentina looked utterly defeated.

I then realized I was making her feel unsafe, so in my naiveté I came up with an absurd idea. "Maybe we can go back, enjoy the Sunday talks or scripture readings, and come home immediately. We won't let anyone know about our business or let them get too close. But I need God in my life, Valentina. We need God." I wish I would have known then that God is found anywhere there is love, grace, acceptance of others, the face of mercy and the simple golden rule under every roof 'Do unto others as you would like others to do unto you."

She bitterly replied, 'This God surely doesn't seem to like us. But," she said, "I will try this for you."

Something inside me told me this was going to be some kind of new search to refind where God really is.

Chapter 12.

Back in Church

It was inevitable what was about to happen. After a couple of weeks of attending Sunday services, the bishop whom I will call Francois, asked Valentina and me to meet with him in his office. We knew the bishop to be a young good-looking Frenchman in his 30s. His sense of style made him stand out in the crowd, his short dark hair sticking up in front from well-placed hair gel, his bright colorful ties and fitted suits. American men don't dress as well as the French. His wife, Ashley, was American but had a great sense of style as well. But she did not need to do much to herself as she was naturally beautiful - slim, blonde, high cheekbones and gorgeous blue eyes. They truly made an astounding couple.

We followed him to the bishop's small office with the usual leather chair in front of a big desk, pictures of Christ, the book of Mormon and the temple hanging on the wall. He took control of the conversation, "I just want to welcome you to this Church Congregation. I heard from a couple of members that you both went to BYU! Ashley and I went to BYU as well. We met there, dated for a year and got married right before we graduated."

I looked over to Valentina and I knew she was not in the mood to engage in small talk. She was not the kind of person to pretend either. I immediately answered, "Yes, thank you for welcoming us here. We are really good friends. We met at BYU and decided to room together in NY. That is a great story of how you met. Do you like New York? How long have you been here?"

"We have been here for over a year and we love the people. We are still adjusting, but overall it is going well. I work for an Advertising firm and Ashley stays home with our two children."

The bishop, Francois, then looked at Valentina, "You are European as well…It is good to have another European around."

She nodded and smiled politely. "Thanks. I am Swiss. I graduated in Classical Studies at BYU," she added.

Francois seemed really pleased to have other people with similar experiences joining the ward or congregation and then inquired more about our living situation and our jobs. But soon after, he switched the conversation to the most common and pressing question.

"The Lord wants you to serve. I want to get to know you a little bit more and be able to extend you a calling so that you can serve the church here. What do you think?"

After the bishop said that, I got a little excited about the thought of teaching again. I loved connecting with our Mormon community in deep spiritual ways. I looked over to Valentina. Everything was happening fast, and this was not what she had signed up for.

We walked out of his office this time without a commitment, but weeks later the bishop called us to his office. "Sisters, I am excited to extend you a calling! The Lord needs you to serve in this ward."

Valentina answered first, "I am not ready to accept a calling." She was never a person to give too much explanation.

I immediately followed, "Yes, Bishop. I think we just need a little more time to adjust and get to know the ward."

He looked puzzled. No one refuses a calling. Saying no to the Bishop is like saying no to the Lord. But Francois was also different, he wasn't like any other bishop I had met. He was cool, modern, perceptive and sensitive. In fact, he looked at us as if there was something that he needed to decipher.

"Thank you for your honesty. It will be great to have some follow up conversations, so I understand more. Why don't we have regular check-ins?"

Valentina and I just nodded and couldn't wait to exit the office.

While we attended the ward, I became really good friends with a Jamaican girl named Tiara. Tiara was one of the funniest people I had ever met in my life. Being black in a church that is full of white people is always peculiar. In this particular ward in Queens there was more diversity, Latinos and Filipinos primarily, but there was a scarcity of black people, but that didn't bother Tiara. She seemed to be extremely comfortable in her own skin and always happy. Her personality made things more exciting in this ward. She was passionate about the church and the community and her life revolved around it. She was a person of poor means, so when she lost her job, I asked Valentina if it was ok if we hosted her for a couple of months in the second bedroom in our home.

Valentina wasn't excited by my generosity. "If she finds out who we are to each other, which she will if she lives with us, what do you think will happen?"

My desire to live both lives, be part of a church I revered and be with the woman I loved, led me to this reckless, illogical and unthought out path. I started to rationalize this senseless decision, "But she will have her own room. We will have our privacy. We just can't hold hands in front of her." I cannot imagine how Valentina felt. I wonder what kept her with me as I continued taking us down this conflicted and tormented path for months.

I accepted a calling as a teacher and stopped being intimate with her. The next argument I made to her was, "If we know this church is true, then why don't we try obeying the rules? We could still be together, but maybe we can decide what our boundaries should be. Perhaps we can still kiss and not sin."

Believe it or not, Valentina stood by me. She and I would read the scriptures, particularly the book of Mormon together and try to find a way to live both lives somehow. All she wanted was to not lose me and all I wanted was to find a way to keep our relationship intact while still communing with the Latter-day Saints. It took some more growing up to know that that was an absurd delusion.

Tiara stayed with us more than 3 months. She seemed to constantly have money problems and spend what she didn't have. Valentina had become friends with her and wanted to help her, but we both wondered if we were enabling her behavior. My partner and I were so careful about how we spent our money, we never bought ourselves any brand name clothes or things, but suddenly, we would hear Tiara walk into the apartment bragging about the Gucci glasses she had just bought, only to complain weeks later how she could barely afford anything. The church used to help her with food; thus, she always had what she needed.

Eventually, we asked Tiara if she could find a place to live. Finally, Valentina and I had the place back to ourselves, but we were more apart than ever. My discomfort with being gay started to creep in the more I was surrounded by members of the church and the doctrine of the gospel. We started to become more like roommates than lovers. Not because I didn't love her. I always did, but one cannot go on living with a divided soul. It becomes like a thick heavy fog creeping into your whole being, just as smoke in a fatal fire creeps in through a door. Sooner, rather than later, one can, devastatingly, lose even one's own soul.

Chapter 13.

The Breakup

After a couple of years of living together, I took a trip to Paris and as we landed and were getting ready to get off the plane, this charming French guy who worked at the airport came in to the airplane to ensure all controls had been followed. He took a look at me and he was magnetic. He was wearing a grey suit with a pink shirt and a bright turquoise tie that contrasted the color of his shirt. He smiled not only with his mouth but also his eyes and he approached me to introduce himself. His name was Philippe. After speaking for a few minutes, he asked if he could invite me to dinner. I gave him my number, he smiled again and left.

We went out that night and kissed. He was smart, very knowledgeable of world politics, but also very sensitive. He took the time to ask me questions about my life. One of the first questions he asked that started a connection that would last for many years was, "Tell me about your mom's death; that must have been so hard."

I opened up to him in the way I had not opened up to anyone for a long time besides Valentina.

We spent time together every time I flew to Paris. He loved to work out and take care of his body, so we had fun going on runs together. I also enjoyed his ability to discuss complex philosophical ideas and his passion for arguing politics. He would start by dissecting everything that was wrong with the United States and how much better the French political system was. He would say, "France really cares about the human being and not just the bottom line. We have access to education, health care, basic human rights that you don't. If you are poor in America, you are doomed. We do not need mansions or exuberant Hollywood lifestyles. We live simple, but meaningful lives."

He also awakened my interest in the state of affairs between Israel and Palestine. He would draw pictures of a map of these two countries and tell me what happened throughout history with the territory, the wars, the unresolved dilemmas and the challenging dynamics of all their neighboring countries. I became fascinated by this long-standing political issue.

I told Phillipe that I was a Mormon and that I couldn't have sex before marriage. His reaction was calm and supportive. He would ask me to explain why that rule was important and did not try to argue against it. He never asked me to compromise any of my values. I felt respected by him in so many ways. He was an atheist whose character was unquestionably honorable and admirable, not like anything I had been taught to believe about atheists.

One sweet thoughtful act on his part was that once he learned that Mormons do not drink coffee, he replaced all the coffee he had in his apartment with hot chocolate. I was introduced to all his friends and we would have dinner in his garden at a long wooden table where we all mostly discussed world politics. Although my French was good, I had to make a concerted effort to concentrate so that I could follow the discussion.

In other words, I started to live a double life. When I was in NY, Valentina was my love, but when I was in Paris, Philippe was my refuge and escape from my tumultuous confusion back in NY. Phillipe, though, was not only an escape, he was a soul I connected with in significant ways and, at this time of my life, he made sense.

My life seemed to be going at the speed of light. Valentina could sense that there was something different in me...and one time she found a note that Philippe had given me when he bought me roses. That is how she found out that I was emotionally cheating. Since I was not intimate sexually with either of them, my mind rationalized this delusional life of mine by telling myself that I was not "really cheating."

I did not even know who I was anymore, so how could I even begin to explain any of my actions to anyone else? I was devoid of any feelings, suffocating from the fog that had now inundated my life. I was hurting and it is said that, "Hurt people hurt others." Well, that is what I did, I hurt Valentina in ways that I wish I never had. I just did not know how to balance my faith, my love for a woman and my desire to also live a normal life with this wonderful man.

Even with my betrayal, Valentina decided to stay in the relationship. After several arguments about my cheating, I had promised her that I was going to stop seeing Philippe. But Valentina never trusted me again. Her eyes never looked at me the same way and, from that moment on, our love took a downward spiral, especially after I decided to get involved with someone else a few months after.

The way I managed my delusions was that when I got involved with a guy, I made sure that he understood I couldn't have sex because I was a Mormon. This is how I shielded myself from stepping deep into the mud. My actions became reckless, my character flawed; it seems as if I was determined to self-destruct my life and sabotage one of the greatest loves in my life.

"Valentina, I think it is time for us to separate. I cannot continue living like this. I think we need to try to find a way to live normal lives." I said all of this without much emotion, forgetting what this woman had done, following me from Provo to live this unconventional life with me. I was incapable of love for anything or anyone in my life as I could barely love anything about myself. I was dying inside at a rapid pace and nothing seemed able to resuscitate me. I couldn't even see how far gone I was.

Valentina's heart broke in a million pieces and I was never able to put those pieces back together. She tried to convince me to not give up on us. But I did, so she moved to Manhattan to rebuild her life alone. Ironically, she found a Mormon church in that area and she built a community of friends who helped her make it through this painful transition. She also had a close friend from her fashion company who was gay and knew everything that happened and became her confidante and best friend.

After Valentina moved out, I ended up leaving Philippe. I decided to go back to the church and give it all I had again. I committed myself to a single life as the church would want from me with the consolation that God would fix me in the next life.

Throughout the following years, I missed Valentina and I tried to reconnect with her, but she wanted nothing to do with me. I tried again and again until she let me back into her life as a friend. She was not completely devoid of any romantic feelings for me, but she would not allow herself to open her heart to me again. I could see the emptiness, the distrust, and disillusion in her eyes. I realized that it is possible to destroy the most profound of loves.

I wasn't clear either about what I wanted as I was trying hard to live a celibate life, but at the same time, I was craving the intimacy and affection of a loving relationship. Even describing this now brings me deep sadness. When I see couples in a happy relationship, I can't help but ask myself, "Why is it so easy for some to love freely and almost effortlessly, while for others, love feels like falling into difficult and torrential waters?"

I now had been in New York about six years and I had been working in the top financial services firm in the world, as an analyst.

One day, the Head of Sales at this firm approached me, "Congratulations Veronica. I want to promote you to financial sales." I was of course thrilled to receive this promotion, but then he surprised me, "There is only one small detail, the role is in San Francisco."

I was astounded, "San Fran. I have lived all my adult life here. When do you need me to make a decision by?"

He answered, "I need someone there yesterday. Could you move to San Fran in three weeks?"

"Three weeks?" I said. "I have my lease agreement till the end of the year, and I have so many things to pack and move if I say yes. How could I do that in three weeks?"

"We will take care of everything. We will settle your lease contract and a moving company will pack everything for you, even your pencils, and deliver it to your new apartment in San Francisco. You will stay in corporate housing for 2 months to give you time to find an apartment. We will pay for everything."

I went home and, as I sat by myself in my empty apartment, I thought, Why not? I do not have anything left here. Just a life that I want to leave behind.

The next day, I accepted the offer and a few weeks later I was on my way to San Francisco.

Chapter 14.

San Francisco

Since I felt lonely there and did not know a soul, I joined the Mormon ward in a prominent wealthy area of the city. The bishop was an investment manager at Morgan Stanley. Many of the men in this ward were in finance or were dentists or going to dental school. The Mormon women who attended this ward were astonishing. Every Sunday I felt that I was in a fashion show filled with beautiful women. Many of them were married to these driven and accomplished men.

I enjoyed a lot of church activities that connected all of us in meaningful ways either through spiritual discussions or by demonstrating our crazy, fun competitive side when playing sports. We went all in- win or get killed. I felt fully in synch with this magnificent group of women.

There were just a few single women who were part of the congregation, which is often the case in the Mormon church. But there is usually a lot more single women than single men in the church. Being a single man in your 30s is almost a disgrace in the Mormon community as men are commanded to marry in their 20s right after they finish their mission. They have the control as there are plenty of young ladies in the church who are waiting for a worthy young man to ask them in marriage. On the other hand, women in the church have it harder as they have to wait until a worthy Mormon man shows interest and ultimately wants to marry them.

So in some way, single people feel like outcasts. They don't really fit in the plan as the most they can aspire to be in the next life is to become angels serving those who got married in this life or becoming one of the many wives these worthy Mormon men would be granted in the next life. It is a privilege becoming one of these men's many wives as this is the only way you can earn the Celestial Kingdom and live with God, the Father. You can only be a God if you are married and sealed in this life to your family in the Mormon temple for time and all eternity. But it is better to stay single than to marry outside of the faith.

What a privilege it is to be a man in the Mormon church! I thought. They get to choose who they marry, when to marry, and only a man can talk directly with God. They are the ones who have the authority to lead the church, become a Prophet and, at the end, they get to have multiple wives in the next life saving the women from eternal damnation. "Does God really favor men?" I asked myself for a long time. Maybe this goes back to Adam and Eve where God intentionally created a man while it seems that the woman was more like an after-thought. "It is not good for man to be alone…I will create a helpmate," the bible says and then just like that "Abracadabra" and a woman shows up.

There was one single girl in the ward who caught my attention as she was exceptionally kind, funny and spiritual. She was engaged to a Mormon guy from England and was only a few months away from getting married. I will call her Giovanna.

Giovanna was 5'8, blonde with big green eyes and big teeth. She was very active so she had a fit physique. I was immediately drawn to her. We laughed a lot together and no matter what I said she found it amusing. We had a lot of profound conversations about the church, Christ, and shared some of the same liberal points of view.

After a couple of months in San Francisco, I heard she called off her engagement. I approached Giovanna at church, "Are you ok Giovanna? I heard you decided to call off the wedding."

"I just didn't feel it was right. The closer I was getting to the wedding date, the more awful I felt. I decided to end it."

I did not question her but found it brave of her that, in her 30s, she chose to be single rather than get married as everyone expected. That hardly ever happened in this community.

Giovanna and I spent more time doing fun things with the singles group and then, on occasions, we would spend time alone just talking and as usual laughing. I had started to become attracted to her, but I had left New York to escape my life and I couldn't think of repeating the same scenario again.

One evening, Giovanna showed up at my door close to 11pm on a Sunday and asked me if it was too late to talk. She looked nervous and, at first, we had a senseless conversation that did not lead anywhere. My heart felt close to this beautiful human being and all I wanted at this point was to be with her. It was as if we were having a hard time approaching the unavoidable. Without any explanation, we started to kiss and then there were no words; she spent the whole night at my place.

After a night filled with tenderness and passion, I could barely get up the next morning. My job was only a few blocks away as I lived right on the border of North Beach and the financial district is one of the most beautiful hilly areas in San

Francisco. My town house was right on a hill overlooking the Bay bridge and the water.

Giovanna and I became an item. Every time Giovanna would stay overnight, which happened often, I struggled to get up in the morning. I was supposed to be at work at 7am – I would get out of bed around 6:30am and get ready in a matter of minutes, run the ten blocks down the hill to get to work on time.

Rushing to work became a pattern, until one morning, a neighbor I had never talked to before, who lived on the corner of the block right before I had to turn down the hill to head to work, screamed at me from his second- floor bedroom window, "Hey You! Why don't you start getting up earlier? If you got up earlier, you wouldn't be running like this every day!"

Giovanna and I tried not to talk initially about the shame and guilt that comes with this type of relationship within our church. It was her first time falling in love with a woman. She seemed more at ease with it than I was. She had a strong, open upbringing and her mom was her confidante and best friend. Giovanna's mom was German, a psychologist, and although she was also a convert to the church, she held a healthy outlook on life and did not subscribe to the church's extreme doctrinal beliefs. Giovanna spoke to her mom about our relationship and her reaction took me by surprise, "As long as you are happy, Giovanna. I do not care who it is, a man, a woman, I just want you to be happy."

When Giovanna shared this with me, I was dumbfounded, I had never experienced someone loving me unconditionally the way her mother loved her. If I would have told my family or any of my Mormon friends that I was in love with a woman, I would have been repudiated, shunned and that was mostly what I experienced with church leaders when I sought help. There was no one in my life that I felt I could go to for emotional support or advice. I do not think I realized how much of a heavy burden I had been carrying alone, enduring the painful shackles of shame that had been placed around my ankles as I walked a life-time sentence for something I never chose to feel.

Giovanna and I tried to contain our two lives- being in a gay relationship and sitting at church on Sundays. It felt as if we were squaring the circle of our split existence. However, something was different with this relationship. Something in me started to open up more to the possibility of envisioning myself in a serious long-term relationship with a woman. There were moments where I felt no pain, no darkness, only the freedom to love.

However, on one occasion when Giovanna and I were at church during a sacrament meeting, an older single woman in her 40s who had moved from New York was sitting in our row, and looked our way and, with a smirk on her face, whispered, "It is ok you know…whatever it is that you have going on."

I pretended I had no idea what she was referring to. But I knew that we were not going to be able to hide in the shadows, and this incident resurfaced intense emotions of stress and shame for me.

After a few months into the relationship, I walked into the bishop's office, the older investment manager who worked for Morgan Stanley. Up to that point, he had shown a great liking for me. I used to give talks at church meetings and taught a few lessons in the relief society. I have a gift for teaching spiritual concepts and that helped me build some real friendships in the ward and gain respect from the bishop.

"Hi Veronica. Good to see you. What can I do for you?"

"I am good, Bishop. But I came to share something that I think will make you feel very disappointed in me."

He looked at me a bit startled, as he did not have the slightest idea what I was going to say.

I wanted to get it over with knowing that what I was about to tell him would make me fall from grace. "Bishop, I am struggling with homosexual feelings."

He looked stunned. His face turned pale and stony.

I paused as I knew I had not said it all. I swallowed the bitterness of the moment and continued, "I am in a relationship with a woman." As soon as I said this, his face could not contain his disgust.

"Who? Is it someone I know?" he asked as if terrified of what I would say next.

"Yes, it is Giovanna."

He seemed now beyond shock and outrage. Giovanna was one of his favorite people in the ward.

I knew this was not going to go well, but I wasn't prepared for what he was about to say next.

"Listen, I am taking away your church calling. But also, here is a book on pornography addiction."

"What do you mean by pornography addiction? I have never watched pornography in my life!"

"It is all the same. What you have is an addiction and it is no different than pornography. I really believe this book will help you." And he slid the book across the table towards me.

I looked at the book that he had thrown my way for a second, then I threw it back to him and said, "I do not have a pornography addiction. That is ridiculous. How can that be the same!" I was irritated and fed up at this point. I got up and left his office.

I had told Giovanna that I was going to seek help from the bishop, but she tended to be positive and thought the exchange with the bishop might go better than expected.

When I told her what happened, she said, "I am not ready to speak to him. But now that you have gone to him, I feel like

I need to figure out what this all means and what I need to say to him."

I had gone through this too many times in the past and was becoming more and more disillusioned. I was done with bearing my soul to these Pharisees who were ready to stone the adulterous women to death and also kill the very Jesus because He did not fit the façade of what they expected the Son of God to be.

I was simply exhausted and, when I went the next day to work, I contacted the CEO of my company whom I had a really good rapport with, which was surprising to a lot of people as everyone else seemed to be terrified of him. He was a force to be reckoned with, loud, intense, direct, and overpowering. He was this tall bald eccentric Englishman who often dressed in a purple suit, almost out of a Batman movie. While most people feared him, I loved him. He was one of those leaders who are refreshingly authentic, trust-worthy, creative.

This CEO had a big impact on my career, and I was able to do some amazing things in the company because of him. He was not afraid of honesty, he was not afraid of people who challenged him or pushed limits and he pushed all boundaries himself during his legacy at the firm.

But this time, I had a unique request. I had been in San Francisco for only 18 months and my contract said that I had to be in this city for a minimum of 24 months. When I had told the Head of Sales that I wanted to go back to New York, he denied my request, "I can't bring you back to NYC now. I am not even sure I can bring you back after the 24 months as it all depends on the needs of the company."

Therefore, the only next thing to do was to go to the CEO. "I have been here for 18 months. I appreciate the opportunity, but I really want to go back to New York." As I paused to reflect on the argument I needed to make to persuade him, he said,

"Consider it done. You are leaving in two weeks and we will put you in corporate housing in New York with all expenses paid for a couple of months to give you time to find your own place."

That day after work, I went to see Giovanna to share the news. I wasn't sure how she was going to receive this. But knowing Giovanna, I knew she would make an effort to listen and understand.

"Giovanna, you are one of the most beautiful caring souls I have encountered in my life, I am in love with you. But I do not want to confuse your life. If this church is true and if God does not approve of this lifestyle, then I do not want to be responsible for your eternal unhappiness. I care about you too much to not think about the impact that this relationship will have on your life. I am leaving San Francisco."

Up to this point, I thought I was saving her from eternal damnation and that if I had to be alone and sacrifice love one more time in my life that it was all worth it in the name of God and for the love I had for Giovanna.

Giovanna cried, "I am not sure life is black and white like this. I am not even sure God feels the way the church has taught us. I think there must be a way to have this love and still be able to go to church. I am willing to do this with you and tell the whole world we are together. My family accepts me and that is what matters most. I would even move to New York with you if that is where you think we should be."

I was not willing to do this again. I had already hurt Valentina. I knew that although I had taken some steps forward in this path of self-acceptance, I still had a long way to go. As much as I tried, I couldn't get rid of my feelings of unworthiness. So, I stayed with my decision that I needed to leave and that it was best for us to say goodbye. Instead of feeling sad at that moment, I felt relieved as I felt I was escaping the axe of justice constantly hanging over me. Two weeks later I was gone.

Chapter 15.

Back in New York

Back in New York, determined to live the principles of my faith, I wanted a clean slate, a new start, a chance to redeem my life to God. What this meant was that I was resolute to stay single and to never experience the tenderness of a true love. This way I could be worthy of belonging to my faith. I had never struggled with any other vices, so this was the one.

My cross was falling in love with certain extraordinary women who had crossed my path. Up to this point, I had only been in a relationship with Mormon women. It was easy, we understood each other's beliefs, values, upbringing, struggles and there is a certain innocence because of the way we grew up that made me feel safe.

Interestingly, when you transfer from one geography to another, your church records need to be transferred. When the bishop in New York asked for my records, the bishop in San Francisco went out of his way to contact the bishop in New York and outed me and told him to keep an eye on me. "She cannot be trusted." This did not make church safe for me, but I was determined to stay despite my new bishop's mistrust.

I spent most of my time and energy at work. It was the only other way besides church that I could fill my life with something productive and uplifting. I worked for a fascinating financial tech company which had a wonderful culture at that time. As with any other financial firm, there is a lot of pressure to perform and be the best. I spent a lot of time studying the markets, understanding how to analyze financial instruments so that I could be effective with customers, gain their respect and, therefore, exceed my revenue targets. All of this busyness helped me forget any deep needs of the soul, any desire I could have for romance in my life, or the need to dig deeply into my wounds so that I could uncover the depth of my essence, my true self.

My company made my church life bearable and I started to connect with some wonderful people outside of the church for the first time in my life. I used to be a public figure at work, often giving presentations to hundreds of people and this made me well-known within the firm. It made others want to get to know me a little more. However, while on one hand I appeared extremely outgoing, dynamic, and confident because of my public persona, on the other hand, I experienced anxiety if I was asked to connect with someone one-on-one.

I did not know how to relate in a personal way with those who were not Mormons. When you grow up in a religious institution, your whole life revolves around the members of this institution, you tend to speak their unique language, and psychologically, you feel that you can only relate to those of your faith. Dogmatically, you are taught that you are the chosen people and those outside of your faith are 'gentiles' who do not share your values. This dogma subconsciously or consciously creates a separation, an abysmal distance between you and those who do not share your beliefs.

How did I navigate both worlds? A financial world where most people would not understand my Mormonism? And Mormonism where I had to trump the very essence of who I am? Somehow, I managed to perform in both worlds when, in truth, I didn't feel I fully belonged in either of them.

What some people find hard to understand is that when you are a public speaker, you are performing. It is an art. Although it is an act of love towards the audience, it doesn't have to be intimate or personal. You do not have to become fully vulnerable or open to any one person.

I was representing my company at a group of non-profit organizations the company had donated money to. On one occasion, they brought a group of young people of color who belonged to a non-profit which helped young people with mentorship and ultimately guided them to do well in life. I was the designated speaker and we had an uplifting dynamic discussion about the financial markets. I made sure the presentation was engaging and exciting for these young people. I have always felt a special love for young people as they remind me of how I came to this country, without much direction, support or guidance. I feel that it is my privilege to be in front of them.

After my presentation, the Director of the Non-Profit, a tall young lady still in her 20's approached me to thank me. I exited the conference room quickly and did not stay to chat more than to thank her for her thoughtful feedback and I left right away.

A day later, the head of the non-profit at my firm forwarded me an email that this young lady had sent about me thanking my firm for my "Amazing presentation." Her email was quite elaborate and thoughtful, so I had to reply thanking her for her wonderful feedback.

She told me later that this was her strategy to get hold of me. She knew if she wrote such an elaborate email, it would be forwarded to me and that I would have to answer!

Needless to say, after I contacted Monique to thank her, she asked if we could meet for coffee. After our coffee date, she asked if I would give her classes on the financial markets. I found out later that she detested the topic.

The first time she came to my apartment in midtown Manhattan, we slept together, and the next morning after waking up, I knew I couldn't go through it again. I was still attending church and I was not going to go through the humiliation with a bishop ever again. So, I showed up at church to inform him that I was never coming back. I did not give any explanation, maybe he didn't care.. All the authorities in this ward by now knew that I was 'gay' and I felt their hatred staring me in the face all the time.

I walked back home with the image of the bishop's disdain for me. When I made it back to my small studio in midtown Manhattan, I barely saluted the doorman. I went as quickly as I could to the elevator. Every step I took, I felt as if I was lifting orbital pounds of sadness. I had nothing left in me.

A myriad of thoughts invaded my mind, "I have walked away from God. I have walked away from His church." I could hear the Mormon Temple ceremony pound my head, "If you walk away from these covenants, you will be destroyed."

If I allowed myself to break down and cry, I was terrified of where that would take me. Suddenly, my mind entered a state of emptiness, with an inability to feel anything except a bitter resolution to end it all. There is no point in continuing to live, I thought. Who would care if I am gone anyway?

When you enter into this state of darkness, any love you may have in your life becomes invisible. In that moment of Gethsemane, you feel utterly alone.

The only solution to this is to terminate my life, I decided. I went to the kitchen and I grabbed a knife and put it right to my stomach. I could feel the sharpness of the blade on my skin. I was trying to find the courage and strength to just end it all. I tried once, twice and three times and, as I tried to gain the strength to push harder, I couldn't. I didn't have the courage to go through with it.

At that moment, I screamed and threw myself on the living room floor. On my knees with my head down to the floor, I started to sob uncontrollably and shouted to the heavens: GOD, I HAVE DONE IT YOUR WAY ALL MY LIFE!!! I HAVE DONE IT YOUR WAY ALL MY LIFE. I HAVE NOTHING MORE TO GIVE! I CAN'T DO THIS ANYMORE. I CAN'T DO THIS ANYMORE!!!!

"God, do you hear me? … Help me Please!!!" I wept inconsolably for close to an hour.

Then, with a weary body, drained from the psychological warfare that I had endured for so long, I collapsed on the floor and suddenly I heard a soft but strong voice inside of me, almost like a powerful whisper,

"Your life is so much bigger than the Mormon church."

The voice repeated, "Your life is so much bigger than the Mormon church."

I had met people who had shared that they heard the voice of God at a pivotal moment in their lives and I think I had doubted it. However, this time, a healing, mighty and undeniable holy whisper rescued me.

I got up from the floor and the unbearable darkness that was overpowering me left me, almost instantly. I felt as if heavy chains were lifted from me that very moment. My body and soul experienced a lightness that I had not known existed. I knew I would never go back to the way my life had been.

After this experience, I walked over to my bed, too exhausted from everything to leave my apartment. I lay down, not understanding what I had just experienced meant or what my life would be like after that moment. All I knew was, that in order to survive, I had to take life moment by moment. I fell asleep thinking about all of it and I slept for a long time that night.

The next morning, I got up to work and felt like a person who had been placed on a different planet. My mind started to think, So, if I am not a Mormon anymore. Who am I?

I proceeded to put my energy into work – I applied myself to understanding the markets and asset class valuation. I studied the art of sales and made sure I was one of the top salespeople in my department and I was highly successful. I had no friends besides my Mormon friends and now that I'd left the church, I had nowhere to go on Sundays and no Mormon visiting teachers assigned to check on me. All I had was my job Mondays to Fridays and my relationship with Monique.

Not everything changed. If there was a company event, I still wouldn't drink alcohol or coffee or engage much in small talk. In New York, it is normal for people to curse as a way to emphasize a point, "That is Fuc##% hilarious!" Or curse when someone is really mad! "Get the Fuc#$ out of my way." Just go on the subway and you will learn immediately how to speak this language. But Mormons do not curse and, although I was now free to do whatever I wanted, nothing outside of the rules that I had lived by felt normal. Inside of me, I was still a Mormon living in a world I was taught to exclude myself from. "If you entertain yourselves with people who are not of the covenant, you can be tempted and fall off the path of righteousness..."

I was now free to go out with my first non-Mormon girl-friend without any reservations, any hiding or feeling that I was living a double life. Regrettably, though, I still couldn't feel free about it. Although I had a powerful experience with God that saved my life, I did not realize that the road to healing, reconciliation and wholeness can take a long time. It would take an excruciating effort to erase years of a dogma that had taught me that something was deeply wrong with me.

It was especially hard because I had no one to talk to. I did not know any women in my circle who were openly gay, no one that I could look up to for guidance. I could not fathom speaking to my new-found friends as they were all straight. I thought if they knew, they would leave me.

I still did everything I could to hide from the world that I had a girlfriend. I made Monique invisible and she suffered through it for over two years. Why did she stay with me so long? In some ways, I made her happy and she was truly invested in the relationship. She introduced me to her lovely family, we traveled together, but she could have given me the world and it would have not been enough because I was not enough myself. I still did not accept myself as gay as she had come into my life just as I left the Mormon church. Although I was almost 10 years older than her, she had a lot more experience in love than I did. I was still learning about anything that had to do with a gay lifestyle.

She, on the other hand, had been out as gay since she was 18 years old and we met when she was 28. She'd had plenty of love affairs while my only experience with love was, in reality, with my two ex-Mormon straight girlfriends.

Monique moved in with me after a few months of knowing each other. I told the doorman she was a friend. I would never hold hands in public. I remember celebrating my birthday with a dear group of friends at a Peruvian restaurant in Manhattan. I had invited about 20 friends who were all seated around a long table. My closest friend Shilpa sat next to me on one side and Monique next to me on the other. Everyone else filled the chairs around the table. I still insisted on keeping Monique at arm's length so none of my friends would suspect. Sadly, Monique complied. Because of this lie, I barely enjoyed the celebration. Monique was someone to be proud of, she was a beautiful smart girl who taught mathematics at one of the best private schools in Manhattan. She was a respected artist as well. But I could not see her, I could only see myself.

"We live together now! How long are you going to keep this up?" Monique said when we got home from my birthday celebration.

I reacted angrily, "Why are you trying to push me to do something I am not ready for? Why are you so insensitive? My friends will not understand!"

She replied sarcastically, "Then, maybe they are not real friends."

I used to become angry at her when she would question me about my coming out. The longer we stayed together, the more this became a problem and Monique started to change gradually. The person who would run to meet me at the door with a hug and kiss every time I came home from work, became less excited to see me. She started to lose the light in her eyes when she looked at me. I believe she had high hopes that I would evolve faster into accepting our relationship. But as we hit our two-year anniversary, I believe she realized my wounds were too deep and that there was nothing she could do to help me heal.

"I met someone at a work event," Monique said when I got home one evening. It was small talk that for some reason did not feel insignificant.

"Tell me about it."

"This gay woman who seems very nice and she has a Vespa so she gave me a ride home. It was fun! Especially now that it is summer."

I was so into my own world that I could not see what this meant.

During this time, I went back to work one afternoon after visiting one of my clients. It must have been around 3pm and I was consumed in reading my emails. Suddenly a salesperson, a Latin man who was about 6'4, stood across from me and said out loud in an unfriendly tone, "I never met a woman like you."

The office was an open environment where we all sat next to or across from one another and only the monitors separated us.

I stopped what I was doing and looked up, "What do you mean you have never met a woman like me?"

He quickly answered defiantly, "You know what I mean."

"What are you trying to say?" That was all I could say and, although I could feel his hostility, I wasn't sure what he was about to say.

He vomited his words, "A woman who goes out with other women!"

I did not dare look around to see who was around. I looked away from him and fixed my eyes on the computer for a couple of minutes, grabbed my bag and walked out and left the building. I went to see one more client that afternoon and walked for several blocks as I thought, He must have seen me somewhere in the city holding hands with Monique. I wasn't careful enough.

I was devastated as I had never come out to anyone at work. During my walk back to the office my devastation turned to anger, and I stopped to send him a message, "Don't you dare talk about my personal life in front of people like that. It was unprofessional and unacceptable."

I walked into the office building to pick up some of my belongings and I saw him waiting for me.

"Hey, can I talk to you for a couple of minutes?"

I didn't answer but looked him straight in the eyes with a volcanic fury. There was no one around as it was late and he proceeded to beg, "Please don't take me to HR. I have a family... Can we put this behind us?"

I didn't answer and walked away. But as I was leaving the building, I remembered his wife and child whom I had met at some company event and I thought, They are not guilty of his ignorance, and I decided to stay quiet, but I could hardly look him in the face after that.

One evening I came home from work, and Monique was chopping vegetables in the kitchen making dinner for us. I stood by the kitchen door and although I was engaging in small talk with her, I was not fully present. Monique looked more withdrawn. Suddenly, we started to have an argument and all I remember are these words coming out of my mouth, "I do not think I can do this anymore Monique. I do not think our relationship is working." What I wish I would have said is, " I do not think my being is working. "

She did not look at me, she kept on chopping the vegetables with an air of disappointment, anger and sadness while I stood by the door just watching her. I wanted us to have a conversation about our relationship, perhaps for her to convince me that there was something more to fight for. But I couldn't verbalize the possibility of an ending, and she was not ready to discuss the possibility of us not being together anymore.

A few weeks into Monique's friendship with this new-found friend, she had a love affair with this woman, and we split up. What was incredibly sad about this was Monique saying to me about her affair, "You pushed me to this. If you would just tell me you love me and tell me you want this, I would leave anything to be with you."

I was angry and delirious and told her to leave.

This was around the same time that I decided to do a marathon and was training for one with an organization called Team In Training. The day that I found out Monique "cheated" on me, which in my deranged mind I saw as cheating, when in reality, I was the one who had left her first because I made her feel invisible and empty inside, that day I had to run 15 miles in Central Park with the team. I ran in a brooding silence next to this Asian gay guy whose name was Andrew. By the time we were finishing our second loop in the park at mile 10, I broke my silence and said to Andrew, "My girlfriend just told me that she slept with another woman." The more pain I felt, the faster I ran so that my physical pain would outdo my internal pain. He tried to keep up with me, and after reflecting on what I had just told him, he said these words in a calm, reassuring tone of voice, "Don't do anything. Let her go. Never control anyone. Always let people be free. If this is what she needs to do, let her go in peace." We stayed together the rest of the run, but I remained quiet, my mind racing and my thoughts physically hurting. As we finished our third loop in Central Park, I returned to the apartment. She had not moved out yet.

When I got back, she asked me to forgive her and, defeat-edly, as if it was hopeless, asked for us to stay together. Never-theless, I did everything except what Andrew advised me to do. I made her feel guilty and diminished. I wanted to make her feel all the pain that I was feeling for what she did. In my mind, she still lived with me, she could have waited to sleep with anyone else she wanted after she left. In retrospect, I do not blame her in any way for whatever she did. In life I wish many times I could go back and redo certain parts where I could have been more understanding and acted with more compassion, more love. But, with time, all these hard lessons have taught me wisdom and they became ultimately a gift.

Chapter 16.

South Africa

Outside of work, all I did was RUN. I took up endurance running as if it was my religion. It didn't feel like a huge effort to train for this sport that I had grown up with. However, in my 30s, I started to push my body to its limits by taking on marathons. Breaking through physical pain and suffering helped liberate me from my trauma and limitations, and it unbolted a life of healing and unlimited possibilities. Overtime it gave me purpose, confidence and peace of mind; it was truly my saving grace. Given everything that life had unfairly thrown at me, it was a miracle that I never had to rely on any anti-depressants, drugs or alcohol. Unknowingly, exercise helped me avoid all of it. All I needed was to run. It also gave me a community of athletes whose stories of survival helped rehabilitate me.

I continued to thrive at the financial firm I worked for. I became a well-respected professional as the global voice for one of the company's key products, giving a continuing series of presentations to all of the sales teams. These were televised real-time and shown to all employees round the globe. I was described as a self-assured, passionate and dynamic speaker. And when it came to sales, I was one of the top sales executives in the firm. I had everything going for me, except for a meaningful personal life and I was not the happy, confident, self-assured person everyone thought I was.

This was how I had met my good friend Shilpa, an Indian woman in her 30s, who had joined our sales team, and sent me a compliment via email. She asked if I would be open to have lunch with her that week. I did not answer right away and then she stopped by my desk and I agreed.

Lunch was the following day and all that time until the next day, I thought, what will I talk with her about for a whole hour? I do not think we have much in common… I should just cancel. My uncomfortable feelings grew as the time got closer for us to meet.

I decided to go any way and she suggested we picnic in Central Park. Once we got to the park, I managed to be present. I told her that I grew up as a Mormon and that God was very important in my life. Then Shilpa went on to explain her faith, Hinduism. "Truth is eternal. It is the very essence of the universe. Truth is one but the wise express it in a variety of ways," she said. Then she explained that she married her husband after her MBA and that he is the only person she had ever slept with and it was the same for her husband. I learned through our conversation that integrity was everything to Shilpa. I felt a warm connection with her at this picnic and that meeting was the matrix of one of the most beautiful friendships of my life.

The company had many social events and team activities that allowed me to get to know other employees at the firm who became part of my close circle of friends over time. In fact, these people and I had now known each other for over ten years and shared vacations, secrets, weddings, divorces, tears, laughter and a lot of dancing, and the profound joy that comes with true friendship.

I had now dedicated myself to training for longer distance running. One afternoon at work, I decided to look for a marathon vacation outside of the United States and I found, "The Big Five Marathon in South Africa." An agency planned everything for the athletes who came from all over the world. I was in the best shape of my life and, shortly after, I landed in Johannesburg. The agents were waiting for me and a couple of more people at the airport to drive us for four more hours or so to a town called Entabeni, which is a game reserve where the marathon was to take place. We were told the Big 5 animals that we might meet on the marathon route were the African lion, African elephant, buffalo, giraffe and rhinoceros.

When we arrived in our jeep, the African people- men and women from Entabeni dressed in white – greeted us with songs and dance in their local language. I got so excited that, as we were driving in, I jumped off the jeep and joined them in the dance. I can still remember this feeling vividly. I absolutely love South Africans.

This was my first time in Africa and one of the most amazing experiences of my life. I took time to develop friendships with the locals and, one morning, I got up for breakfast and all the men who worked at the hotel were dressed in a white shirt and tie. There was always a certain dignity to the way they carried themselves, but especially today, they were looking sharp. I asked, "What is the occasion?"

One of them answered me with a kind smile on his face, "Today is the birthday of Nelson Mandela, and to honor him, we all dressed in our best clothing."

We had a few days to visit the game reserves and discover the majestic sights and make friends with the other athletes who were either Europeans or Africans, and a few also came from other places in Latin America, such as Mexico. My neighbor in the lodge was Alfonso. I took time to ask people around me so many questions about their lives that Alfonso nicknamed me "The Journalist."

Then, one day while we were sitting outside of our hut looking out at the African Savannah, I asked him, "And what is your story?"

He gave me a warm smile, "So now you are going to drill me with questions?" and then he laughed.

He started to reflect as if he was trying to travel back in time. I wasn't uncomfortable with the silence, but after a moment, he started to talk. "I became a runner after an incident where I almost died."

I was looking at him attentively.

He paused and then continued, "I had just turned 61 and my wife of 30 years and I had an argument about how much money she was spending. It was about $5K a month on things she didn't need! She would tell me that it was not only for her but also for our daughters who were in their early 20s and going to college.

"She would continue to spend enormous amounts and, although I was a successful architect and we owned a beautiful home in a prestigious area in Mexico City, I began to be concerned about her financial recklessness. Then, one Saturday, I was cleaning her car and I found a jewelry box with a diamond necklace in the trunk.

"I had not bought that for her. I had a restless eerie sensation. I looked inside the box and I found the credit card receipt, I put it in my pocket and closed the car."

"Oh Alfonso! This is like a movie, what happened next?"

He looked deep in thought. "I went to a friend who worked at a bank and asked him to look at the records of the credit card receipt. My friend refused initially as he said he could lose his job. But I became furious. I held him by his shirt, and I told him that he owed me many favors and he gave in."

"Did you find out who it came from?" I asked.

He nodded and said, "It was my best friend's credit card. My wife was having an affair with my best friend!"

I could tell that relating the story called up deep sadness for him and I told him he didn't have to continue.

However, he went on, "My wife proceeded to file for divorce, made up some story and kicked me out of the home that I'd bought and the guy who was supposed to be my best friend moved in."

Alfonso ended up moving to a small apartment in the city and he had to now prove to lawyers that there was infidelity, but she made it really hard for him to prove it.

He then looked at me with tears in his eyes and exclaimed, "I lost my home, my daughters, my financial stability…I was enraged and I wished their deaths! I was bitter for months and then this emotional brutality took a toll on me. I started to feel extremely tired, I realized I was not feeling well. I decided to go to the doctor, and he ran some tests."

"What happened then, what did the doctor say?"

"Well, the doctor told me that I had cancer and that I only had 3 to 6 months to live.

"At that moment, I had nothing else to lose. I was bitter and I was upset at God. I became depressed and stayed mostly inside my small apartment. Then one day, one of my close friends who was a runner, stopped by, saw me in my state of depression and asked me if I wanted to go for a run with him and our other friends who were waiting outside. I told him, 'Are you mad? I am about to die! Why would I run?'

"My friend replied, 'But it may make you feel better and it is better than you spending time alone in this place!'

"I bitterly declined, 'You are mad if you think I am going for a run.'"

Alfonso then looked at me and laughed, "Those sons of a gun kept stopping at my apartment before they went for a run and they never got tired of asking me, 'Are you coming?' I just continued to decline, but I started to feel that perhaps I should give it a try. I was for sure tired, but probably I could walk.

"Then one morning after many times of my friends coming, I told them, 'Ok, I will go with you guys. I may have enough energy to walk, but we will meet at the end.' My friends smiled and gave me an initiation hug.

"From that day on, every morning, I went on a run. I started very slowly; my body felt really weak as if life was seeping away from me. But the more I made myself run, the more energy I gained and eventually after a couple of months I started to keep up a little more with them. Then suddenly I realized I had been running for close to 5 months and I went to the doctor to find out how much longer I had left.

"The Doctor ran some tests and then he came back with the results.

"'Alfonso,' he said to me, 'I am confused. I do not know what to say… I do not see the cancer anymore. I do not under-stand!' He was ecstatic to tell me that I had a second chance in life, even though he said he had no explanation.

"Since then, Veronica, I have never stopped running and now I run a race in different countries all over the world. Here we are in South Africa about to run together."

These stories gave my trip to South Africa more meaning. I was so proud of Alfonso for rebuilding and transforming his life. We were almost inseparable during our time there. The day we ran the marathon we started together, but we had one of the worst windstorms that the town had ever experienced, and the coordinators were even contemplating canceling the race. I told the other runners, "I came all the way to South Africa, and I am running no matter what!"

I had read the book, "Running Hot" by Lisa Tamati, before traveling to South Africa, and it helped me understand that running is a not just a sport, it is a healing experience where you shed all your fears. Lisa had run in some of the most extreme weathers in the Sahara, so I told myself, I can do this. This is nothing! I am ready. So, I covered my eyes with glasses to protect them from the sand, then put on a running scarf around my neck and mouth so that I could resist the wind and I wore some warm clothes and I started to run.

Alfonso was complaining about how difficult the weather was as he ran next to me and, to be honest, it was annoying me. Negative self-talk has always bothered me, so I told him, "Alfonso concentrate. Stop thinking about how bad the weather is. Focus!" Even though I loved him, I started to run faster so that I could leave him behind so I wouldn't have to listen to him.

I was one of the front runners for quite a few miles and there were about three stops. I loved the sight of the African Savannah and the wonderful African people standing in the middle of nowhere waiting with water, singing and playing the drums.

I had a great pace for 16 miles trailing the top runners all the way, but then there was a very steep 2-mile hill and I had not trained for this. Most of my runs had been in Central Park which is flat and has tiny hills. I walked the steep hills as fast as I could but, as I was finishing the two miles, I reached towards my back to my waist band where I had placed some of my running energy gels and, when I tried to bring my arm back, I couldn't. My arm was stuck due to cramp and fatigue. I kept on running with my arm stuck towards my back. Another runner finally caught up to me and she jogged next to me and helped me bring my arm back, gave me some water and off she went. She was a runner from Belgium who ended up finishing the race right before me.

When I crossed the finish line, I was the 10th woman. I felt this incredible sensation of triumph, of satisfaction like no other feeling in the world.

The race had been extremely well organized, with a couple of doctors along the race and they made sure I undressed a bit as I had dressed very warmly at the beginning, but the weather got warmer as the race progressed. They held my clothes and found me at the finish line. The whole experience was magnificent. Only one of my friends finished before me and we waited for the others to arrive. We relaxed after the race since nighttime we were going to have a major outdoor celebration. We built a bonfire; had great food and drinks and they played some house music. People couldn't believe that I danced all night like a maniac! Alfonso looked at the rest of the athletes sitting around us and said, "Where does she get all that energy! We just ran a race!"

What Alfonso may not have understood is that a marathon meant so much more to me than just a race. It was the beginning of seeing the world in a bigger light, a world of vast possibilities and indescribable joy. For the first time I felt, outside of my life in the Mormon church, a joy that I had never realized existed. The physical pain and fatigue that I experienced during an endurance race became a way to transcend and rise above my past hurt. I began to realize that we humans have no limits except the limits we place on ourselves.

Chapter 17.

140 Miles

After that race, I returned to my regular job at the financial services firm. At this time, I had been moved to the trading solutions department. We had just hired a new girl named Amanda. She was thoughtful, kind, warm and we instantly became really good friends. To my surprise, after two days of meeting her, she told me that she had done an Ironman and that it was one of the most transformative experiences of her life and then she said, "You should do one."

"That's so funny, " I responded, "I met a Spanish couple in South Africa and he said the same thing."

Amanda asked, "What did you say?"

"I told them I can't," I laughed. "I do not know how to swim."

Amanda said, "Oh, that's nothing. I trained with some of the best Triathlon coaches in the US, the team is called TriLife. You will learn how to swim perfectly and bike. You are already a really good runner. I know you can do this. If you want, I can speak to them about you."

"Not now. It is ok. Thanks for the confidence." This time my negative response felt a bit different. It was as if I was not giving her an absolute No. This time, Amanda made me wonder whether I should look into this crazy triathlon business.

It wasn't too long after this conversation that Amanda invited me to travel with her to Lake Placid to watch the Ironman race being held there and meet the TriLife team. I went because I liked Amanda and I would learn something and, no matter what, I would have a great time with her.

We arrived at Lake Placid a day before the Ironman competition. We walked in to the 5-bedroom home rented by a few triathletes and Amanda and I shared one of the rooms. That day I met Nicole, the best cyclist in the team, although I did not know that at first. A lot of triathletes do a somewhat difficult ride or run the day before the race if they are not competing the next day and, for those who are competing, they may do a very light ride or run.

Amanda walked into our bedroom and asked, "Do you want to cycle about 60 miles today? We can try to do Whiteface mountain."

"Whiteface mountain! I don't know what that entails!" I said.

Amanda looked hesitant, "Well, give it a shot. If you can't do it, you can wait for us at the bottom of the mountain."

I accepted without knowing what I was getting into. We cycled part of the Lake Placid loop for cyclists and then we headed to Whiteface mountain. What I did not know was that Whiteface mountain is the fifth highest mountain in the State of New York with an elevation of 4,867 ft. We cycled part of the loop and I followed them. I soon realized that they were shifting gears depending on the elevation of the curves or how flat the roads were. Nicole and Amanda were riding smoothly at a similar speed. I was trying hard to keep up with them in only one gear; however, I quickly realized that serious cycling is not just about peddling forward. I needed to learn quickly how to shift gears and all the strict rules that avid cyclists follow. My shifting was clunky, with squeaks, creaks and clicking noises as I attempted to shift gears and climb the mountain. Amanda and Nicole were quickly leaving me behind.

I think Amanda had just realized that I wasn't by any means an experienced cyclist, so she looked back and said, "V, you do not have to go up. This is one of the hardest climbs. You can wait for us down here."

I was breathing a bit harder, "No. I am going to ride up with you. I will see you at the top."

Amanda nodded for support and then she began to climb the steep hill behind Nicole. I lost them in a matter of minutes. My legs have always been muscular and strong, so I used all the strength of my legs to push forward slowly and steadily. Halfway up the mountain, I saw Amanda lying on the grass underneath a tree taking a break next to another cyclist. Nicole had left her behind. When Amanda saw me, she looked astonished as if she did not expect me to have got this far. I waved to her and kept peddling forward. All I could feel was the exhaustion and sweat all over my body, but I was determined to climb to the top, as it is in my nature to never give up.

Amanda immediately got off the grass, got on her bike and started to climb again. I could sense that perhaps it would look bad if the newbie made it to the top first. We got to the top at the same time and met up with Nicole who gave me a big supportive smile and said, "You did it! This is incredible! You have barely ever ridden a road bike and especially this distance and you managed to climb the entire Whiteface mountain! Unbelievable!"

Then Amanda turned to Nicole, "She needs to do the Ironman! We will introduce her to the coaches this weekend after the race!"

I, on the other hand, had no understanding of the difficulty of what I had just done. Cycling up Whiteface mountain without any training! I only knew that when I start something, I work my damn hardest to finish.

The next day, I watched the Lake Placid Ironman and witnessed the perseverance, fitness, and courage that was beyond inspirational- I watched the athletes- men and women- after being out there from 6 am and now close to midnight, still pushing forward, even limping. I could see their determination that, no matter what, they were going to make it to the end. It was glorious. I told myself, "This is me! I am not meant to be on the sidelines; I am going to do this!"

The next day, I talked to Amanda's coaches. One was a very likable Canadian, Scott, and the other, a tough Russian guy, Ross, and, after doing so, I crazily signed up for the NY City Ironman for August 12, 2012. I did not have any idea of the arduous year-long training ahead of me, especially because I did not know how to swim.

Training started and I remember getting into the Olympic size Asphalt Green pool on the Upper East Side. This pool is well-known to most triathletes as it is one of the biggest and best pools to train. Each lane is assigned different speeds and I started in the first lane where the slowest swimmers jump in. But it turned out I was even too slow for this lane.

I had to learn how to float, tread water which I never became comfortable with or adept at. My body just wasn't buoyant. Scott, the Canadian coach, met us at the John Jay pool in Manhattan at 6am on Saturdays and he usually started with something like this, "Everyone get in the water as I give you the instructions. Today, we will do several drills and then swim free style for the next two hours. To start, you will swim with only one arm one way and then the opposite arm coming back. This will help you with balance…" Everyone started to tread water as Scott spoke. I would try to get close to a pool divider as I could barely last a minute in the water without sinking. I was the only one who could not hold myself above water. The goal was for me to be able to swim 2.4 miles free style to survive the first leg of the Ironman. I told myself, maybe I do not need to learn to tread water in order to finish the 2.4 miles of free style.

There were many instances in the pool when I panicked, could barely breathe, and felt as if I was drowning. I would see irrational things in the water, blood and dead bodies floating as I was attempting to swim. I would stop, hold on to the pool dividers and hold back my tears. However, on one occasion, when the pool was not as filled with triathletes, I allowed myself to cry wholeheartedly and, afterward, I said to myself, "These fears are not real! You are going to overcome this!" From that day on, whenever I imagined blood and dead bodies in the water, I would tell myself, "It is not real. It is just a matter of time for these horrible images to go away."

I hired a swimming coach as I needed a lot of help if I ever wanted to finish that race. I went religiously every week and swam for hours three times a week. My coach was to help me overcome my panic attacks and help me develop swimming technique. I went from barely being able to float to swimming laps for 2 hours non-stop. I often struggled with my speed, but I knew that I could last the time now to finish the race if I managed to do it within 2 hours.

Then, one day, he told me, "Let's work on your fear of the water and how you are going to survive this leg of the race. I want you to swim underneath the water without breathing all the way to the end." The pool was 25 yards so swimming underneath the water without breathing all the way to the end felt impossible.

Nevertheless, despite all my deep insecurities, I had to jump in. If there was a 1% chance I could ever do this, I held on to that atomic seed of hope. I took a deep breath and jumped to the bottom of the pool. After a few strokes under water, I felt asphyxiated and rushed to the surface. My coach was standing at the side of the pool watching me and I yelled, "I CAN'T DO THIS! I JUST CAN'T." He would yell back, "TRY IT AGAIN! IT IS ALL IN YOUR HEAD!"

After many failed attempts, I got tired of failing, I got tired of feeling powerless and hearing the voices of defeat in my head. I talked to myself, "I HATE BEING AFRAID! I HAVE TO DO THIS!" Nothing made me feel more like an imposter than swimming. So, I jumped in the water and went deep in the pool and started swimming one stroke after the other, not breathing, all the way to the end. And like that it just happened. I touched the end of the pool and when I floated back up and took my head out of the water, I smiled, free of all my sabotage. How can we explain that feeling when we push beyond limits that we place on ourselves? When we start to realize that perhaps there is something more than all our doubts and fears? I trained myself to think that although I could not breathe, I just had to keep on going. That was all I had to do even when I felt that I was dying.

I now knew you either drown or you keep on going and, no matter how low you sink in the water, somehow you have to believe that you will come out on top.

While I was learning how to swim, I also had to learn how to cycle like a true cyclist. I had never thought cycling would be difficult. I had enjoyed cycling since I was little, but this was not by any means a nice ride in the park.

The first time I met with the Triathlon bike team was in Central Park at 5am in the morning. The group was split in three - beginners, intermediate and advanced. I started in intermediate as I was expected to cycle faster due to my fitness level, but I soon find out that there were quite a few rules I needed to follow. We cycled in pairs in a straight line keeping the same cadence and pace as the pair in front of us. If they shifted, I shifted. I also had to keep a distance of about 10 meters from the bike in front of me. There were hand signals and verbal cues that I had to learn and the hardest lesson for me to learn was nutrition. I did not understand that I needed to be equipped with specific energy drinks and electrolytes in order to have the stamina to last for hours cycling nonstop. The closer we got to race day, the longer were the training rides, especially on the weekends. I knew I had to practice a 7- hour ride for over 100 miles without stopping because, if I could not do that, I would get disqualified.

Cyclists are a serious bunch. They love their rules and I learnt, with time, to understand that it is a matter of safety. But besides all the rules, cycling is extremely challenging, especially when you are going full speed for miles, trying to keep up with your team and you reach a hill, where you feel as if someone is sucking the life out of you. Our training went through the winter where I would still show up at 5am in a dark and freezing Central Park. I wore a scarf and a warm hat to cover my head and ears underneath my helmet and also wore special winter gear for this time of year. We wore lights on our helmets so that we could see each other as we rode around the park until it was about 7am and we could see daylight. That was just the beginning. As time went on, training moved to the roads. We left Central Park, headed towards the west side highway, rode along the west side of Manhattan all the way to George Washington bridge and then across to NJ. From there the route took us to 9W all the way to Bear Mountain. The only moment we stopped after cycling full speed was when we got to the top of Bear Mountain to refuel. I barely took any time to refuel, maybe 5 to 10 minutes, as I would tell myself, "In the real Ironman race, I have to cycle 112 miles non-stop so I cannot afford to rest. I need to mirror race day. I'd rather learn how to suffer now and endure the distance." We also had weekend camps in New Paltz, Lake Placid and trained in all kinds of weather, rain, snow, heat, everything.

I was probably the most unprepared athlete on the team. One training morning on a Saturday, I fainted on the bicycle while riding on 9W as a team. Why? I only had Coconut water in my water bottles, which I had no idea was not enough to help me survive the long grueling training rides. Right before I fainted, all I heard was my Russian coach, Russ, scream at us, "FASTER, FASTER, FASTER!!!" I was already feeling weak, famished, but I still pushed hard on the bike. I never wanted to let myself or my coach down. The next thing I knew my vision was getting dark and I found myself on the ground. I came back to consciousness in a matter of seconds, but for those who have fallen at a high speed on pavement, you can imagine the lacerations on my skin, particularly my fingers which were pretty badly damaged. Most of the athletes had gone ahead of me, but one of them saw me and stopped to help get me off the ground. "Oh my gosh! You are bleeding. We need to get you back. Do you need an ambulance or are you ok to ride back until we get to the bike shop close to the George Washington Bridge and clean you up?"

I was used to the pain so I said, "I think I can make it."

My teammate said, "Ok. I will follow right behind you. We have about 10 miles to go until our next stop."

I nodded and got on the bike, carefully touching the handles as I saw blood kept falling from my fingers. I left a blood trail until our next destination. We made it to the bike shop and, while my teammate held my bike and belongings, I went to the bathroom to clean myself up, put soap on my wounds and get ready for my next 20 miles back to Manhattan.

The only part of my training that was relatively easier than all the craziness I got myself into was running. I could run faster than most women in my team, but I wasn't quite as fast as the fastest men in the team. So, during training, the coaches made me trail behind the fastest men. This made me better. I was running spurts of 6 minute miles. We had weekly training in Central Park and met the team every Tuesday at 7pm to do drills for over two hours. I can still hear my Russian coach scream, "FASTER, FASTER! LOOK AT YOUR FORM. KEEP YOUR HEAD STRAIGHT. GO UP THE HILL! AGAIN!" Running was the only part of the race that gave me some confidence, the only part of the Ironman training that didn't make me feel like a failure.

I often felt that the other athletes could see right through me, that maybe I did not have what it takes to finish the race, that I was an imposter. Thus, I exhausted myself in anything I embarked on so as to feel worthy, that I belonged.

Chapter 18.

Open Water

Whatever training I had endured in the pool didn't prepare me for the ocean. My coaches took us to Coney Island and asked us to swim away from the shore until it was deep. The whole team of 20 had to swim from one side to the other to complete 2 miles of training. I could not see anything, I could not see my stroke, I was afraid I was just going to get further and further away from the shore into the deep ocean where no one could rescue me. I started to panic, "What the hell am I doing? I am going to die!" My breathing got fast. I felt like no one cared! My coaches were monitoring the crowd, every athlete was looking out for him- or herself, and I was barely swimming. Who am I kidding? Why don't I give up? I felt rage overtake my body and all I wanted to do was quit. I managed to get to the shore on my own and sit down on the brown sand, defeated. I watched the team continue to swim, flawlessly, fearlessly and I was resentful, envious and a million thoughts filled my brain. Why is it that some people just have it easy! NOTHING! NOTHING! has ever come easily for me! Nothing! How is this fair? At times

I thought God must not like me. He had given me too many deficiencies from the start: an unstable family, no mom, no dad, no affection and I'd had to hustle and figure things out on my own all my life. Always alone. I hated this.

When I got home, I sat down, and tried to regroup. I reminded myself of how far I had come and that this was not the time to give up. I just needed a gentle hand to help me get over what seemed to be an insurmountable task. Soon after, I looked for a second coach who could train me individually.

I met a wonderful guy from Toronto, Martin Russocki, who'd tried out for the Olympics in his day and I hired him to help me conquer the open water. He asked me to swim right along with him and said, "I am right next to you. I will not let you drown. You have to trust me."

I tried to nod. I would make every stroke, my heart beating fast and, every time I took my head out of the water as I made another stroke, I would check to make sure he was next to me. When we got to the middle of the ocean, he stopped, treaded water and asked me to stop, "Look around. Feel the sun on your face. Feel the peace around you," and then he asked me to repeat after him as he screamed out loud, "I am having fun. Life is beautiful." I was having a hard time treading water. He watched me with so much kindness and compassion and then he exclaimed, "Stop being afraid, that is why you are sinking, relax your body and enjoy! We are here in the middle of the ocean, it is sunny. Let's go! Scream after me." And I did, "The ocean is my friend! I am having fun. Life is beautiful." I had never thought of the ocean as my friend. How could I think of anything scary as my friend! But I was floating and, for the first time in my life, I felt so much peace, so much joy and, amazingly, I was no longer afraid.

We then went to the shore and he asked me to take off my wetsuit.

"I can't do that. My wetsuit is my security blanket. I will drown without it!"

He said, "It is time to give up everything to have everything."

I took off my wet suit and swam next to him for over 1 ½ miles and, as I got out of the water, I had a big smile on my face. I felt so much gratitude and was reminded how, in life, we sometimes need patient, generous souls who are miles ahead of us to show us a better way, to help us see what we cannot see in ourselves.

It is interesting how life teaches us. It is when you feel that you are breaking, that you are actually breaking through into new possibilities. This was not just about swimming. This was about the only life I had been given. I asked myself, "How am I going to live the only life I have!"

Around this time, one morning, one of my colleagues, a single mom from Trinidad in her 40's, came to greet me, "Hey Veronica. I have been thinking about you! I took my son to a swimming class at Asphalt Green on the Upper East Side this past weekend and I met this girl from Barcelona who works for our company and she is lovely! She speaks four languages like you. She is training for a triathlon! She has fun energy and you both seem to have the same vibe! I think you could become great friends. Her name is Daniella."

I had never had anyone approach me about a colleague so enthusiastically, but I didn't pay much attention. Then, later that afternoon, I had problems with my PC, so a very gregarious guy from our technical support team, came to my desk to fix my issue. As he was fixing my computer, he was chatting away and then surprised me by saying, "Hey, have you met Daniella? She works in a different division; she is so cool! I think you women should meet." The experience was a bit surreal, two random people who do not know each other talking to me about the same person. No one at the company knew or thought I was gay, for them I was just that "perfect Mormon girl," so the intent was to introduce us as friends.

The next day, I couldn't take my mind off this mysterious woman whose energy I could already feel from the description of these two people. I was sitting in my office and suddenly I found myself Instant Messaging her, "Hi, my name is Veronica. We haven't met, but it seems that other people think we should." She immediately acknowledged the chat and wrote, "LOL! Yes, I have had people telling me that I should meet you. It seems that people think we have similar energies. Thank you for taking the initial step. "I then asked her when she was coming to my building as she worked in a different office in Manhattan. Daniella replied, "Why don't we meet Thursday lunch time? I can come to you."

Thursday came and we met on the 6th floor of the modern, majestic building, full of light and lots of bustling. The sixth floor is where the company broadcasts the Financial News. She sent me an instant message to let me know that she would wait for me underneath the main marble stairs. I had seen her picture on the chat function, so I quickly spotted her. We said hi enthusiastically and it was wonderful to hear her Spanish accent which seemed so sexy to me.

Nevertheless, I thought that she probably wanted some professional advice as I was a manager and she was in a more entry level position.

"Are you happy being in Global customer support?" I asked her, as we sat down.

"Well, I learned what I needed to learn but I am ready to move on. But it is hard to get out. The opportunities to get promoted are infrequent. Everyone is competing for the same roles."

"But what would you like to do?" I looked at her with sincere concern as I knew she was not the only person who wanted to leave that department. People get tired of answering phones all day.

Daniella started to look scattered. She would look at me and then look away as if she was distracted or nervous. I thought, she seems a bit all over the place.

Our conversation ended a few minutes after that as she had a company meeting, but right before we said goodbye, she said, "Let's have lunch next time." I nodded but had no intention to follow up. She seemed flighty.

As I was walking away, I get a text from her: *It was so wonderful to meet you. Sorry I was a bit nervous. Can we see each other again?*

I had not given her my cell number. She must have got it from our internal system, I decided, and, also, I thought the tone of her note a bit unusual.

I had to go away that weekend to do the half Ironman in Connecticut. I was staying in a hotel with other athletes. The night before the race, I got a suite of text messages from Daniella.

I hope you are having fun. I would love to see you soon.

I was enjoying the attention and texted her multiple times in response to her questions. But right before we were supposed to say goodnight she wrote: *I have something to tell you, but I am afraid to say it.*

I got excited, but I was also a bit uncertain. She was a gorgeous woman from Barcelona with red hair, an amazing body as she had been a professional dancer for many years, extremely talented, and, as I got to know her a bit in the texts, she had a charming personality. It can't be what I am thinking…There is no way she could like me, I thought. And then I read: *I like you…I was so nervous when I met you that I could barely make any sense with what I was saying. Didn't you notice?*

I was staggered. *I am happy to hear this. I think you are beautiful…*

When do you come back and when can I see you? Daniella continued.

I come back on Sunday. What if we see each other on Tuesday?

Her answer was short and quick: *Ok. See you Tuesday.*

The half Ironman went very well but, as I immersed myself in the lake, all I thought about was how eager I was to meet Daniella again. This made me forget the anxiety I experienced every time I threw myself into the water. Instead I felt a calming peace and bliss. The 70.3 miles of this race was a complete joy; I was in my best shape ever. Although many athletes talk about how difficult and hilly the bike path is, I felt strong and, when it came to the run, all I remember was smiling widely and running fast toward the end, passing some guy whom I overheard comment to other athletes after we crossed the finish line that he couldn't believe I passed him like that. For the first time in a while, I had something to look forward to when I came back from the race.

When I went back to work on Monday. I got a text from her: *Why do you want to wait until Tuesday to see each other? Why don't you want to see me today?*

I was thrilled by her persistence and agreed to meet her Monday evening after work. As I waited for her, my heart pounding, I heard the bell and wondered if I looked good enough and what she was going to think when she saw me again. When I opened the door, she looked more beautiful than what I remembered from the first time I saw her.

She came in wearing a green elegant dress with oval lace around her neck. We sat on my dark brown leather living room couch. Since I lived in a studio, I did not have a lot of things adorning my apartment, just the grey living room carpet and a small dining table with two wide leather chairs and, to our left, the window facing 2nd Avenue and 69th Street. It was as if all the pieces around us were framing the beginning of a fairy tale love story. I sat somewhat close to her; I did not know what to do. I have never been comfortable on first dates; I lack either courage or confidence or both. After a few minutes of being together, she got close to me and then we kissed. That is all we did the rest of the night until it was time for her to go home. My apartment was on the 15th floor, we took the elevator down, passed by the concierge and then proceeded to call a cab. We kissed on the lips again and I was filled with ecstasy. It was as if my life had changed magically.

After our first rendezvous, Daniella and I were inseparable. All I thought, breathed and dreamed of was Daniella. We worked in the same company so as soon as we got into work every morning, we utilized the company Instant Messaging system.

Hola Amorcito! Daniella always called me and never stopped calling me. "Amorcito," those words were my nest of love.

I would always answer, *Te quiero Amorcito.*

When we walked in the streets, we held hands or hugged so tightly, it was as if we didn't want the air to separate us. When she would stay over at my place, we would wake up, look at each other and say, "Not even death will separate our love." One morning I opened my eyes and I couldn't believe I was waking up to such love and, as I was looking at her, my eyes swelled with tears, my heart exploding with a joy and gratitude I had never felt in my life.

Daniella was also training for an Olympic triathlon; it was a shorter distance than mine. She belonged to a different team at "Team In Training" but, coincidentally, we had the same coach. We realized one Saturday we both had to train in the ocean at

Coney Island; her training was at 8am and mine at 10am. We decided to go together and I would wait for her and then she would wait for me until our swimming drills were done.

As we were approaching the beach, our mutual coach, Scott, the friendly Canadian, looked at me confused and said, "Why are you here? Your training doesn't start until 10am."

"I am just here with my friend Daniella. We came together."

He looked at both of us, smiled and said, "Ha…ok! I will see you later!" As soon as the coach walked away, Daniella and I continued walking towards the area where I was supposed to meet the other athletes. I was not holding her hand as I was used to hiding. However, I immediately sensed Daniella's disappointment. In fact, Daniella had tears in her eyes. I asked her, "Baby, is everything ok?"

Then Daniella started to cry and spoke to me in a way that took away any desire to hide or cover up, "Don't you ever tell anyone that I am just your friend! I am not your friend. Do you hear me?!!! You are not going to hide us!" Seeing Daniella crying broke my heart.

How could I love someone so much and think that I could hide her? Any shame I had lived with all my life felt senseless now. Daniella was the love of my life and I had to now rise up from the ashes of those long gone oppressing dogmas. They were so entrenched in my consciousness that it had always seemed like an impossible feat. But now there was Daniella. For the first time, I had something that was bigger than all of that.

My intense Ironman training continued during my relationship with Daniella, but I never had to choose between my relationship or training. Daniella dedicated herself to my training as much as I did. When I had to go to weekend camps in Lake Placid to swim, ride and run for hours, she would come along with me. We would stay in a small shack and spend our early nights being intimate in the many senses of the word. We had long conversations, we laughed a lot and spent the most tender moments together. Then, the next day, I would wake up before sunrise to start training with the team. I swam in Mirror lake in Lake Placid for close to 2 hours, then rode over 90 miles, arriving at the transition area after 6 hours, intensely tired, but there was Daniella waiting for me with water bottles or sports drinks so that I could have enough fuel for my run. While I was off to a 15 mile run, she would monitor how long the run would take me and make sure she was back at the finish point to embrace me and help me get back to our rental place so that I could take a shower and then we could eat together. In the evenings, we would walk the streets of Lake Placid, hugging so tightly as if we were one body. We were like an old couple whose love had no beginning or end, whose souls had indeed been together from the awakening of the first star, when the universe came into existence, where the first thought that ever entered consciousness was us.

As part of my preparation for the real race, I participated in a few half-Ironman races, one of the most memorable ones at Tupper Lake. Daniella drove with me to the race and she planned to wait for me at the finish line. Right before starting the swim, she walked with me to the starting point and as I was putting my goggles on so I would be ready to jump when they called my age group, my goggles broke. I looked at her with panic. I was only a few minutes away from the siren. I didn't need to speak, she just looked at me, ran to our car, got a second pair and ran back to me just in time for me to hear the whistle blow. I put on my goggles and jumped. The swim went relatively ok. I was part of the last group that came out of the water. As soon as I left the water, I took my wet suit off as I ran to the bike transition area. I immediately put my helmet on, cycling shoes, sunglasses and off I went. Tupper Lake was very windy that day. I had to cycle about 56 miles, which is the bike distance for a half Ironman, but due to the strong wind, I felt myself losing control of the bike in the first few miles. I crashed and fell to unconsciousness. But even in the depth and darkness of this blankness, I said to myself, "Get up! Daniella will be so worried if you don't come back." I then started to wake and, as I opened my eyes, I saw people around me and heard one of them saying, "She needs to be pulled off the race." One of my teammates, Amanda, asked me, "Are you ok? Your helmet is cracked."

I couldn't speak coherently right away, but the first thing I was able to say was, "I am ok. I am going to get back on the bike." I heard others surrounding me say, "We should not let her continue. We should get her off the race." So, before anyone could take a decision for me, I gathered all the strength in me I could to get back on the bike and take off. Initially, I could barely see clearly. I felt faint. I kept going slowly while other cyclists kept passing me. However, as time went by, I regained my strength and I got faster.

Surprisingly, as I kept riding and trying to gain ground, I noticed some cyclists would take a second look if they were riding by me. I had no idea why I got a few stares.

When I finally finished the 56 mile bike ride, I took my helmet off and put my running shoes on. As soon as I started running, I felt strong, but the unusual stares of those running around me became more obvious. When I got to the finish line, I saw some of my Trilife teammates look at me surprised and Coach Scott said outloud, "For heaven sake, you have blood all over your face!" A couple of my teammates laughed and said, "She is indeed the 'Terminator.'" I then saw Daniella immediately running towards me. "Amorcito, I should take you to the Doctor." Luckily, the doctor said that although I suffered a concussion that I was going to be ok. He did warn me that next time If I fall and hit my head that I should stop the race as it could be dangerous to continue under these conditions.

On another occasion when we were at one of my training camps, Daniella, knowing I still struggled with being in the open water, offered to swim next to me, and she did. Every stroke I took, I would see Daniella next to me. She had indeed become my everything.

My Ironman training was now coming to an end. I was now weeks away from the biggest and most arduous race of my life: Ironman Race in NYC, August 12th, 2012.

In one of my final training sessions, I swam for 2 miles, cycled for 100 miles and ran for 15 miles all in one day, not quite the full distance of the actual race, but it was an accumulation of many training sessions over an entire year. This last training session gave me greater confidence that I could finish.

I was in love with Daniella more than ever. She and I had shared an intimacy that few couples have the privilege of in a lifetime. But as soon as the race was over, I went back to a "normal life" and, without the demands of an intense daily training schedule, I felt a little lost. Yet there was always Daniella to focus on. She was enough to fill my world, I thought. However, other things surfaced in our relationship. She had never been in a serious relationship with a woman before and her mom was completely against our relationship. On top of this, we faced some significant challenges in our professional lives because we came out publicly as a gay couple. We felt that people were watching us and some of Daniella's colleagues started to treat her differently. On my side as a manager, I also felt that I had a lot to lose. A leader at the firm stopped me once on my way to a meeting, "Listen V. I am going to talk to you as a friend, some people are just not comfortable with this partner situation of yours." I did not know what to say. But one thing I knew for sure is that the discomfort of the few did not represent the values of the company I worked for.

One afternoon when Daniella was working, she was on her way to the bathroom when she passed a glass conference room, and as she looked in, she was shocked at what she saw. There were a bunch of guys in the conference room looking at a big screen of pictures of us that they must have found on the internet. It was as if they set up a watch party. She shocked them as she opened the door and said, "Gentlemen, can I help you?" Some got nervous, others started to laugh. She closed the door and then called me panting, "I just caught a bunch of men from my department looking at pictures of us!"

I listened to her not knowing what to do with all of this information.

When I shared with HR that Daniella was facing some uncomfortable situations at work because of our relationship, HR dismissed it. When I told the HR woman about the conference room scene, she obviously didn't understand how this made us feel and said, "If I had your arms, people would probably be looking at a picture of me too!" She laughed and I smiled, yielding to a situation that I felt I had no power to control.

All of the pressures that we started to feel being in this openly gay relationship overwhelmed both of us. Daniella started to become extremely depressed. She had big aspirations for her life, her career, she had worked hard in her life to be the best at whatever she put her mind to, and she felt that some of her peers were stonewalling her and ridiculing her for being in a relationship with a woman. We were both now dealing with a whirlwind of confusing and painful events.

After a few months, Daniella and I started to become like strangers to each other. She still had not received the promotion she had been waiting for and she was becoming more and more discouraged. I, on the other hand, would come home exhausted from a work environment I felt unsafe in, and we barely talked to each other. Instead, she spent a lot of time on her iPhone texting other people and talking to friends. I would talk to Shilpa about my day and how shaky and fearful I felt about my relationship with Daniella. I have always dealt with an unfathomable fear of loss since the death of my mom and having to lose other people in my life, but I could not possibly endure losing Daniella. Not Daniella!

My biggest fear came to life. One Sunday evening, we had gone out to meet some of her dance friends who were visiting from another country. In front of me, she started to flirt with one of them. When I approached her and asked her what was going on, I felt belittled.

I waited until we got to the apartment to ask her, "Daniella, do you not want to be in this relationship anymore? Just tell me! Just let me know and I will let you go!"

She answered with a despotic attitude, "Leave me alone! I don't want to talk."

"Daniella, we must talk! I cannot continue like this anymore."

She lashed out and said and did the most hurtful things. Out of respect for the love I have for her, I will not repeat them, but it was enough for her to leave and for me to let go.

The following weeks and months, I could barely get out of bed to go to work. You could see the pain in my face, and I was often seconds away from crying. Some of the people that I had managed for over a year were loyal to me and reached out to ask me how they could help. I will never forget this. Marshall was one of them. Any manager would be fortunate to have someone like him. He approached me several times and called me on my cell to tell me, "V. You have been so good to me, whatever I can do during this difficult time of your life, I am here. Whatever workload I can take from you, I am here. I will do anything to support you."

One day on a Friday, a friend of mine came to visit me at my apartment where I used to live with Daniella to check on me and she took one good look at me and said, "I am not leaving. I am going to stay the weekend with you to make sure you are ok." She slept on my couch, cooked for me and tried to get me to talk.

The next person who checked in on me was Shilpa. She also took a good look and said, "You are coming to stay with me in my apartment in Hoboken. I have one extra room; my husband and I will be happy to have you."

I declined her offer, but she did not accept my answer, and showed up at my apartment to help me pack so I could stay with her for a few weeks.

I remember her getting up at 4am in the morning to try to get me up. "V. Do you want to work out? It will help you feel better!"

"No, Shilpa. I can't. I just can't."

"V. It will make you feel better. Just give it a try."

My body felt as if getting up was the most difficult task I had ever done. My drive for any type of physical activity was gone. I was devoid of the will to live.

When Shilpa would come back from running, she would then go to my room and ask me to get in the shower or help me get dressed so that I could be ready to leave with her for work. One time as we were riding the train to our Manhattan offices, I broke down crying. Shilpa reacted desperately, "Stop V. Don't cry. Everything will be ok."

But nothing felt ok in my life. It felt as if my grief would never subside. I remember speaking to God, "I cannot bear waking up feeling like this one more day. God I cannot. Please take this pain away from me because I cannot live like this anymore." I needed a miracle.

I am not sure if it was my supplication to God that did it or the help I received from all my friends, but most likely it was all of it that helped me climb out of my hopelessness and deep sadness. There was also one life changing conversation with a colleague from work that hit me so hard that I had no other option than to rise from the ashes.

This colleague of mine had lost his fiancée over a year ago to a car accident a couple of days before their wedding. He had bought a beautiful big house where they were both going to live. The wedding was all set and I remember him, with a big smile on his face and eyes shining, telling me as we were walking together to a client meeting that she was the love of his life. But the unfortunate news left him in such shock that he had to take a leave of absence and was not able to work for months. I reached out to him to tell him that I was there for him and that he could call me anytime he needed to talk.

I remember him answering one of my texts: *I am living in the house we were both supposed to live in together. I check my cell often to see if I have a text from her. I cannot sleep, I don't feel like getting out of bed. I sometimes think that I hear her…that I see her and I keep looking at my cell to see if she has called…*

I prayed for him in my heart that he could be ok one day.

This same guy, a year later, saw me sitting at my desk after my breakup with Daniella and asked me, "Can we go to lunch?"

I nodded as if I had no strength to do anything more. He took me out of the building, and we went somewhere to talk. "Listen Veronica. I know what happened to you. I need you to get better. When my fiancée died before our wedding, I went into a deep depression. I wanted to die. I was taking pills, nothing or no one seemed to be able to help me. Until my psychologist asked me once, 'What is the biggest and most painful loss that any human being can go through?'

"I did not know what to answer," he said. "And then the psychologist proceeded to explain, 'The biggest pain someone can ever go through is the loss of a child. That is the most terrifying loss anyone can ever endure. But we must learn how to dig deep, find purpose and meaning again in the midst of our sorrows. We must choose to live.'"

Then he proceeded to share the story his psychologist told him. "I had two patients, both mothers. Both of them lost a child through death. One of them could not function anymore. She lost her job and eventually her marriage. She was never able to rise from her ashes. My other patient also lost her child. But after giving herself some time to grieve, she used her deep sadness and struggle to find meaning by helping others deal with their pain. She volunteered with a nonprofit. She eventually went to work and created a closer relationship with her husband. Of course, the sadness will always be there, but she found solace, purpose and meaning in her suffering. She chose to live."

Then, my colleague asked me, "Which of these two women do you want to be, Veronica?"

"I am going to tell you one more thing," he said. "It is the story of the train."

At this point he had my attention. The story of the train? I thought.

He continued, "I want you to think of your life and those who are in it as if you are all on this train sharing a ride to a destination. Some people come in at different points and suddenly someone sits next to you. The train gets full, you get accustomed to the people around you. You get really close to the person sitting next to you, you share some meaningful conversations, laugh, and you cannot possibly imagine being on this journey without them. But suddenly after hours and days, the train stops. And that person who was sitting next to you, gets up, turns around to take a look at you, walks to the door of the train, waves at you goodbye and then leaves.

"You may ask yourself," he said, "why did this person leave? Why do people have to go? But Veronica, some people come into our lives to share part of our journey. But suddenly the train stops, they reached their destination and it is time for them to go. We must honor their journey and we must let them go!"

By the time he was finished with the story, I was weeping. It was as if all the sadness I was carrying inside of me could no longer be kept inside. I cried out my loneliness and, with the wisdom found in those words, I found some instant healing. The type of healing that allows you to start your life again. In my case, I felt that this train of life had a different destination in mind for me no matter who left me along the way. I had other places to go, people to meet, lessons to learn and there was no other choice but to go on. Today was definitely not my STOP.

IRONMAN PART 3.

I was good at running and good at endurance. This part looked like it would be not as difficult. But nothing worthwhile is ever straightforward.

I arrived on my bike to the same transition area in Palisades Park and got off the bike to change into my running shoes. I continued wearing the same tight shorts and sports bra. The average time to change from your cycling gear to your running gear is about 3 minutes. Just enough time to take off my biking shorts, my helmet and gloves and put my running shoes on.

I felt that there was something wrong. My level of energy was lower than what I was used to at the start of my run. As I started going uphill at the beginning of the running path at Palisades Park, I heard some of my teammates from TriLife who were not competing in this particular race scream, "Go V! Running is your strong suit! You got this one!" But I didn't feel that way. I started to feel sick to my stomach. I had read about it in Chris McCormack's Ironman book, "I am here to Win." I had what triathletes call GI Issues or, in other words, major stomach issues. Fortunately, I had read what it felt like and what could possibly help me- coca cola and chicken broth. Suddenly as I ran to the top of the hill, I saw Daniella, "Amorcito, you got this one! I will see you at the end." Just seeing her gave me an extra push. I knew that there was nothing else to do but to finish this race.

My body was not able to swallow the energy gels or take in any more sports drink. I was going on empty my first few miles. I had run about 7 miles when suddenly I felt a pull in my stomach, I started to get the chills, then a desperate desire to go to the bathroom to empty my system. But I was on the route and surrounded by hundreds and hundreds of spectators on each side of the road. I felt that I was seconds away from having a horribly embarrassing accident. I then asked one of the volunteers on the side of the road, "How far is the next portable bathroom?" He screamed his answer to make sure I heard as there was tons of people around us, "IT IS 1 MILE AWAY!"

A MILE AWAY?!!! That felt like an eternity, I nervously thought. I looked around to see if there was any area I could run to and hide to discharge my distressed body of its waste. I started to experience cold sweats, and felt horrible, but I kept on running. I looked down at my stomach and my whole belly was swollen as if I was seconds away from exploding. Then, I commanded my mind, you are going to hold this until we get to the bathroom a mile from now. You are going to do this. Do not shit on your pants!

I just kept putting one foot in front of the other for a good 10 excruciating minutes until I saw one of my coaches on the side of the road as he screamed, "V. Are you ok?"

I shook my head and I pointed to the portal bathroom which at this point was just feet away from me. I could not believe that I had told my mind to do the impossible. I ran to the bathroom on the side of the road and discharged pounds of waste. It had been over 7 hours nonstop out there and my body must have gone through a shock. I left the bathroom and I felt immensely grateful that I had not let go on the road.

However, at this point for all the miles I had run, my body did not want to take any more nutrition. I could barely drink even water and, if I attempted to take an energy gel, I threw up. At that moment, I looked at the heart that Daniella had put on my arm and the very thought of her helped push me beyond my strength.

I kept on going, but unexpectedly, I saw a guy next to me who looked like one of those guys on the front of a fitness magazine, handsome, built, strong, extremely fit, faint next to me. This did not make me nervous, instead I thought, This is not going to happen to me! Go!

I kept on running at a pace of 10 minutes a mile or maybe even more; all I cared about was to run steady. Ross, one of my triathlete coaches trained me to count every time I took a step: One, Two, Three, Four. I did that for hours, almost until the end of the race. That helped me focus on my form.

Around mile 10, I saw some volunteers giving small cups of Coca Cola, which I took. Chris McCormack was right; it made me feel much better. It gave me the strength to continue. Then around Mile 16 or so, I saw another group of volunteers giving out chicken broth and it felt like medicine. I crossed the George Washington Bridge to head to Manhattan and as I was running on the west side highway, I regained more strength and I started to run slightly faster. I saw another of my teammates struggling a bit as expected; we were now in our last miles of the race and, as I passed by her, I said, "Let's go! We can do this." When you see another athlete, who is sharing the same pain and enduring such a race, all you feel is a sense of camaraderie and deep respect.

The end was near, I was now about 6 miles away from the finish line when I saw from the corner of my eye, the face of my most feared and respected coach, Ross. The one whom I hardly ever heard a compliment from. But I saw it in his face, he took a look at me and I sensed his pride. Then as he nodded with his stoic face, he yelled, "Good job V. Keep your form! You are almost there." His affirmation meant the world to me. I'd spent a whole year trying to please this man and I finally saw it in his face. I understood that he was trying to teach me that "Pain is just weakness leaving the body."

I felt a sense of gratitude because I understood at that moment that all that discipline, the demands, his expectations of me as an athlete, all of what I went through in my training, made me an Ironman!

I knew without any doubt at that point that I was going to make it! All the dedication that Scott and Ross and his team of coaches put into me was helping me get to the finish line,

Chapter 19.

Cornell- How I rebuilt my spirit

When managing a team that supported our Trading Solutions platform, I had some late days as something often went wrong with the product. One afternoon as I was working, I saw an email come in from Cornell University inviting me to an Executive MBA Open House in Manhattan. The email read that there was going to be a lecture from one of the top Critical Thinking professors, Risa Mish.

A couple of months after my breakup, this was the first time something excited me. I felt my heart beating again. I had thought about doing an MBA in the past, but I had not done as well as I wanted in my GMAT scores to apply for Harvard. However, life is full of surprises and it has a way of giving you exactly what you need, at the right time.

I read the email and reserved to attend the session at 6:30pm that very day.

It was about 5:30pm and I was getting ready to wrap up. This was one of those days when something went wrong with the platform. Now it was 6:15pm and I had barely resolved the issue. I thought for a moment, It doesn't make sense to go now. I am going to get there too late.

But as I left the office, something told me to walk in the direction of the Cornell Club building. Maybe I can make it to the last part of the session and still get something out of it, I thought.

I got there closer to 7pm and I rushed to get to the right floor. As soon as I got out of the elevator, I saw the classroom door open and the professor giving the lecture. I paused, observed for less than 5 seconds and decided in that instant that I was not going to interrupt the lecture. As I was about to turn around and walk away, Professor Mish saw me and said, "Welcome! Come in!" She stopped her lecture to let me in. As I walked in, I saw a few round tables with people sitting around them. There was one table at the front with an open seat and she directed me to sit there. One of the women at the table gave me a big smile and I felt an instant connection. I could see her name was Marie-Helene. Most of the people in the room had already been accepted to the EMBA program and were about to start in a month; however, there were a handful of guests like myself.

Professor Mish continued her lecture, and in those few minutes, I was able to capture what she was trying to convey with her teaching. She then asked that each table discuss the case and one of us had to present afterwards.

After a fifteen-minute discussion, it was time to present. One person per table. When it was our turn, one of the already accepted students got up to explain the case. But I thought that she was missing some critical information. So, I spoke right after her, explaining passionately other factors that needed to be considered to make our case stronger. The professor agreed and gave me some praise.

After the session was over, the Director of the Admissions program came toward me and asked, "Have you thought about doing an EMBA?"

I answered, "Yes, but today I am just observing."

He then said, "You should apply for the Cornell EMBA. You were really good when you spoke today. I think you will do very well in this program."

Marie- Helene who was standing next to me immediately said, "I feel like I already know you! Can you please apply? I would love to have you as a teammate!"

I looked at her. Then, I looked at the Director of the Program and said, "But your program starts in six weeks or so! Is that enough time to apply?"

He immediately answered, "It doesn't matter. Can you get your application in right away?"

Maria Helene screamed, "Yes Baby! Do it!" Ever since then, she's always called me, "Baby."

The day after, I received a text from Marie Helene: *Baby, did you start the application process? I can't wait for us to do this program together!* That was enough motivation for me to go online and begin.

I had to now find out if the Financial firm I worked for was willing to sponsor me financially. I couldn't see a reason why not. I had been there for many years and had a successful career. There were employees who were not in management who had got their full MBA program paid for. I contacted two guys in the division who had been paid for to find out how they went about it. Neither of them was in management. Both of them said, "We just spoke to the Global head of the division. He didn't ask any questions and approved the finances right away."

I started to get excited! Maybe this is all meant to be! I can't believe that this could all be possible, I thought.

Then I sent an email to the global head of the division and expressed that I wanted to meet with him to discuss my desire to do an EMBA at Cornell University and that I was looking for his support to get my studies financed by the company.

About fifteen minutes later, I got a reply: *Hey V. Good to hear that you want to do the program. I just want to set your expectations as we do not approve scholarships for a full MBA. But I am happy to chat if you'd like.*

I read the email and read it again. I felt a sense of betrayal and deceit. But instead of replying to his email, I went back to the other guys who had just told me that their program was approved by this same leader. I did not tell them that I had just been rejected. I approached the first one, "Hey, I just wanted to confirm that you got your full MBA program approved by our global leader and that the company is paying for everything." His answer was, "Yes! I told you that the global head approved it right away and I am not paying a cent."

I smiled as he answered and thanked him for his answer.

I went to the second man, "Hey, I just want to confirm if everything was approved for your MBA. Who approved it and how long did it take for you to get the money for the program?" He looked at me a bit confused, "I told you that the global head approved everything, and that the money was available right away before starting the program. I am not paying a dime."

I thanked him for his time and walked away to my desk and stared at the email I'd received: *Sorry V. I want to make sure that I set your expectations as we do not approve a full scholarship to pay for a full MBA. Happy to chat about it if you want.*

I set a meeting to speak to him. I wanted to hear from him firsthand that he had never approved an MBA for anyone in that department. We met and he said, "Oh V. Congrats that you are thinking about doing an MBA. Sorry that I do not have any control of this. I have never approved an MBA program to be paid by the company. Even mine, I paid for it myself."

I repeated what he had just told me, "So, not ever in the history of this department have you ever approved an MBA program for anyone?"

He answered, blinking his eyes, "No. I have not."

I smiled, thanked him for his time and politely ended the conversation.

I then went to a very high-level senior executive to discuss the situation. She reviewed my case and my stellar performance in the company. I had been highly ranked as a top sales executive globally for all the years I had worked there. I mentioned to her how different minority groups at the firm had not gotten their Masters' degree approved by their managers and that that is not sending a good message externally. We had a couple of meetings, and after she reviewed my case, she looked at me and said, "On behalf of these men, I am going to ask you to forgive us. I do not know why these men are like this. I am sorry. This does not represent what we stand for as a company."

By the time, I walked out of her office and went two floors down to mine, I received an email from HR making it official that I was getting my full MBA program approved and paid by the firm. I was grateful for this leader who listened to me with compassion and was committed to making things right. I had a sense of satisfaction, but also, I realized at that moment, more than I ever had before, how a certain group of people when in power, may look at others who do not look like them as undeserving of the same blessings and opportunities life has granted to them.

After I got sponsorship, I submitted my application, and a week later I received an invitation to interview with the Cornell Admissions staff in person. The following week, I received a call during the day while I was standing with my team.

"Yes, hello."

"This is Cornell University. We are calling you to let you know that we have many people who apply to this program and as you know we go through a rigorous interview process and we only want to accept the best of the best." I stayed silent. The director proceeded, "But I want to give you personally the news that you have been accepted to the Cornell EMBA program class of 2015."

My heart was swollen with excitement, pride, hope. I screamed by the trading desk, "Yes! Thank you so much!" Then I looked at the team I managed, "Guys, I was accepted into the MBA Program at Cornell!" The team clapped and Marshall, my favorite and most loyal person in the team, had a big smile of sincere joy for me.

My life at Cornell started that July, only a few weeks after being accepted. We were supposed to report to Cornell for a week in Ithaca. Marie- Helene and I made plans to go there together. This was the beginning of one of the most fascinating and life altering experiences of my life.

As school started, my life became intensely busy. I worked during the day, I studied every night and weekends. I had no time to think of Daniella or my pain. My life was filled with infinite possibilities and assignments. Initially, I was overwhelmed with subjects such as Statistics. I was in my early 40s and I couldn't remember when was the last time I had taken a math class. I had to get a tutor to help me. I started to doubt whether I had what it took to do well in this program. Everything required an enormous effort. Economy, Leadership, Accounting, Valuation, Strategy, Finance, Negotiation, Critical Thinking, etc. etc. But the longer I stayed with it, the easier it became. I put in hours and hours of study. I was not the fastest learner, but I was extremely dedicated, and I worked very hard. But something else underneath was also motivating me. I was the only Latin woman in the room, so I felt a need to represent, to leave a good name for my people. I never wanted anyone to say, after interacting with me, that Latin people were not smart, or hard workers and very capable. It is not that I felt I had anything to prove, but I felt that I had to leave a legacy for those who looked like me.

The Cornell Professors were remarkable. I could write a book about them and how they changed my life. Beta Mannix (Leadership), Risa Mish (Critical Thinking), Yaniv Ginstein (Valuation), Justin Johnson (Strategy), Kathleen O'Connor(-Negotiation), Angela Noble (Public Speaking), the innovation professors, etc., etc.

But besides Marie-Helene whom I became really good friends with throughout the program, another teammate whom I worked with for 3 semesters changed my life as well, Henry.

Henry was an intimidating smart handsome guy from Taiwan. He didn't smile much. He was quick to understand any material and had an air of arrogance about him. He almost made you feel stupid for not getting the lesson as quickly as him.

Well, he was my teammate whom I didn't necessarily love from the beginning, but better than love, I respected him. He was someone who taught me the meaning of integrity in your work.

One of our first Statistics assignments required that we work on it in teams. My first team at Cornell was made up of 4 guys and me. Henry and another guy in the team had a good hold of the material and assignments. Another of the guys was simply lazy, barely showed up to any of our meetings or contributed to the assignments. The other guy was just all talk.

For our first statistics assignment, we had to finish six problems as a team. Henry suggested that we all work on the problems and come together on a Thursday evening to review our answers before our weekend classes at Cornell.

I had an incredibly difficult time with statistics. It took me hours to work through the problems and I only was able to answer 5 out of the 6 questions. I stopped trying as I felt that I had already put in so much work and that I had a lot to show as it was. I even felt proud of my work.

When Thursday came, we all got together. Henry led the meeting and asked each of us to share our answers. The two teammates that I referred to earlier, immediately shared that they were not able to work on any of the problems. One of the men said, "I was traveling for work and I never got to it." The other went after him, "Yeah. I had a busy week at work and at home with the family." I then proudly showed my five answers.

Henry then paused and looked at all of us, including me. "I have the 6 answers," he said. "I did what I said I was going to do. The assignment did not say, just try to work on the solutions. The assignment did not say, work some of the answers, but not all of the answers.

"If we are going to be graded on effort, then we all deserve an A. But we are not graded on effort. We are graded on results."

I felt crushed. How dare he put me in the same bucket as the other guys? I really tried and I'd tried my hardest. I had tears of disappointment in my eyes, but as unfair as I felt it was that I was put in the same category of these other guys who did nothing, I thought about it for days. I committed myself to be reliable, to be the kind of person that if I say I am going to do something that I will do 100% of what is required of me. Never again did I show up to class with an assignment half-way done or almost done. I applied myself, got tutors if needed, worked extra hours until school became easier. My mind became quicker and I was more capable of managing the demands of school, work and life, until there were times when in some difficult classes, such as finance and valuation, I got some of the top scores and I was able to help others who struggled with the information. What kept me motivated as well were the professors at Cornell. They just didn't cover information. Every time they stood up there to teach, I felt grateful to be taught by such inspiring, captivating and intelligent professors. At times, I could not contain my tears; I felt a deep gratitude because I knew that being taught by such great souls was a privilege that I did not want to take for granted.

My time at Cornell was almost up. I was doing my last semester and during that time, I was working on a big project implementing a trading platform for one of the biggest Pension funds in Canada. I was directly responsible for the success of this project; these high-level executives, especially a woman leader in a high position, depended on me as her reputation was on the line and I did not want to let her down. I traveled to Montreal almost every other week to manage the project and work with the Pension Fund Consultants and Senior leaders.

However, during this time, I was offered a role for a subsidiary of the company to work in the Equity Trading floor. I gladly accepted as it was a privilege to be accepted in this division. It gave me the opportunity to get the Series 7, 63 and other licenses that could transform my knowledge and career. I was hired to become a trader. Taking tests does not come easily for me. I have to work my ass off. The Series 7 is a test a lot of people fear. If you do not pass, some people get fired on the spot because, if you do not have this license, you have to wait a month to take it again and there is nothing that you are allowed to do while you are sitting at your desk waiting. For me, I knew that because I had been with the company a long time that I may get a second chance, but I could not fathom failing. I had heard that the decision my manager made to hire me was not popular as the men in the trading floor doubted my abilities as

I had never traded before and I did not want to speculate on any other reasons.

To study for this test, I took a class and I was required to take 23, three-hour tests each, to practice. That is approximately 69 hours of just taking practice tests after spending hours reading the material and then reviewing each answer every time I took a test. I would wake up at 4am, go for a quick run, read the Series 7 manual before work. Then go to work, and work on the implementation project in Montreal.

When I finally transferred to my new department, I had to start reading on equity algorithms, asking the traders to help me learn the behavior of each trading strategy. They were too busy to sit with me for too long, so I would get fleeting bites of information from them. I had to get most of it by reading. During the afternoon, my manager would give me time to take a practice test, three hours locked up in a room. Then another two hours reviewing why I only got a 60% on my practice tests initially. The recommendation was that I had to get close to 90% on my practice test to be ready for the real test. At night, I had to work on assignments for the MBA. Weekends I traveled to the Cornell campus located in Palisades, NJ to spend the weekend there taking classes.

I had no life. I felt so much pressure, so much stress, but I knew that I had to just do it. I had no other choice. As I spent more time deciphering what I did wrong on the practice tests, my score got higher, but not high enough. I kept on trying, crying from frustration, and trying again.

During that time of the many and multiple Series 7 practice tests, as part of the MBA program, I also had to travel to China with my Cornell teammates to do a consulting project for an American company. The company was going to grade our performance at the end of that project.

During the night, as my other teammates went out to tour Beijing, I stayed in my hotel room every night taking a Series 7 practice test, which took 3 hours and then some more to review my answers. I hardly saw Beijing; I was lucky to take a break and visit the Great Wall of China, Tiananmen Square and some local areas as a team. We then flew to Shanghai and I was blown away at how beautiful this city was. I wanted nothing else than to tour this city as we only had one day in Shanghai, but I had to prepare a report for our team as part of our consulting project. I walked Shanghai for a couple of hours and then went back to the hotel to write that report.

My time in China felt like a blur, but I was happy to come back to the States as that meant I was now a couple of weeks or so from graduating. Back in New York, it was the deciding time of my career. I took my final exams for the MBA on the weekend and I felt that I could almost see the light at the end of the tunnel. But I still had one major mountain to climb, I had to take the Series 7 test the following week on a Monday and, that same weekend, I was to graduate from the MBA program.

Around this time, the Dean Associate at Cornell, Beta Mannix, sent me an email asking me if I would like to represent Cornell as their Top MBA for Poet & Quants, a Ranking Agency that performs in-depth analysis on business schools. I felt very grateful that she would consider me for such an honor especially coming from her since she is really one of the most remarkable and demanding professors at Cornell. I had to write a paper answering some key questions so people could know my story and how I found the Executive program at Cornell. I woke up at 3am to write my story that morning as I had a deadline and I did not have a lot of time to work on it as I was close to taking the tests for my licenses. I did the best I could to capture the essence of my story and I asked a friend to correct my paper.

The day of the Series 7 test couldn't come any faster, I was extremely nervous. I felt as if my life depended on the results. The test is a 6-hour timed test. I remember doing the math and I think I had no more than 2 minutes per question. The exam was broken down into two parts. The first 3 hours, which took me for a rude awakening, then a short break, and then the last 3 hours where you feel you are fighting for your life. You get the scores right after you finish the test.

During my first 3 hours I started to realize that I was running out of time. I realized I had what seemed like 30 minutes left for 20 questions. Oh my god! I took too long! I started to panic, could barely breathe but at this point I had no time to think, I just kept clicking on answers so that at least I could get some right instead of leaving any question unanswered. The first 3 hours were finished, and I was allowed to leave the room. The first thing I did was to call my girlfriend at that time, "Yvonne…" and then I could not talk anymore. Just silence, which she could tell meant I was not doing well.

"Yes, sweetheart," she answered.

I started to cry. "I am failing the test! I hardly finished the first part and I do not know what I am doing." I kept on crying.

Then Yvonne said in a loving way, "Sweetheart, it is not over yet. It is not over yet. Calm down. Please take a deep breath."

"I can't baby. I am such a failure." I continued to cry.

"It is not over until it is over, sweetheart. You do not know yet. Go back in there and finish the other 3 hours. You got this!" Yvonne inspired.

I had no more time, but her words were the kindest and most supportive words I ever had from a partner. I went back into the testing room and I took three deep breaths and I decided to be more aware of the clock, pace myself and answer each question without doubting myself so much. At the end of the last three hours, I hesitated, but all there was to do was to click SUBMIT. Then the computer started to think and upload the test results, and every second felt like an eternity. I then closed my eyes almost in supplication to God, "Please don't let me fail."

Then I opened my eyes. When I looked at the score, I couldn't believe it- I passed!

I left that room as quickly as possible. As soon as I got out of the building and was out in the streets of Manhattan in midtown, I cried. I cried out of gratitude and because I felt that, given my conditions and how hopeless I was feeling, this felt like a miracle. I immediately called Yvonne to give her the great news and her response meant the world to me, "I am so proud of you sweetheart. I knew you could do this!"

The day after, I showed up at the male-only equity trading floor. I was now licensed so I walked in with my head up high as I had earned my right to be there. That same weekend I had my graduation ceremony for my MBA. I went to Ithaca with a group of friends who expressed interest in celebrating my graduation. I rented a home and they all came. Shilpa, the same dear friend who was at my Ironman, flew from a work training in Florida simply to attend my graduation ceremony, along with her daughter and husband. The joy and sense of accomplishment I felt that week was indescribable. I understood what Paulo Coelho said in the Alchemist, "And when you want something, all the universe conspires in helping you achieve it."

One morning, a few weeks after I started working at the Equity desk, I looked at my phone and I saw an alert from Tweeter, "Veronica Carrera, Best MBA, Cornell University. Poets & Quants."

I couldn't believe it! Poets & Quants selected my story to be featured in their publication. After, a few people reached out to congratulate me, "You make us proud!" Then, I saw an email from Beta Mannix, Cornell Professor, congratulating me. I remember speaking to Beta right after, "I just wish I could have done better…" and I kept on trying to come up with reasons as to why I didn't perhaps fully deserve it. I can't remember her exact answer, but she tried to tell me that I was very deserving of all of it. It made me feel at that second that I was good enough. And she wasn't any professor, she was Beta Mannix! An outstanding professor who everyone respected and feared- who had no problems telling you when your answers were "very shallow." And she was the Assistant Director of the EMBA program. If she thought I was good enough, then perhaps I was good enough. This is a feeling that I try to hold onto.

Yvonne and I were in a relationship for almost a year after this, but I was so consumed with my life that we grew even more distant with time and I ended up leaving the relationship. The reality is that I preferred being in a hectic whirlwind than face the awakened reality of love.

Life at work went on. A year passed and now the 2016 elections came about. Hillary for President! I had taken a picture with Hillary when she came to the company headquarters one day for an interview. She had been coming out of the studio and for some weird reason that I still cannot explain, she looked directly at me and from a few feet away started to walk toward me, extending her arms to greet me. I was in cloud 9. Why is Hillary coming toward me? Then she grabbed me and we walked together a few feet with the crowd following us. For a second I wondered if she had confused me with someone else. Maybe she did, but a few of my colleagues took pictures and I sent one of them to Grandma who was now living in Charlotte with the rest of the family.

My Grandma immediately called, "I love Hillary. I am glad I am still alive to see her become the first woman President." At that point, it seemed that Hillary was the only Democratic candidate who had everything it took to be our President. I couldn't get behind Bernie Sanders, although he was gaining a big following among millennials. And the only Republican candidate whom I thought I could vote for was John Kasick, Governor of Ohio. He seemed a man of principles. There was one bizarre candidate that most people I knew thought was simply a joke, a TV personality and real estate mogul, a man of questionable character and abhorrent behavior. He had no respect for any of the other candidates during the debates. He made fun of disabled people, talked about minorities in a demeaning way. He spoke with very little respect for women and the media exposed him for immoral behavior in his personal life. I thought, who would ever vote for this guy? I never gave it another thought until later when the elections advanced to the final Republican candidate and our reality seemed an appalling abysmal nightmare.

Grandma was now 89 years old and I loved to see her passion for US politics. Her devotion for Hillary made me research more on her and read her book, "Living History." I heard that when I posted a picture of Hillary Clinton and me on Facebook that a few of my connections and family members from Ecuador and here in the US called Grandma to congratulate her that her granddaughter had met Hillary. I heard that my Grandma who had lost a lot of her eyesight was immensely proud to receive these phone calls.

For Grandma, I have always been her biggest celebrity and she always had big dreams for me. Maybe the most important thing I was to Grandma was her friend. In the most difficult times in her older years, when no one could convince her to do something, even her own daughter, they would call me because they knew Grandma would listen to me.

Before Grandma moved to Charlotte where the rest of the family had moved due to the high cost of living in Miami, Grandma refused to join them. Grandma loved the town of Hialeah in Miami. She was surrounded by Latin people and her best friend, an older Cuban lady named Hilda, who lived in the building which was a home for her. Grandma had lived there for almost 20 years. As a woman in her 80s, she did not want to pick up when the family decided to leave Miami for Charlotte. She wanted to stay in her small apartment even if she had to take care of herself. She had help that the government provided. Someone would visit her to help her clean the house and make her breakfast and they would deliver meals.

But then problems came. Grandma didn't only have a heart problem, she also had arthritis in her spinal column. The doctors performed surgery, which left her almost paralyzed. Now she began having a harder time getting in and out of bed on her own. She started using a walker and, as time passed, she needed to use a wheelchair. I started getting frantic phone calls from her helper when she would arrive at Grandma's apartment. "I found your Grandma on the floor and called 911. She was on the floor all night! She is not well. The ambulance is coming."

I was in New York and Grandma was in Miami. Her daughter and sons were in Charlotte. The only person left in Miami was my father, but they were not on speaking terms. My father was bitter and unforgiving because Grandma would not go against another one of her sons, Chicho. Chicho's daughter had faked Grandma's signature and taken dishonest and wrong ownership of the home we all grew up in Ecuador. Chicho never did anything about it and protected his daughter while all of my uncles and my father came together in unity to stir up a bloody fight against Chicho and take him and his daughter to court. My father, being the oldest child, had been like a father figure to his brothers, so Cristobal and Carlos (my uncles) followed his lead with total loyalty.

My father felt particularly betrayed and enraged because he was the one who had to save the family when his father died. When my Grandma lost her husband when they were all children, someone had to help Grandma finish paying the mortgage of the house. Someone had to help Grandma raise his younger brothers and sisters and that person became my dad. My dad is very smart, well read and an intelligent and charismatic man who could have become much more than he did. Instead, my father worked while graduating from high school to help Grandma pay the bills. He did not pursue a higher education because someone had to work to put the rest of his brothers and sister through college. He applied to get a green card to come to the United States and followed the process, got the green card, came to the United States in New York's bitter cold winter, a weather that we never experienced in Ecuador, to create a better life for himself and send money back home. He also took a loan to help pay off the mortgage of the house so that Grandma and his younger siblings wouldn't have to worry ever about having a place to live. It was because of my father that Chico and Carlos became engineers. Jose, the second child, obtained a Business and Economics degree and became a very successful businessman. He died in his 30s in a car accident. Cristobal became a Marine in Ecuador. So that leaves only Mirella, who did not like school, but managed to finish a beauty school degree.

Therefore, given all of my father's sacrifices, he would say to me, "Do you think it's fair that after everything that I have done, after sacrificing my own life so you could all become educated and successful, after doing the paperwork for each person in the family so that you could all come to the United States legally, do you think it is fair for Chico to let his daughter steal our home in Ecuador? The home that we all grew up in? The home that I had to work so hard to pay back a $10,000 loan, which then in the 1960s was a lot of money?! Of course, I am furious. I do not want to ever see Chicho again and we will sue him and his daughter for what they have done! They will pay for this!"

I listened and heard the underlying anger that had been part of his existence most of his life. He continued, "And I am angry at my mom because she turns her eyes away from what Chicho did and talks to him on the phone as if nothing happened. That is an insult to everything I have done for her and this whole family!"

My father was on a mission to destroy his brother for what he did or, as he put it, "I am defending my honor!"

I would say, "Let it go. This hate will kill you."

But then he would get terribly upset at me. Thus, I tried to stay away from my father at all cost. His indignation was righteous, but I knew his hate could destroy all of us as a family.

Cristobal, Carlos and my dad would get together often to strategize how to navigate the murky laws of Ecuador. I knew that because I often spoke to my uncle Cristobal. But even though he was the only son she had left in Miami, my dad did not speak to my Grandma. This was sad because, for Grandma, my father could do no wrong. That was her first child, the boy who supported her through the most difficult times in her life. Every time I called from New York, she would ask, "Have you spoken to your father?" I would answer negatively and then she would say, "I look out the window sometimes to see if he is coming. Or when the phone rings, I think it is him. I think he will come one of these days."

I kept on getting phone calls from Grandma's caretaker, a Cuban woman who worked for the government, saying more and more disturbing things about her health. One of the last times she called, Grandma was unconscious, and they were taking her to the hospital.

Mirella called me crying, "You have to talk to my mother. She doesn't want to listen to me. She can't be there anymore. You need to convince her to move to Charlotte with me. She is my mother and I will take care of her until the day she dies."

Mirella is my only aunt and I have never seen such a pure and immense love and devotion from a daughter for her mother.

When Grandma came back from the hospital, I called Grandma and started the conversation very lightly. She would always get super happy every time I called, "Mijita. I knew you would call me. Y como esta?"

"I am good abuelita. How are you feeling?"

Grandma was never good at sharing when anything was wrong with her; she only wanted to talk about positive things. She would divert the conversation and ask questions about me. "How are things with you at work? Are they treating you well? How is your health? Are you eating? I think you are too thin."

But this time, I confronted her situation. "Grandma, you are having a lot of problems with your health. You are waking up in the middle of the night to go to the bathroom and falling on the floor and then you are there alone all night. You cannot continue to live like this Grandma… This is not the kind of life I want for you!"

She tried to defend herself, "But I have lived here for 28 years, this is all I know. This is my home. My best friend Hilda checks on me. My clinic is here. The doctors are Cuban and speak Spanish. The clinic staff picks me up and drops me off. They take good care of me."

Although we were talking on the phone, I could feel her emotions and understood all her reasons. I continued,

"Grandma, I understand this has been home for you for so many years. I know your friend Hilda is very dear to you. Everything you have known since we left Ecuador is in that apartment and it feels like this is something that is yours- you feel independent. It doesn't feel fair that we are talking about you letting all of this go. But I want you to think, given all the accidents that you have had, what kind of life you want going forward until our Creator calls you home?" I paused, but Grandma remained quiet.

I continued, "Can you see yourself being there, without any help, living alone? I know change is hard Grandma. It is hard for me and I am not even as old as you are. So, I understand, I hate change. But imagine this, what life could you have if you were to move to Charlotte with your daughter and granddaughter? You now will have people who love you with you all the time. If something happens to you, they will be there.'"

There was only silence. At this point, I was getting emotional, but I added one more thing, "And as far as the money goes, you know you don't have to worry about anything, you will always have me. I will take care of you."

When I finished my desperate plea, there was another long silence on the phone. I knew it was a long shot to convince an elderly woman to give up the only life she knew. I let the silence be. Perhaps that silence had wisdom that would turn into answers. Then, Grandma spoke with a sad voice, "Can I take all my things with me? Will you be there with me when I move? Will you go and visit me?" And then she started to cry.

Her cry broke my heart; I didn't see her in that moment as my Grandma. She was more my child; I had become her friend and all I wanted was to protect her. The tenderness I felt for her in my heart was indescribable and it made me realize once more how much I loved her. Once she stopped crying, she said, "Ok. I will go."

With tears in my eyes, I shouted, "Yes!!! And you will never lack anything Grandma! I promise."

She said, "I know mijita. I know you."

A few weeks after that I paid some movers to pack all her stuff so that we could move Grandma to Charlotte with the rest of the family.

Grandma lived with Mirella her daughter and grand-daughter Cynthia, Mirella's daughter, and great grandchild Emilio, Cynthia's son. Four generations all in one house. They became a family unit and although Charlotte didn't provide all the government health care assistance she needed, she now had not only all the love and support at home, but also her son, Cristobal who adored her, living 5 minutes away and he would check on her all the time. My uncle Cristobal's wife, Lourdes, is one of the most noble women I know; she often checked on Grandma as well.

Back in New York, the political environment became heated and a surreal circus seemed to take over. The nation's political debate had grown more toxic and some revolting rhetoric about Latins was coming out, particularly from the shocking Republican nominee. Now, it was Donald Trump against Hillary Clinton. During the debates, despite Trump's negative rhetoric, Hillary remained presidential. She spoke with substance, she knew her facts, she had the experience. She kept her cool. But it seemed that she had to constantly defend the underlying subconscious fact that she was a woman and her long history of being a Clinton. Her opponents tried to discredit her, diminish her, Trump's crowds would scream, "Lock her up." The email server issue during her tenure as United States Secretary of State became the nemesis of her powerful and well-deserved candidacy. "According to Clinton's spokesperson, Nick Merrill, a number of government officials have used private email accounts for official business, including the secretary of state before Clinton." The bloody war against Clinton was fierce and even Bernie Sanders who had a big following made comments against Clinton that impacted his followers' support for Clinton. He created doubt about her ability to lead.

I have a diverse international group of close friends who are Muslims, Jewish, Christians, Latins, Blacks, etc, and hearing this hurtful rhetoric from the Republican candidate, made me angry. I felt powerless, how is it possible that people could hear all of this and still follow this man! It made me lose some faith in humanity.

My life in New York continued and I would visit Charlotte from time to time to check on Grandma primarily. I did not like Charlotte. How can you compare Charlotte to New York? In New York you have access to the most interesting and most diverse people I have ever met in my life. I had built a wonderful community of highly intellectual and spiritual friends. A never-ending choice of restaurants with any cuisine you could ever want is in that city. The night life, live shows, museum, Central Park, Bryant Park, and the East Village being my most favorite spots in the city are filled with artistic and fascinating people. Because of that, my visits in Charlotte would last days or a week and then I would leave, desperately wanting to come home. I felt guilty at times; guilty for not wanting to be there. Nevertheless, Grandma and I had some special times together.

She had started to experience some dementia, so there were moments that she couldn't remember who I was. But then I would hold her hand and search for YouTube on my cellphone and find some Spanish songs from her times. She was in love with Julio Jaramillo and I would play songs for her such as "El Testamento," which speaks about a love that will never die.

"That if the dead can love, after death we will love even more." Grandma would sing along with her faint voice and I would hold her hands for hours just singing quietly next to her to not overshadow her fragile voice. We would talk about the times when she was married to her handsome charming husband. She would tell me that he always wore a suit and, when she showed me pictures, I was proud that my grandpa was so handsome and distinguished.

Then the conversation would turn to me, "When your mom came to introduce herself and you to me right after you were born, I embraced you in my arms and put you against my chest. You have been like my own child ever since."

"I know Grandma. And how was my mom? What do you remember about her?'

She and I hardly talked about my mom after she died. It took many years before I could bring myself to ask her questions.

Grandma would answer, "She was a woman of dignity and a noble heart. Just like you." That gave me something; maybe the only thing I wanted to know as I did not want to dig too much into the past to find out why my mother left her home when I was four. Why did she leave my father or them? Something enormous must have driven my mom out of her house. But I made peace with the thought that whatever it was, every character in the play of our lives operates with the default programming of their own deficiencies. I have chosen to believe that, for all of us, given our own set of circumstances, we are just doing the best we can and, unfortunately, in the process, many times people get deeply hurt. All I felt for Grandma was deep compassion and love. At the end, everything in our lives happens perfectly- Every experience leads us to the next phase of our spiritual evolution. The dark moments accelate our growth if we let them. There would be no stars if we didn't have the night. In other words, the Universe is always harmoniously working for us, for our highest good. Therefore, every character in this play of our lives is playing exactly the role they need to play. Everyone in the end is perfect and we must be grateful we have our opportunity to exist in this grand stage of life.

When I got back to New York, it was time to vote. I volunteered to get Hillary elected. I would talk to friends to encourage them to vote. I was getting extremely frustrated and shocked by how Trump's disrespectful and nasty narratives were not railed against. I would hear some white people at work speaking disparagingly about minorities and I asked myself, what is happening to the world? How is this ok?

My passion to see Hillary get elected became ferocious. I say ferocious because I felt like our lives depended on it.

Grandma could barely move at this point. She had to be helped out of bed and my aunt had a whole system for this. She would put a folded blanket underneath her body before putting her in bed. This was done so that every morning they could pull the folded blanket to help move her and get her closer to the edge of the bed and then lift her off the bed and transfer her to the wheelchair. Every movement would hurt my Grandma's body and she would moan with pain. Every time I visited Charlotte, I had to help my aunt get Grandma out of bed or put her in bed at night and it took us at least 30 minutes to move her comfortably. Getting her to the bathroom or cleaned up was even a harder task. I had deep respect for my aunt who was then in her early 60s, having to do this every morning, every night and every moment my Grandma needed help.

Knowing the great pain Grandma was in, I knew her body and mind were now deteriorating daily. There were moments she would watch me as If I was a stranger and then I would say, "Grandma. It is me Veronica. Your granddaughter."

She would look at me with great suspicion and mistrust, "You are not my granddaughter." Then, she would come back to normalcy and we would hold hands and talk about life and I brought up the topic of death. I wanted Grandma to be ready for death. I was afraid that she might be frightened.

It wasn't easy to ask what I was about to ask her. "Grandma. How do you feel about dying?"

"Estoy Lista," she told me with a soft voice – she was ready to die.

I had always been terrified of death, this mysterious cruel unfair fate for all of us that leaves me in constant fear.

I asked her, "No Tienes miedo?"

"No. I am not afraid," she replied with a faint voice as she looked away with those almost gray eyes that come with age.

Her answer gave me some relief. It didn't matter how I felt about this unfortunate separation of our existence, I wanted to give her hope by digging into the only hope I had about death. I held her hand and I started imagining anything good that could come with death.

"Grandma, you will have angels around you helping you transition out of this life and guiding you to the light-filled place of perfect peace where God lives. I heard that that is what happens. That we are called to this infinite light where there is only love." I paused…and I felt myself believing all of it. My eyes started to get teary. I looked over to Grandma and she was looking away as if she was envisioning everything I was saying. She held my hand a little firmer.

I continued, "Also, your second son Jose and your husband will be there waiting for you. And if you see my mom can you please make sure you both take care of me and when it is time for me to go home to our God, could you be the ones waiting for me to cross this veil of existence?"

Grandma did not hesitate to react, "Of course Mijita. I will be there waiting for you. Your mom and I will be waiting for you." Then, we stayed in silence holding hands as I sat next to her reflecting on our conversation and realizing that one day, I would not be able to feel her warm hands again. I placed her hands on my cheek and, although we were not comfortable saying I love you, I said, "I love you Grandma."

"I love you too Mijita," Grandma responded as if she was coming to a place of peace and a profound realization about her end but, at the same time, of our unbreakable bond.

Chapter 20.

Time To Vote

It was voting day and my uncle Cristobal got Grandma ready so that she could vote. "Every vote counts," we would say to each other when we spoke on the phone. Knowing how much work it was to get Grandma out of bed and how painful it was for her to move at this point, I was inspired by her determination to get out and vote. I was immensely proud when my uncle sent me a picture of them at the ballot box.

Most people in my circle thought Hillary would win; we turned on the TV to watch the results and suddenly, my eyes could not believe it, states that we thought Hillary had, were turning "Red" and voting Republican. Little by little I saw how one state after another that was supposed to be Blue "Democrat," turned Red and my heart sank. I did not watch the rest, I went to bed and hoped that somehow when I woke up in the morning, that this was just a nightmare.

But it was not so, the Republican candidate became President of the United States. I got myself ready to go to work and, as I was taking the ferry from Weehawken to Manhattan, tears rolled down my cheek. As I approached my office building, I remembered that some of the guys whom I worked with were rooting for the candidate who had just won. I cringed at the thought of having to go into the office. As soon as I walked in, a couple of men started to congratulate each other, thumping their chests and saying, "We are going to Make America Great again."

I felt enormously out of place and sad.

Four years later, 2020, although this has been a challenging year due to a global pandemic that has shaken us to our very core, it has also been a year of immense victory when this Republican President lost the election after a long week of counting and recounting votes. We have now elected a decent man, Joe Biden, as Elect-President and Kamala Harris, the first woman and woman of color as Elect-Vice President.

A few days later after the results of the 2016 election, while I was at work, I got a call from my uncle Cristobal, "Your Grandma is in the hospital. She had a heart attack." Then his voice crumbled, "They are giving her just a few days to live. They said that this was one too much for her. They don't want to do anything else for her. They are sending her home to die."

Later, he face timed me from the hospital and put the camera on Grandma.

"Mijita," Grandma said when she saw me. "I almost died." And she smiled. "I made it! I am ok now."

"Si abuelita! You escaped death again! They don't want you in the other life."

She laughed and I laughed. It was our family's ongoing joke as Grandma always had some illness and she always came through the other side. I was determined to think that this was no different.

"I am going to take a flight tomorrow and come and see you Grandma." She smiled big. "And when I get there," I said,

"I will finally buy us the home that you really want, and you and I are going to live there together. It is going to be your home!" I wanted to say all the things that she had wanted and that I should have done a long time before.

Grandma smiled excitedly, but she looked pale and weak, and I got scared. I wanted to believe Grandma's words that she was going to be ok instead of the doctor's.

I asked my uncle when he got back on the phone, "She is going to be ok right?"

My uncle Cristobal adored his mother. He just looked at me through the video as if he wanted to believe that as well, but his eyes were red. I sensed his sadness, his silence spoke the truth.

I took the flight the next day and Grandma was already at home. When they transferred her from the hospital, it was too rough on her body and her health declined significantly from that moment on. The hospital had arranged for a nurse to check on her every day for a couple of hours; this was a hospice situation.

Grandma was still talking, but as time passed, I witnessed her body and strength withering away. She and I made small talk. I would put on the Ecuadorian songs she liked that we used to sing to distract her. This time, she didn't have the strength to sing them, but she would open her eyes, looking up, as if listening intently. I tried to sing for both of us and, during those moments, she would not complain of any pain in her body.

Then the nurse came to tell me that someone had to be in charge of giving her the morphine to help with her pain and, eventually, help her die. My aunt started to cry, "My mom is not dying! We are not giving her morphine!" My uncles, Cristobal and Carlos, echoed her words and refused to believe their mother was leaving them.

I took the nurse aside and, with my chest full of sadness, I asked, "Is there any hope Grandma will not die?"

"No, Veronica. Your Grandma has only a few days to live."

"Do we have to give her this morphine? What if we don't?" I wanted her to give me some hope.

The nurse answered softly, "I know you love her. I know you don't want to see her go. But the best you can do now is to help her die without pain. If you do not give her the morphine, her pain will be excruciating. You need to give her a dose every 2 to 3 hours."

I looked at her and surrendered, "I will give her the morphine."

My aunt and uncles were upset that I was giving up on Grandma. I understood their resistance; she was their mother. So, if someone had to do this, it was me. I loved her the same way they did, but I had to be strong for Grandma and for them. If someone had to suffer and do the most difficult thing, I'd rather take that upon myself so that they would not have to. I hadn't realized until those moments how much I loved them too and I wanted to ease some of their pain, especially Mirella's & Cristobal's. They were the closest to Grandma, the most affectionate with her and they were taking it hard. My uncle Carlos, I could hardly figure him out. He was Grandma's youngest child; he did not show what he felt and I'd never felt as close to him. I saw his sorrow, but he was good at keeping it all inside.

That afternoon as I sat in the dining area, Carlos, Cristobal and Mirella were standing up around me. It was time to discuss the funeral and burial. I knew already that I was going to have to take care of things as I was the one who was the most financially able and willing. I was single, making a great salary, and living in New York. I had significant savings, so I never even questioned whether I was going to take care of Grandma. I had promised her that, in life and death, I would be there for her.

After we discussed the funeral arrangements, I immediately began to think, "What would Grandma want to see happen before she dies?" And it became very clear to me what that was. I decided to take charge, directing my statements primarily to Cristobal and Carlos.

"Your mother is dying. She may have one day or two days to live. The best gift that you can give her is to see all her children together in one room. I am going to call Chicho and ask him to come say goodbye and I want to see all of us in one room together. If you love your mother, you are going to make this happen."

Both of my uncles stood paralyzed, quiet, struggling with their feelings. I knew I couldn't show any weakness in front of them, so I kept my eyes fixed on them. Then Cristobal, glancing at Carlos, turned his eyes toward me and said,

"What about you? You are not even talking to your father? Are you going to speak to him and ask him to come?"

"I would never ask you to do something that I am not willing to do myself! I will call my father and ask him to come as well."

Then Cristobal looked at Carlos and said, "I will do it for my mother."

Carlos complied.

Mirella stood in awe as she never thought the day would come when her brothers would all be in one room. She thought this would be a miracle. She didn't speak, but immediately went to call Chicho, the brother she loved, and asked him to come. I also had to make an additional call to convince Chicho that the encounter with his brothers would be civil. I gave him my word.

My other aunt, Marianna Carrera, Grandma's stepchild, also came from New York to be there for her brothers and especially Mirella. They were close growing up, so Marianna served as an incredible emotional support for Mirella. When Marianna, Mirella and Cristobal got together they, even in these dark moments, found something to laugh about and this gave me some relief.

Now I had to call my father. "It is me, Veronica. "

My father already knew what was happening but had decided to stay in Miami.

"Si. Como esta?" he asked.

I had avoided his calls for over 3 years so I could sense his humility in listening to me, after yet another rejection from me.

"Papi, your mother may not make it through the night. Could you please come to the airport now?"

"Ok, I have to check how much the tickets are this last minute. Maybe I can check a flight for tomorrow."

"No No…Tomorrow may be too late. Come now. Just go to the airport and call me when you are there, and I will give you my credit card so you can pay for the flight. Please come now."

He complied, "Ok Mijita. Putting clothes on and I will head to the airport now."

I felt a sense of relief. First, I had called my father after years of not speaking to him, refusing his calls, certain that I would never speak to him again. My resentment towards him had been so immense that I never imagined that I ever would ask him anything. But my love for Grandma and the integrity of my words were worth much more than my hate. Secondly, I had made it happen. All her sons and daughter were going to be together in one room. This is what I knew Grandma longed for. What a pity, I thought, that we wait until someone is on their death bed to show them that we love them, to show affection and to yield to the desires of their hearts.

After making the call, I knew now would be the last moment I was going to be able to have alone time with Grandma. Everyone was in the living room and I went in and held Grandma's hand and asked her the question that I most desperately wished I could have asked her my whole life, "Grandma, do you love me the way I am? Do you love me the way I am?" I repeated.

I wanted so much for her to know what I meant. She was still able to listen and say a few words, but now they were faint, "I love all my children exactly the way they are."

I wanted more clarity. I think I wished for her to say, "I love you Veronica the way you are." But she mentioned all of her children.

Perhaps that made me take the attention off me and realize that this was about all of us.

That day, in the late afternoon, Chicho showed up with his son at the door. Mirella and I escorted them into Grandma's room. I could tell Cristobal's and Carlos' initial discomfort. I gave them a look and said, "You promised me." They just nodded in agreement.

Then, my father showed up. Carlos and Cristobal immediately welcomed him and stood by his side. I thanked my father for coming and then said, "Your mother may have tonight or the next day according to the nurse. I asked Chicho and you to come so that we can all be here to say goodbye. It doesn't matter how flawed or imperfect you think your mother has been; she is your mother. With the life that God gave her, she did the best to raise you all…. Now this house that you are fighting about, is it worth it? We do not take any of this with us…Let life take care of the injustice, the Universe has a way of taking care of things. Your mother could not pick sides. You have been asking her to side with one child against the other. She loves you all equally… Now go to that room and stand in the same place as Chicho and everyone else; and surround your mother with love. This is the best way you can thank her for giving her whole life to you. She raised you and she raised me as well. Go to that room now… and let us all be together."

One by one, each man in my family entered the small bedroom my Grandma was in and then Mirella and then me.

Grandma was still semiconscious and called my father's name as if she was waiting for him. "Adolfo…Adolfo.."

My father replied with a broken voice, "Si mama. I am here."

She did not say anything more. His eyes swelled with tears.

Then all of us shared this space of grace and talked and laughed together as when we were young children. I had called in for a Catholic priest to come and give her a final blessing. But they did not have a Spanish priest in that area in Charlotte, so they sent a Chinese Priest.

When the priest showed up, he walked into the bedroom where Grandma and all of us were and, in a serious and strict tone, asked, "Who is in charge here?"

I said, "Me." Then, he took a good look at me and said with disgust, "No. You are not Catholic!" and from that moment refused to talk to me. I couldn't help but feel that he'd figured out instantly that I was gay and that he may have thought a gay person couldn't be Catholic.

The Priest then questioned my father and aunt, "You are Catholics, right? When was the last time you took your communion?"

My father then pointed at a picture my Grandma had in her room when he was a little boy and said, "That was the last time I went to church."

The priest took a good look at all of us with such wrath and said in his Chinese accent, "I cannot administer the communion to any of you." He barely blessed my grandmother and left in a rush. I heard that on his way out, he stamped his feet by the entrance as a sign to wash his feet from the house of sinners.

My family defaults to jokes in bad situations, so my aunt Marianna started to laugh out loud and everyone else followed. All of us around Grandma's bed made jokes, imitating the Priest and repeating everything he said to each of us. Some were laughing so hard that they were almost on the floor as if it was the biggest joke we had experienced in our lives. It occurred to me that in the oddest of circumstances, we had all become one.

I had an alarm that would beep every 3 hours so that I could give Grandma the morphine. I slept on blankets on the floor next to her bed so that I could accompany her through the night and administer the morphine. Grandma made it through that night and two nights after that. At this point, I had not slept for three days and I was beyond exhausted.

My half-sister, Fernanda and my cousin Yeimmy from London, had flown in as well and, given the kind natures of their souls, said, "Give this to us. You have done enough. We will give Grandma the morphine now and you can go to sleep." Then, Chicho also watched my Grandma all day. My Grandma was completely unconscious at this point. We were told that we should not give her any food or barely any water. It was now clear that I was assisting her in dying.

That last night, I decided to go sleep at my uncle's house which was 5 minutes away so that I could get a good night's sleep. I had just put my head on the pillow when I got a call from my cousin, "Grandma died. Grandma died."

I shouted to my uncle Cristobal and his wife who were also getting ready to go to sleep. "Mi Abuela… Mi abuela…" I started hyperventilating…. They knew.

We got into my uncle's car, got there in 5 minutes, and we walked into my Grandma's bedroom. Mirella, my father, my half-sister and cousins were already there, completely quiet, as if they did not know what to do or say. Then, I saw her lifeless body. I went next to her and got in her bed and hugged her….I felt her cold body next to me and I started to cry, deep from within my being. I felt my heart being cracked wide open. The pain I felt was like something I had never experienced; it was unbearable, and I threw myself on the floor next to her and howled in desperation and part of me refused to ever get up.

Then I heard my father speak, "She is not ok. She is not going to be able to take care of the funeral. Who can help?"

Then my father said to me, "You are not alone Veronica. You are not alone. Now your Grandma will take care of you from above more than ever."

Then I heard Mirella say, "You are not alone Veronica. We are your family too."

I didn't answer. I felt utterly bereft.

As I was on the floor, I thought, "I am the only one who knows what to do next. I have all the information." So I commanded my body to get up and said in a raspy voice, "I can do it. I can do it."

Then I made the call to the funeral home to come and pick up her body. They came almost immediately and put Grandma's body in a bag and carried her in a rolling bed out of the house to their car. I followed them outside, barefoot, until they put her in the car and drove away. I stood there as that little 9-year old child who had been told her mom was dying. I stood there as if everything was happening all over again.

The next day I woke up and there was a small part of me that felt that Grandma was no longer suffering. I got up and went for a run because that is the way I deal with life; I go for runs. When I came back, I asked my cousin Fernando who is in the Navy, Mirella's son, and my cousin Yeimmy from London to come with me to the cemetery to make all the burial arrangements and to negotiate pricing.

Having a sales background, I was dumbfounded to find out that even funerals and cemeteries have a quota to meet and, since Grandma died February 28th, which was the end of the month, they had hijacked the rates for me. I couldn't believe that they would take advantage of people during unfortunate circumstances. Luckily the funeral owner had the decency to see what the cemetery people were trying to do, and he called them out in front of me and told them, "Just because you have a quota, you cannot take advantage of these people. You are trying to charge them for something they do not need to pay."

The cemetery then agreed to dismiss the additional charges and I gave them my credit card. I thanked the owner of the funeral parlor for his decency and for being there for a stranger.

The next day, the funeral was beautiful, and the cemetery people went out of their way given what had happened and we had a tasteful and dignified burial where the whole family participated. We got her a plate on her tomb that says, "We will never forget you." And I realized this book is my way to tell not only my story and heal many hearts, but also to keep Grandma's story alive.

The next day, I returned to New York. I didn't realize how much Grandma's death affected me. I went to the office the next day and informed the CEO of the division and my director that I wanted to leave. They tried to convince me to stay stating that I was making this decision due to my Grandma's death and that I needed to take a week for myself, think things through and then decide. I took a few days, went back and, still told them, "I am leaving."

I am glad I took that time. Grandma's death haunted me for months. I would have dreams where I would see Grandma telling me how much she misses us. I would cry out of nowhere. I distanced myself from close friends, I became functionally depressed. I stopped racing all together; my body barely wanted to work out. My aunt, cousins and even my father would check on me constantly, but I made sure to hide my suffering as I was more worried about their suffering, especially Mirella's. I wondered how she was handling not having Grandma around.

One time as I was sleeping, I heard Grandma whisper, "Go and check on Mirella." I woke up that morning, booked the first flight out and went to Charlotte and stayed for a few days to make sure Mirella was ok. Mirella had Cynthia her daughter and her grandson, Emilio. I think this is what kept her going. I started to feel more at peace for her. With my uncle Cristobal, I saw the pain in his face every time I visited, but he had his wonderful wife by his side, so I also started to take the weight of that suffering off my shoulder.

Then I started to feel guilty for having helped Grandma die. I started to question myself, "What if Grandma didn't want to die? What if there was a way to keep her alive?" I was driving through the Lincoln Tunnel one afternoon and these terrible accusatory thoughts that I gave up on Grandma were crippling my spirit so I started to scream at the top of my lungs and hit the steering wheel, "I killed Grandma…I killed Grandma!" Of course, no one could hear me.

That made me know that I was not okay. I called my friend Lynn who is a psychologist and pastor. I had met her at Middle church in the East Village when she used to be a minister there and we have been friends ever since.

"What's going on Veronica?"

"I killed my Grandma. Maybe I was not supposed to give her the morphine. Maybe she was not supposed to die. I watched a documentary titled, "HEAL" where people share stories of how they all healed, even after a fatal diagnosis. I gave up on her and maybe there was a way to save her!"

Then Lynn answered me in the most unexpected way, "What if you killed her Veronica? What if you did? You followed the doctor's advice, and even if she wasn't supposed to die, if you would have been able to keep her alive longer, is that the life you wanted for your Grandma? Full of pain? She was in pain constantly. You did the most compassionate thing for her and I am proud of you."

That shocking response gave me a strange peace. Lynn saved me.

The following week, I received a call from my cousin Cynthia that the family was planning a visit to Ecuador. Mirella, Cynthia her daughter, Emilio the grandson, Cristobal, my uncle, Fernando, Mirella's son from the Navy, and my cousin from London Yeimmy. I decided to go back too; it would be the first time after 31 years. I contacted the only cousin, Patricia, that I had left in my hometown whom I had been very close to as a child and told her I was coming. She was beyond excited. I also said, "I want to find my mom's sister. The same sister that picked me up at school the day my mom died."

"I will help you find her," said Patricia.

Marlene Mendez was her name and that was all I knew. Some relatives on my mom's side had found me on Facebook, so I tried to contact them to find her whereabouts. She lived in a very poor area where it is difficult to find someone by their address. When we got to Ecuador, I left the rest of the family to enjoy the city of Guayaquil, while Patricia and I drove around making phone calls to find my Aunt Marlene.

First, we drove to the same neighborhood I grew up in as a child. When we parked, Patricia said, "Here it is!"

I told her, "Here is what?"

"That is your Grandma's home and that is my family's home across the street."

"You've got to be kidding! This does not look like the block we grew up in." Everything looked old, desolate, lifeless. The homes had deteriorated as if someone took the spirit completely out of our neighborhood.

Patricia then explained, "Yes, the young generation got educated and left. The older folks stayed, but never renovated and this neighborhood became an unkempt and unsafe place."

My uncle Chico's daughter, who had faked Grandma's signature and now was in possession of Grandma's home, had rented the home to strangers. I knocked on the garden door and introduced myself, "Hola. I am the granddaughter of the woman who owns this home. You probably know my cousin who rents you the house, but I am her family. Is there any way I could take a look? Sorry to bother you like this, but this is for memories. My Grandma just died, and I want to see the home we all grew up in."

The people declined and asked me to go away. Patricia and I drove off and then we went to the Mormon church we were both part of when we were young. She was one of the few cousins who got baptized after me and we shared a lot of memories that happened there. We went in and checked the church and took a picture together; we laughed as we were now outsiders. Neither of us were members of the faith, but we chatted and said that we were grateful for all the good things we had learned there.

Patricia finally got a hold of another relative who gave her a more accurate address as to where my aunt might reside. In fact, she was living in another city, the city of Duran, just 45 minutes from Guayaquil. We drove to Duran into a neighborhood with dirt roads and poor looking homes.

She made an abrupt stop and said, "I think this is where your mom's sister lives. This area is not as safe, so I will give us 45 minutes here and then we have to leave. People may see my car and notice that we have money." Patricia had become a successful model and businessperson, so even her car could draw attention to us.

I knocked on the home that had a cement gate and a lock on the small and very old door. An old and beautiful dark skinned lady came out, and I stood outside looking at her and she looked at me speechless as if she knew who I was immediately.

"Veronica. Veronica. No puedo creerlo. I prayed so much to be able to find you one day." She started to cry.

"Tia. Si soy yo! I am so glad we found you." I did not know what to say.

She instantly asked us to come in. Her home was small, the living room/bedroom and kitchen were separated by a thin curtain. She had a small stove and she said, "I make some really good Yuca bread. Can I make you some?"

"Siii!" I said enthusiastically as if I was trying to remember my Grandma on my mother's side when she used to make me "maduros." I tried to study her face and wondered, "Is this what my mom would have looked like if she was still alive?" If so, she would have been so beautiful. My aunt had dark skin and cheek bones that made her a beautiful masterpiece. Her light hazel eyes reminded me of mom's eyes. She was also in good shape and I was not surprised when she told me she bikes everywhere. I guess that is the reason why I love to bike everywhere, it must be in my genes.

My cousin Patricia gave us some space and stayed in the living room, while my aunt Marlene and I talked in the kitchen. As she baked the yuca bread, I sat on a wooden chair, asking about her life and what happened after my mom died. I found out that when I went to live with Grandma, they were not allowed to contact me, and that Grandma did a good job at keeping me away from them.

I could sense her resentment and told her, "Let's not talk about this. She is dead now and I do not want to go back to things that happened and judge."

My aunt agreed and held back any further comments.

Then, I heard Patricia speak from the living room, "Veronica, it is time to go now. You should thank your aunt for everything she did for you." And she was right, being there was so surreal that at times I did not know what to say. But when I heard Patricia, I knelt down on the floor in front of my aunt who was now sitting on the wooden chair, held her hands and said, "Tia. Thank you. Thank you for everything you did for me! Thank you for picking me up from school when my mom was dying…" My voice started to break, and I could barely finish the rest, " I was alone sitting on the sidewalk by myself for hours." I couldn't hold my pain anymore and my 9 year-old heart wept as I put my head on her lap as she held me and caressed me.

Then she said, "Your mom loved you so much. She loved you Veronica. I love you too. Don't ever forget that." I did not want to let go of her. She was the only thing left in my life that reminded me of mom. It made me wonder what it would have felt like to have a mother in my adult years who could have held me when life got tough. I embraced her tighter and she held me until I couldn't cry anymore.

Then Patricia interrupted softly, "Prima. It is time to go."

I stood up, put my hands on my aunt's face, gave her a hug and we said goodbye.

I will forever be grateful to my cousin Patricia for making this moment happen.

The rest of my time in Ecuador was filled with joyful moments where we, as a family, enjoyed the beach, the warm weather, the local food, so many healing moments that became a healing balm for all my wounds. I felt closer to my family than I had ever been. This was the gift that Grandma left me.

Chapter 21.

The ashes begin to rise

When I came back from my trip from Ecuador, I discovered Marianne Williamson's lectures, "A Course in Miracles," in Manhattan. A dear friend, Celest, could not stop talking about how powerful these lectures were and, because I valued her opinion, I started to attend Marianne's lectures. I also started to read her book, "Tears to Triumph." Marianne Williamson became my spiritual teacher and my saving grace. After going through "Tears to Triumph" and immersing myself in the words of A Course of Miracles, I started to feel more peace in my heart. Also, the realization that there are universal spiritual truths bigger than what I had ever experienced felt like an awakening in my soul. For example, two statements from Ms. Williamson's book struck me, particularly, "Miracles are natural signs of forgiveness. Through miracles you accept God's forgiveness by extending it to others." "The Holy Spirit will help you reinterpret everything that you perceive as fearful and teach you that only what is loving is true."

The people I met at Marianne's lectures became my tribe and we would get together often to speak about these deep

Truths, the biggest one being, "Only Love is Real, Everything Else is an Illusion."

I believe that there are no coincidences in life, the Universe had been orchestrating all of this to help me get to my soul. One day I came home and said to Grandma, "Grandma, I do not want you to come to my dreams anymore." Up to this point, she had been in my dreams every night. "I want you to go in peace now. I will be ok. I will learn to be happy. I will not be alone. I will find someone beautiful who will be by my side. I will form my own family. You can go now." Grandma never came again into my dreams after this.

All of this happened while I did not have a job; everything was happening perfectly. Although I had significant savings, I also had significant bills to pay. I own a home in New Jersey and also in Charlotte. I was doing AirBnB in Charlotte, but not every month was steady. The mortgage and maintenance fee for my apartment in Weehawken are high. Health insurance was something else that I needed to worry about. Thus, I had more than enough to live on for three years or so, but I hated to see my savings decrease on a monthly basis, so after a few months, I started to look for a job. This time it was going to be a place that I felt was aligned to my soul, to my values and something that would excite me. After a few rounds of interviews, I took a job at the top research company in the world, Gartner. I was deeply grateful for my experience there, but after a year, due to the fact that I had friends working at LinkedIn who couldn't stop talking about the amazing culture there, I decided to start looking into the company and, eventually, I met with the Senior Director of Talent Solutions and we spoke for a few months until they had a leadership position open and I was hired!

The people at LinkedIn are, indeed, wonderful. My first team helped me from day one to feel at home. I also learned what great leadership should look like. In fact, one of the main reasons why I joined LinkedIn was because of Jeff Weiner, then CEO, philosophies on "Compassionate Leadership.

Although many things were going well in my life, my relationships were still a mirror of the lack of self-love I still faced. Throughout all these significant events in my life, I would go out with someone and it would start by me being super excited and thinking that this must be it, only to realize later that I needed to give myself time to get to know a person before I jump in. I was flummoxed how I have a great gift of discernment for people in general but "Why then, I asked myself, am I not in tune when it comes to my love life?" Maybe because I so desperately wanted to be loved that I would overlook any signs, words or behavior that should have been red flags from the start. I walked into disguised chaos again and again and again until I started to question more and more my self-worth as a lover. Not as a human being, as I have deep relationships with friends, but as a lover, I seemed to gravitate to these complicated affairs. But at the end, everyone we meet are the hidden unresolved parts of our soul.

At this point, Seneca, who is a scientist and one of my closest friends from the Marianne Williamson tribe, called me and said, "Veronica. I just came back from this place called Rythmia and I want you to go!"

"What is Rythmia?"

"It is a spiritual retreat In Costa Rica that heals your soul. They perform Ayahuasca Ceremonies with the Shamans. It is so powerful, Veronica. It will change your life."

"What is Ayahuasca? Also, what are Shamans?" This was such a foreign concept to me.

Then she went on to explain, "Ayahuasca is a divine medicine made out of two plants that the ancient indigenous people have used for centuries to heal their souls and illnesses. One of the ingredients is a hallucinogen so you can have visions."

"Wow wow, Seneca. Wait a minute. Remember that I don't even drink alcohol. How in the world do you want me to take this plant? I do not think this is safe for me. This is a drug?"

"No Veronica. It is a medicine of nature- a Vine of the Soul. It was given to us by our Infinite Creator because we need it now more than ever. People get healed from depression, addiction, traumas and in some instances even cancer. And the Shamans are light warriors. God has chosen them to lead us to the light."

I was skeptical. I'd never heard of shamans. I would never, even in my dreams, dare to try hallucinogens. And then I heard the price to stay at Rythmia for a week and told myself that I would never waste my money on this.

Seneca is a loving friend so she understood my hesitations as she knew my whole Mormon upbringing and just let me be.

Later that month, another ex colleague from my time at a financial service firm, Badou, called me and said, "Veronica, I have something to talk to you about."

"Yes, Badou?"

"I went to this place called Rythmia and it changed my life."

"What? Rythmia? The place where people do Ayahuasca Ceremonies?"

"Yes. That is it! Do you know about it? It is incredible Veronica!"

"My friend Seneca just talked to me about it. But what did this do for you?"

"I cannot even begin to explain the experience I had there. I feel more at peace. Some people go there with cancer, depression, addictions, traumas and they get healed.

"Ok. Enough of this, Badou. Are you serious? Do you believe this? What happened for you!"

"I had issues and traumas to deal with Veronica that are very personal, and I felt the plant working through all of these. I have never felt more connected to God and more at peace in my life."

I thanked him for his call and moved on with my life. However, it was now Seneca and Badou, two highly educated and smart people whom I respect immensely and are dear to me, so those stories stayed in the back of my mind.

I immersed myself at work and was experiencing great satisfaction with my new experiences in my professional career. However, at this point, I had started to date someone whom I had feelings for, but the relationship was heavy, confusing and not working. Again, I started to lose myself but still, I was surprised with a wonderful party that my close friends arranged for a big birthday celebration. As always, my friends sustained me, but feeling the weight of the relationship and the reality that I was now becoming older, I was even more contemplative of my circumstances.

I was at breakfast at work, and a dear friend, Johanna, who had just started at the company approached me, "Hey. Do you remember our friend Mary?"

"Yeah. The one who just had a horrible break up. You also told me that she found out she has cancer. Is she ok?"

She smiled widely and said, "Yes. She just came from this place called Rythmia in Costa Rica and she is so full of life, Veronica. I have never seen her happier. She still has to go to the doctor to confirm, but she doesn't feel as sick as when she left."

"Are you serious?!!! Gosh, this is the third time someone has talked to me about this place! Should I go? I feel like sometimes we need something radical. Maybe this is what I need!"

"Vero, I've known you for years. Maybe what you are seeking is also seeking you."

I now seriously started thinking about going. This cannot be a coincidence that all these people are coming to me. Yet a part of me still doubted.

Then one more friend, Marianna, who knows me well and who is also friends with Johanna, said to me, "You should go."

"Maybe I will and just do the classes, the meditation, but not the plant ceremony," I told her.

Of all of my friends, she is the most radical. "So you are going to go all the way over there to listen to people tell how this ceremony changed their lives, but not experience it yourself? If you are going to do something, do it all the way."

She was right. That is how I am anyway. But, this was a big decision. That night, as I was deeply contemplating whether I should do this or not, I watched the documentary, "The Reality of Truth," directed by Mike "Zappy" Zapolin, which explores the relationship between spirituality, plant medicine and healing. This film features top spiritual leaders such as Deepak Chopra, Ram Daas, Marianne Williamson and Hollywood actress, Michelle Rodriguez. The documentary was incredibly fascinating and it tipped me to the other side. I picked up the phone, called Rythmia, and booked my trip for the following week.

A couple of days before I left, I googled "Ayahuasca" and this is what I found: "Ayahuasca is a tea that is made by combining the "*Banisteriopsis caapi* vine and a DMT-containing leaf, most commonly *Psychotria viridis* leaf (chacruna). The word "ayahuasca," based in the Quechua language, can be loosely translated as "vine of the soul." Historically, the brew was used by peoples of South America, notably in the Amazon, for ceremonial and religious purposes."

For some reason, it just made sense to me.

Before, I left for my trip, I became really congested to the point that I wondered whether I should postpone. However, I thought, If I do not go now, I may find excuses to not go later.

Friday afternoon I had a terrible cold. When my flight landed in Liberia, Costa Rica, my ears felt that they were about to explode. I felt miserable. I picked up my luggage and looked at my email to find the instructions that Rythmia had sent to locate the staff people who were supposed to pick me up at the airport.

As I stepped outside the airport, I saw a white van with Rythmia on it, and I walked toward it. A nice Costa Rican man asked, "Usted viene aqui para Rythmia?"

"Yes, I just arrived," I replied.

"Welcome! Come! Here are the other people in the group. We were just waiting for you. Give me a couple of minutes as I need to get something else before we leave," he said warmly and enthusiastically.

A group of four pleasant Canadians immediately introduced themselves.

"I have a bad cold, guys, forgive me, I am not too chatty." I started to cough. They said, "We hope you get well soon," and left me alone for the whole trip to Rythmia.

The driver took about an hour to get us to the resort. As we checked in, the Rythmia staff gathered us together. "Welcome to Rythmia. This is a life advancement resort. People come here for Miracles. We are grateful that we get to work here and change people's lives. Here is something to read to help you prepare for your spiritual classes. You have some wonderful spiritual instructors that are going to guide you and help you understand your experience while here."

I looked at the printed notebook with its spiritual lessons. As I am known to be impatient, I started to glance through it as our host kept speaking.

"Please see on the board your schedule for the next 7 days. The first day, you will have a class with a spiritual light worker and instructor, Paola, and also John. Then, you will have a breathwork ritual in the evening. Your plant ceremony does not start until Tuesday. Before the plant ceremonies, you will have some classes with other instructors to help you understand what you should expect from the experience."

I started to cough and asked a member of the staff if someone could bring me some hot tea so that I could make it through the end of the welcome tour. I was surprised how quickly someone brought me some natural ginger tea. It felt like heaven and helped me breathe better and stopped my coughing attack.

I looked at the board for the rest of the week and I noticed that we were also going to have a spiritual instructor from Agape, a church found by Michael Beckwith. I knew Michael Beckwith from reading his book, "The Secret," and from watching him on the Oprah Winfrey show. He was someone whom I always wanted to meet as I have always been fascinated by these enlightened souls.

I then saw more and more people showing up. Since I had done little research, I had no idea how many people came on a given week. As I was getting my room key, the host told me that they were expecting over 70 people.

Suddenly, some staff members showed up in different golf carts to take us to our room. I was taken to room 56, the room that was to be my home that week and saw me through the most difficult and most powerful experience of my life.

Early that evening we went to dinner. Everything was fresh, healthy. Our detox from toxic worldly elements started that day. I ate only vegetables, rice and asked for more of that amazing ginger tea. I asked the staff who worked in the kitchen to add lemon and honey, which they gladly did. They showed sincere concern for me to get well. Every time they would see me approach the kitchen, they would ask, "Should we make you the tea?" It was refreshing and remarkable to encounter such kind souls.

As I was having dinner, I tried to stay away from chatting or being too friendly as I was congested and was still coughing a lot. However, I met a couple, two European women, Maiccu and Ingela. They were dressed in white and there was something very special about them – an unusual warmth and light in their eyes.

"Is this your first time at Rythmia?"

"Yes," I said. "It is. I just made a decision to come a few days ago and I know very little about this plant medicine. In fact, I am a little scared."

They looked at me with such gentleness and said, "Why are you scared?"

"Because I have never done anything in my life that had hallucinogens. I have never done any drugs or even drank alcohol."

They acknowledged my concerns and tried to reassure me. One said, "This is a natural plant medicine. It is Mother Ayahuasca. The divine infinite spirit has brought you here because there is healing to be done. Trust that the plant will do what it needs to do with your soul. "

I looked at them and there was only purity surrounding them.

Then the other one said, "We are actually facilitators, light workers. We will be in the ceremony all week and we will be there to help you."

This gave me such relief. I immediately felt trust and safety just knowing that they would be there.

The night before the Ayahuasca ceremony, I joined everyone for some breath work. I felt such strong emotions while doing the breathwork and as soon as I breathed through my mouth, I remembered Grandma's last breaths before she died. I had tears in my eyes and then I became overwhelmed by a feeling that I wasn't alone, that my mom and Grandma were here with me and that they had guided me to this place. That throughout my life I had been worried about everybody else, but that I had forgotten myself. That what I was about to go through was all for me, to heal my soul. I can't explain how all of this came to me, but these were the strong impressions, thoughts, and emotions I felt while doing the breathwork.

The next day after breakfast, we had a spiritual class which explained the most important part of the Ayahuasca experience. The instructor said, "I know that you may have come here with many questions and needs, and this is going to change your life. You can never be the same after this. Through this ceremony you will raise your vibrational frequency. We live in a three-dimensional world, but we can transcend to higher dimensions and vibrational frequencies where love is the only reality. But it is important to go into this sacred ceremony with intentions. We believe that if you have the intentions that I am about to share, everything else in your life will fall into place. The right people will come into your life, the people that do not bring you light will leave. You can overcome the most difficult things in your life and be healed. "

Then the teacher read off some intentions:
- Show me who I have become
- Merge me back with my soul at all cost.
- Heal my heart.

As the spiritual teacher shared these intentions, I reflected on each word. My eyes were fixated on, "Merge me back with my soul AT ALL COST." Yes, coming here to this place I knew I was ready to do this at all cost.

At around 5pm, we were all there, about 70 of us standing outside this glass yoga meditation/ceremony large room, in the midst of mother nature, to get ready for our Ayahuasca ceremony. The vast, forest of trees surrounding the place made me feel connected, made everything feel so real.

From the few conversations I'd had, I understood that, for most people, it was their first time, so I wasn't alone. And for those who had done it before, they had already received powerful miracles in their lives, and they were there for further peace, love and guidance and to be part of this spiritual community of light seekers.

When we walked into the room, I saw Maiccu and Ingela and I lay down on a mattress in the back of the room close to them. Seeing them made me feel like I was cared for. There was one mattress next to me, where a woman, a dentist from Arizona, lay down next to me.

A few feet away from the entrance to the large glass Ceremony room, there was a standing fireplace, with big pieces of wood and two cement benches on each side. This was a sacred fire where the shamans start each ceremony with prayers and blessings before they got in a line of two in the middle of the ceremony room towards the front. They were wearing their indigenous shaman clothing which gave them an air of sacredness, purity and majesty. I felt as if I was watching the movie "Avatar", but this time, I was in it.

Across the room, there were beautifully neatly placed white mattresses with white sheets and pillows and a thoughtfully placed mustard blanket. The mattresses were arranged in twos or threes around the room. What was peculiar though was that, at the end of each mattress, there was a white bucket, placed there for those who purge during the ceremony by vomiting.

"Perhaps the most well-known effect of ayahuasca is its purgative effect—hence the bucket next to each participant's mat.

According to traditional belief, purging can occur through a number of means also including diarrhea, shaking, crying, and sweating," says Evgenia Fotiou, assistant professor of anthropology at Kent State University, who has interviewed shamans and ayahuasca ceremony participants around the world. "This tea made from a hallucinogenic Amazonian plant and consumed in shamanic ceremonies often makes people purge the vileness within themselves."

We end up purging whatever is stuck in our system or soul since we were children, such as anger, depression, sadness, and fear, which resist leaving the body. It can feel like we're throwing up thoughts, emotions, or experiences that no longer serve us; a physical and spiritual cleansing. The most interesting part of the Ayahuasca ceremony that I heard from people who had been there before is that some of them see extraordinary visions that help them heal either their emotional wounds or physical ailments.

I wasn't sure what to expect for myself. All I knew was that I was already here in Costa Rica and I was ready to go through this strange experience "At All Cost."

After, the Shaman spoke some words of wisdom at the start of the ceremony, words that I do not recall as the whole experience felt surreal. All I remember is lying on a mattress and suddenly they asked us to get in two lines to receive our brew of Ayahuasca. I got in the line where the woman shaman, Sara, was giving the tea. Since the moment I'd first seen her, I felt this power coming from her. I eventually got to the front, was given the tea and went back to my place and lay down on the mattress. I waited to see if I would have any reaction, but I did not feel much, perhaps just a little drowsy. But as I was lying there, I started to hear people vomiting, a few others started to moan and whimper. I just lay there trying to absorb the whole experience. Then, they called out for the second round of brew. I got in line and was almost half-way to the front, when my body started to shake. I had never experienced this tremor in my body and suddenly, before I reached the Shaman, I was bending forward, holding my body by putting my hands on my thighs. Suddenly, I saw Maiccu and Ingela who ran to me to make sure I was ok by holding me.

Now, in front of the Shaman, shaking, I managed to speak, "I was not feeling anything until now. I am shaking and not sure if I should take a second cup of the brew."

The Shaman looked me directly in the eyes and said, "Take a little more." And I did. Maiccu and Ingela helped me get back to the mattress and they told me, "Breathe, breathe. Let the plant do the work."

As soon as I lay down, my arms and legs moved as if I was running. I did this for a while and suddenly my body started to shake quietly in different directions. I never felt pain or was scared, but I was in awe of how my body could move without any will of my own. Ingela and Maiccu checked on me throughout the evening, "How are you feeling? I think your body is moving this way because it is trying to move the energy within you."

I would just nod in agreement and follow their instructions and breathe deeply. Two hours later, the ceremony was over, and my body stopped moving. The Shamans called for everyone to listen to their closing words and then suddenly the woman next to me, the dentist, turned to me and started to laugh and said, "Girl, you ran a freaking marathon! Are you not tired?" as she kept laughing. This made me laugh as well. I needed to laugh after this unusual and intense experience. It was a beautiful moment as we were both laughing like children and bonded as kindred souls do. Suddenly, it was all ok.

The next day, although I was not fully healed from my cold, I got up at 6am to go for a run in the majestic green countryside of Costa Rica. I ran for 45 minutes and made it on time back for breakfast where I sat with others at the long table where we were having breakfast. I was still closed up, so I did not share much about myself, but I sat there listening to other people's experiences. Some talked about their purging experiences, how they vomited and what it felt like. I couldn't relate as I had not purged that way and I was glad I didn't. I told myself that I could probably go through the whole week without vomiting. Then others said that they saw "Aliens" that did surgery on them, others heard a voice that spoke to them. Other saw visions of colors and were shown things from their past.

I just sat there in silence as I was going through my own experience that I was trying to assimilate.

I got ready for the second day of the ceremony and I approached Uma, a girl who had Cerebral Palsy. I was humbled every time I saw her walking around on her crutches, devoted, hopeful and committed to this experience.

"Uma, you inspire me. Just seeing how much you try."

She looked at me as she was lying on her mattress, and with pure generosity and light in her eyes, said, "I hope you get your miracle tonight."

I couldn't hold my tears, as she was there hoping for a much-needed miracle of her own, yet she was wishing me to have a much-needed miracle.

The ceremony started as usual. I got in the line, took the brew given to me by the Shaman and then went back to my mattress. As I lay down, I immediately heard people purging and, suddenly a few minutes after, my body started dramatically shaking. It was as if someone was pushing me from one side of my back and then the other. My legs, arms, everything started to move uncontrollably. This time, I started to feel an intensity of emotions inside of me that I could not fathom.

Ingela and Maiccu rushed to my side, "Breathe, breathe." They looked serious. I was wondering if they were concerned or if I should be concerned. "aaaa uffff." I took one breath after the other, but my body kept on moving all over the place, side to side, arms and legs as if they were kicking. The shamans also came to be around me and used feathers "to move my energy." It felt as if they were there to help me through the experience, but never intervene.

All of a sudden, my mind took me to the time when I was a 9 year old child, the day I came out of school and my mom never showed to pick me up. I saw myself sitting alone on the sidewalk for hours waiting and hoping for my mom to just come. Suddenly, I was overcome with sadness, and tears started to fall from my face as my body kept on intensely shaking. Out of nowhere, Ingela put her hand on my heart and said, "Love that little girl." This made me cry more, but I also thought, How docs Ingela know that I am seeing myself as a child in my mind?

Two hours later, my body was still shaking, it was as if I was running away from something, as if my body was living all my traumas all over again. My body threw me from one side to the other and, at one point, I was thrown off my mattress.

I reminded myself, Merge me back with my soul AT ALL COST. AT ALL COST. I am willing to do this. And then one of the other women shamans, Waleska Moya, came and put her hand on my heart and said, "Who loves you unconditionally?"

I looked her in the eyes as I shook even harder, as if my body reacted to that question. I could not think of anyone who loves me unconditionally and I started to cry.

She said, "Cry. You need to cry. It is ok." I just nodded and cried even more.

Then she asked, "Do you have children?"

I said, "No." She looked at me as if she could pierce my soul.

"What about your mom?" she asked.

"She died when I was little…" I felt that I had no one in this world. She looked at me again with such depth and understanding.

I was overcome with great sadness and there was not one part of my body that did not feel empty, desperate, and full of sorrow. I wept and it occurred to me that this was the answer to my first intention, "Show me who I have become." I had become this person who feels alone and unloved.

My body still trembling, my head started to hurt. I shook my head from one side to the other. Every sound was hurting my body, even the sound of the background music they had in the room. I managed to get up from the mattress and started to wobble to the exit door of the ceremony room. As I got to the entrance, my body was so unstable and trembling and the pain in my soul so profound, that I fell on the grass right outside the entrance.

Ingela and the other Shamans followed me. They put a blanket on top of me and brought a pillow so that they could help me feel as comfortable as I could, but also they respected whatever the plant medicine was doing with me.

As I lay on the ground trembling, feeling suffering and torment building inside my body as a pressure, I kept on looking at the stars, the trees and the sacred fire that was a few feet away from me. Then, the same woman shaman who had asked me earlier, "Who loves you unconditionally?" came to me, blessed my heart by putting some sort of oil over me and then said, "I want you now to go to the fire and give whatever is in your heart.

Say your name, then your father's name, then your mother's name and then give the fire whatever is in your heart."

She helped me get up as I kept on shaking and helped me sit on one of the cement benches right in front of the sacred fire. I could see the people inside through the glass walls. A few others were outside praying and having their own personal experiences. I saw the trees, the stars, the moon and then proceeded to talk to the fire.

"My name is Maria Veronica Carrera. My Father is Adolfo Fernando Carrera. My mother is Maria Victoria Mendez." Then, without thinking, every name of anyone who had hurt me since I was a child until now came to my mind and I was divinely guided to repeat after each name I saw, "Forgive them for they know not what they do." Then the next name came, as if someone was downloading these names in my mind and I repeated the same words after each name, "Forgive them for they know not what they do."

Interestingly enough, the first names that came to me were my mom and my dad. I didn't realize that I had felt abandoned and, even though this was not mom's fault, my young soul needed to forgive. I forgave the troubled relationship I'd had with my father and his wife, as if I was letting all of it go in an instant and I was filled with compassion. Then, others who had hurt me deliberately because of their own wounds came to my awareness and I forgave them, one by one. That included relationships that had scarred me. At that moment, I wasn't aware of the enormity of the moment. It was cosmic forgiveness. As I forgave all, I was also being forgiven, redeemed, and healed.

Then, surprisingly, a sudden rush of anger moved through my chest and I looked at one of the Shamans walking softly close to me and asked, "Where is God? Where is God in all of this?!"

The South American Shaman, with long black hair wearing indigenous clothing, looked at me with her dark native eyes and said, "God is everywhere." I cried. I cried because I had felt at times abandoned by God in my life and I'd seen so many others who suffered needlessly. It was the first time I had allowed myself to say out loud, "Where is God?"

At the end of this experience, I walked to the grass and lay my feeble body down on the ground where I collapsed. I was conscious, but I was spiritually, emotionally and physically exhausted and done.

The ceremony lasted for about 4 hours. At the end, almost every participant had left. I couldn't get up. A kind woman from Australia who was also participating in the ceremony came and asked me, "Can I help you get to your room?"

"Yes," I answered feeling deeply grateful. She called a member of the staff and they held me so that I could get to the golf cart and then drove me to my room and proceeded to help me get in my bed where I lay down, fully depleted. In the back of my mind as I was lying there, I told myself, "I cannot do this one more night. I am going to change my flight and go home early. I am not a quitter, but I cannot do this anymore." I fell sound asleep after this and my soul finally rested deeply all night.

The following day, I woke up around 6am. I had not expected to wake up that early. I felt well rested, but hungry. I was embarrassed to show up to breakfast after such a rough night only to tell people that my intention was to go home. But I made myself head to the cafeteria. As I entered the area, one beautiful lady from Iran, Poolak, who was one of the partici-pants of the ceremony, looked up and said to me, "Hey, you had a rough night last night."

I was uncomfortable but said, "Yes. My body was shaking uncontrollably. Don't know what to think of it…This is hard."

She then looked at me with dark and intense eyes, "You inspired me. When they said, 'Merge me back with my soul AT ALL COST." That is you. I was lying down hesitating whether I should take a second cup and then I looked at you standing in the line, struggling, so I got up to take a second cup. Veronica. You are a warrior of light. Remember that THE UNIVERSE REWARDS BRAVERY."

Those words echoed in my mind, "The Universe rewards bravery."

For the first time, I took real interest in hearing other people's stories and I sat on a table next to some young lovely men in their late 20s and early 30s. I asked, "So what brought you here?" Their answers amazed me.

One sweet young guy from Sweden, Alexis, who was often so positive and trusting, said, "I was sexually abused for 11 years since I was a baby and I became a really depressed young man. I considered suicide and nothing seemed to help me get out of this heavy darkness. Neither therapy, nor pills, nothing. Until I found out about this place and I told myself, 'This is my last chance at life.' I have felt a love and peace that I had not felt before."

The other young men shared their stories with depression or addiction and how their connection to the Universe, our Creator, and the plant ceremony had changed their lives. These young men were filled with wisdom beyond their years and, as I sat there, I felt so much love for them. I had asked the Shaman last night, "Where is God?" I was reminded of her answer, "God is everywhere," and I thought, yes, God is here in these young men, in all these powerful stories of tears, triumph, of love, of freedom. I felt so connected to every person around me and I was filled with love for them.

I left breakfast and decided to head to class not knowing what I was looking to get out of it, since I still wanted to leave.

Paola Castro, one of the Rythmia instructors, taught some spiritual truths that spoke to me, "In a relationship, expectations are premeditated disappointments." "All relationships are a mirror of the relationship with the self." Then, she talked about energetic boundaries, "When you are operating at a higher vibrational frequency, nothing below love can touch you." I decided to stay after class to get her guidance and wisdom on what I was wrestling with.

"Paola, I had a very difficult night last night," I proceeded to explain all that had happened, how shattered I felt, the sadness, the emptiness, the pain, the shaking.

And I ended, "I am not sure I want to continue with this, Paola. I am contemplating going home."

Paola listened with reverence and did not take her eyes away from me. Compassionately, she said, "Veronica. The intention is Merge me Back with my Soul At All Cost. That is exactly what you are doing. And Remember that the Crucifixion comes before the Resurrection."

I was pierced to my soul with the power of those words, "The Crucifixion comes before the Resurrection." I had no doubt that I was going to participate in the ceremony that evening.

I got to the ceremony room two hours early. I wanted to prepare myself for the moment that was to come. No one was there and I lay down on the cement benches facing the fire, meditating and saying out loud, "Trust, Trust."

Two hours later, the shamans showed up and started to light the fire. I stayed there and others whom I had never taken the time to talk to before showed up. We had some meaningful conversations about the three-dimensional world, which is where we were. Then they talked about the 4th and 5th dimension, which is where the Divine Spirit is, where there is only love and light. I listened intently and it instilled in me so much calmness, so much peace and once again, I felt strangely and wonderfully connected to these young men. I saw them as my brothers, nothing less than my brothers.

The ceremony was about to start, I picked the same location every time and lay on the same mattress close to Ingela and Maiccu. My dentist friend came to lie next to me and I said to myself, "This is perfect." She didn't know that I felt safe when she was around; she had a way of making things seem normal.

As the ceremony started, Sarah Saso, the majestic woman Shaman, dressed in shaman clothing, started to speak, "We have disconnected ourselves from nature. People are empty and we have forgotten who we belong to. We must learn that we are love, that we are light. We have to go back to that. The Infinite knew that there would be a time that we would feel so disconnected as humanity that we would need this plant medicine. That we would need to merge back with our souls at all costs and heal our hearts." Her presence was powerful and sacred, and it helped me to trust. Then she continued, "This is a path of integrity, and self-respect. Remember this. Our thoughts, words and actions should be aligned. When you live with integrity, you are aligned with yourself and the Infinite. We have to eat with intention. Ask yourselves, Is this food going to nourish you? What we put in our bodies will feed our thoughts and bodies, so we have to be mindful. Junk food, junk mind, junk body."

This night was the feminine healing ceremony so there was a special indigenous dance to the rhythm of the drums and rattles. Sarah danced along with other Shamans. There was smoke, light, and the room was filled with Joy.

It was now time to take the plant medicine, Ayahuasca. I got in line again, most of the people were dressed in white. Sarah handed me the brew, I drank it and went back to my mattress.

There was beautiful rhythmic shamanic music in the background and, just a few minutes after I lay down, something remarkable happened. My body, without any control of my own, started to move to the music. My legs, back, and arms started to dance as If I was interpreting the divine shamanic music in the background. I looked over to Maiccu and Ingela and they smiled at me. From time to time, my arms also moved rhythmically as if I was flying and then I went back to dancing. I got off the mattress and danced all night. I felt light, joyful, free in the conviction that I am loved, I am loved! That love does not depend on any one body. I am love and love is infinite, and it is there regardless of any one person. It is there. And this is God. Just Infinite Love, Light, Wisdom and Compassion. This is God and this is me and all of us are connected, we are part of the Oneness. I cried, but this time I cried because my heart was filled with so much love and so much happiness.

Ingela approached me after my body danced for almost three hours and said, "Let's go to the Shaman Sarah to see what she has to tell you."

Ingela walked over to the front of the room with me. I still couldn't stop my body from dancing and my arms again made a movement as if I was flying. Sarah looked at me with those magnificent piercing eyes and said, "You are free now. You are free. You can fly now."

When I came back to NJ from Rythmia, I received a note from Lory, a war veteran, who was part of the Ayahuasca ceremony, "Sister V. you did it sweetheart! I would go to battle with you any day to fight the darkness! You are a light warrior and so very glad you are in my tribe."

Her words, coming from someone who had experienced the ugly face of war, reminded me of the enormity of our experience at Rythmia. And I was reminded that the Universe is always good. Barbara Marx, speaker & author said, "The Universe may not always be kind, but It is always good. It gives us the experiences that we need to evolve to a higher consciousness and be awakened to more freedom, more joy and a more loving order."

The whole experience reminded me of Emily Dickinson's poem:

> This is the Hour of Lead –
> Remembered, if outlived,
> As Freezing persons, recollect the Snow –
> First – Chill – then Stupor – then the letting go –

Chapter 22.

I Am Enough

I visited Rythmia a year later for a second time with a few close friends during November 2020. Rythmia had been closed for several months due to the global pandemic. When I arrived, it felt that I was arriving home and I shed tears of gratitude. Maiccu saw me walking into the meditation room and started to scream with joy and gave me a huge hug. I wanted her to know how sorry I was that she didn't have Ingela in her life now. But I had no words. Her death this year was a great sadness for this community as she was true healer and a special human being.

On my second night of the plant ceremony, I was in the ceremony room. This time there were only 35 people participating, half of the number of people last year, all due to Covid precautions. Still, it was the same setting, the open meditation room, neatly arranged mattresses set out around the room and their corresponding mustard color blankets, a pillow and a bucket in front of each mattress as it is expected for one to purge.

During this ceremony something powerful happened that I saw as a closing of the circle of healing within me. As I drank the plant medicine, I felt nauseaus, just terribly nauseaus for a long time to the point that I could no longer withstand it.

Suddenly, I started to relive all in one moment, time and space doesn't seem to exist, all those years of rejection in the Mormon church for being who I am. The deep hurt of feeling rejected and unworthy overwhelmed my body and I called out in distress as I lay on the mattress, "Why did I allow myself to be treated like this for so many years of my life? I was so belittled and I lost so many people who truly loved me because I was ashamed of who I was! I allowed them to treat me like this for so long" and I started to cry. Then suddenly, my mind showed me my mom dying alone in the hospital in a white bed in a white room and I cried out loud, "Mami, mami, I am sorry you died alone in the hospital. I did not know. If I had known, I would have been there with you, no matter how little I was."

Then, after I wept for sometime, although I had already forgiven him, I was brought to an awareness of how unconsciously unloving and hurtful my father had been with me and the ceremony brought out other things in my childhood that were difficult. There was something else beyond forgiveness that I needed to realize. Subsequently, I started to feel unbearably nautious and I moaned outloud, "This is so hard…This is so hard…This is so hard!!!" The light worker in the back heard me and came over to me and held me and I wept, wept and wept as I continued to say, "This is so hard…This is so hard." At the same time, his embrace allowed the pain to feel more bearable. The Shamans also came to me to blow smoke and move the feathers around my body to move my energy and assist in the healing process. Again, the majestic Shamans Sarah Sasso and the loving Waleska Moya came several times, put oil on my heart, blessed me with words and observed me as the plant worked on me.

At that point, I started to purge profusely one time after the other, about five times. And as I lay back down in bed feeling some relief from the nausea, my tongue was making an effort to speak, but it felt numb at first. It wasn't me trying to speak, there was a unrecognizable raspy deep voice coming out from some place within my soul and I uttered these words, "I AM ENOUGH...I AM ENOUGH...I AM ENOUGH..." That voice was speaking for me and I was in awe just witnessing this voice that I couldn't recognize speaking through me, "I AM ENOUGH...I AM ENOUGH...". And suddenly, it said, " I AM...I AM...I AM.." and repeated this multiple times until my soul rested and I lay quietly on the mattress with an indescribable peace, healed from deeper wounds. Then Sarah came towards me, touched my head lightly and said, "You are a Goddess."

The next day, I felt so much joy, just pure joy and I had the privilege of meeting the founder of Rythmia in person, Gerry Powell. He was sharing with the group his powerful healing story and at the end of the class with deep gratitude in my heart I went to shake his hand and he said to me, "I feel like I know you. Are you sure we have not met?"

"I don't think so Gerry."

Then, he looked at me with those penetrating eyes,

"Your eyes look so clear. You just look so free." And that is exactly how I felt.

Chapter 23.

The Universe Reward Bravery

After being out there in the triathlon race for close to 13 hours, I started to see, within a short distance, the finish line. The crowd got bigger and loud. There were many people on the sidelines, and I spotted some friends in the mass of people. With the only energy I had left as I ran, I extended my arm sideways to touch hands with all those who were cheering. I touched the hands in gratitude for those who had travelled far and had waited long hours to see us finish such an arduous and grueling race.

Seeing my friends in the crowd reminded me of all the love I've had in my life and the many times they have shown up to lift me up and cheer for me even in those moments when I felt I had nothing more to give. As I was coming closer to the end, I saw all the different faces of humanity in the crowd and I understood what Ram Dass meant when he said that ultimately, we are all here to help each other walk home, get to our truest and most real destination, which is that place of healing, wholeness and love.

I saw the clock above the finish line read: 13 hours 12 mins then I heard the announcer say the words I had so much wanted to hear, "Veronica Carrera! You are an Ironman!"

"I am free. I am free." For the first time I knew that I could fly.

The first person I saw waiting to hug me was Daniella! She had a huge smile on her face, "You did it Amorcito!" Then I saw Shilpa and a rush of other friends who had gathered to see me through the end. I do not even know what I smelled like, what I looked like, I had been out there for 13 hours, swimming in the Hudson river when there was a sewage spill the week before, but regardless, they all hugged me and kissed me and expressed how proud they were of me.

I still felt the adrenaline flowing through my body and I had enough strength to chat, laugh and absorb the moment. I felt a prevailing inner joy that you can only experience when you have gone beyond your fears and you begin to understand that as humans, we are limitless. Just like other events in my life, once again I had been given the gift to overcome and accomplish the impossible and realize the truth of those words, "The universe rewards bravery."

The journey towards healing has taught me that at my core I am only love. As Rumi said, the wound is the place where the light enters you, and, I might add that the light is the only place that can heal our wounds. When I go into a place of stillness, and contemplate the light and the shadows inside me, it is comforting to know that in the presence of light, the darkness disappears. But even the darkness has a mission to propel us forward and as we embrace the shadows within us and love all of who we are, the light and the dark come together in this complex but harmonious dance of life to move us towards a more loving conscious evolution-to Our Higher Self. After hating myself for so long for not being able to fit into this "illusion of perfection" that I had been taught was the way to God, I now realize that perfection is exactly as things are. We are all a spark of the Perfect Divine Loving Source or Universe. We come from this Greater Light, the Great I AM so how can we not be perfect exactly as we are! Recently, I looked at myself in the mirror and for the first time I saw a deep contentment and a calm peacefulness in my eyes that spoke to me, "I can live with you for the rest of my life."

As one of my heroes, Glennon Doyle, said, "If you let yourself shatter and then you put yourself back together, piece by piece, you wake up one day and realize that you have been completely reassembled. You are whole again, and strong, but you are suddenly a new shape, a new size. The change that happens to people who really sit in their pain- whether it's a sliver of envy lasting an hour or a canyon of grief lasting decades- it's revolutionary. When that kind of transformation happens, it becomes impossible to fit back into the old, dead skin or a butterfly trying to crawl back into its cocoon. You look around and see everything freshly, with the new eyes you have earned for yourself. There is no going back."

I pray that no matter how hard life may get, that you may find the gift that has been given to you and, at any moment, be able to ask yourself, "What is trying to emerge out of my struggle and chaos? What am I being taught? How can I use life circumstances to birth a more conscious, more peaceful and joyful version of myself?"

And as you continue to travel along all the miles of your life, may you find your bravery and enjoy your path to live and love deeply. May you continue to move forward in your personal sacred journey and touch hands in gratitude with those who love you best and know that you are never alone. And lastly, may you touch hands with those whom you must forgive, so that you can be free.

May you know that your wildest dreams are yet to come.

Acknowledgments

I wish to thank Gay Walley for her tremendous belief in me. You are a beautiful, gifted writer, and I am deeply grateful for your inspiration and support.

To my family, Dad, I love you. Thank you for all the sacrifices you made for all of us, even the ones I couldn't see. To my aunt, uncles, sister and many cousins, you are some of the most wonderful, fun and kindest souls I know.

To all my dear friends who have blessed my life with their kindness and unconditional love: Shilpa, Fabienne, Johanna, Marianna, Lynn, Seneca, Paola, Badou, Lincoln, Emanuelle, Henry, Hemanth, Atika, Sirin, Mehwish, Daniela, Hiroko, Heewon, Houda, Celest, Gia, Julia, Alicia, Marilyn, Camilla, Amie, Alexis, Rhina, Elma, Phyllistine, Sean, Patty, Ilana, Matt, Hill, Debbie and Sharon and all those who have blessed my life with their presence.

I also want to acknowledge those special souls who have impacted my life through their gifts and life purpose: Zainab Salbi, Marianne Williamson, Jada Pinkett, Oprah Winfrey, Mike

Zappy, Gerry Powell, Dr Jeff McNairy, Paola Castro, Shamans Sara Sasso & Waleska Moya, Ingela & Maiccu.

About the Author

From the moment she became a motherless child in Ecuador, Veronica Carrera became intimate with adversity and uncertainty.

This touching memoir tells the story of an immigrant child who grows fiercely independent and defies the odds to make a place for herself in the world, though she is made an outsider again and again.

All hell breaks loose the moment Veronica Carrera, a leader in the Mormon church, falls in love with a fellow female student at Brigham Young University. Battling her innate feelings for many years after, the devout missionary confesses her temptations to the Bishop in a futile attempt to hold tight to her spiritual home.

After her church shuns her, a shocked Veronica embarks on the hardest endurance triathlon race in the world to reclaim her power, inadvertently beginning a much more important, internal journey of healing and self-love.

This inspiring memoir will have you cheering for Veronica as she embarks on a journey to dig deep, defy all limits, and accept who she is by competing in the 140-mile Ironman race.

140-Miles to Self-Acceptance and Love tells the story of overcoming childhood and religious trauma as a queer, brown-skinned immigrant. It also issues a clarion call to recognize the realities that drive far too many LGBTQ youth and adults to commit suicide under shame from their churches and families.

Veronica's story of triumphing over adversity, not only offers hope and inspiration for readers to discover true inner wisdom and acceptance but may save lives!

Hers is a story of love, loss, courage and healing.

Today, she is an avid triathlete and passionate advocate for human rights, a highly sought-after speaker and a successful sales leader at one of the top tech companies in the world. She is also the creator/producer of the LinkedIn Live show 30 Minutes of Wisdom-Rising in Consciousness & Mindfulness.

Veronica holds a B.A. in French from Brigham Young University and an M.B.A. from Cornell's Johnson Graduate School of Management, where she was honored as "The 2015 Best Executive EMBA." She recently completed the Inner M.B.A. (conscious leadership program) at New York University and is currently pursuing a Life Coaching certification with Jay Shetty.

Made in the USA
Las Vegas, NV
10 December 2021